The Reading Edge

He that reads and grows no wiser seldom suspects his own deficiency, but complains of hard words and obscure sentences, and asks why books are written which cannot be understood.

—Samuel Johnson

Reading is a very elaborate procedure, involving the weighing of many elements in a sentence, their organization in the proper relations to one another, the selection of certain of their connotations and the rejection of others, and the cooperation of many forces to determine final response ... the act of answering simple questions about a simple paragraph ... includes all the features characteristic of typical reasonings.

—Edward L. Thorndike

Reading was the most important subject in our early American schools, and it has continued to be the most important subject all through the years of our national growth.

—Nila Banton Smith

Ben E. Johnson
University of South Florida

The Reading Edge

*Thirteen Ways
to Build
Reading
Comprehension*

D. C. HEATH AND COMPANY
Lexington, Massachusetts   Toronto

For Elsa.
Intelligent, talented, beautiful, loving.
A great investment.
With thanks and love.

Cover: "Pertaining to Yachts and Yachting" by Charles Sheeler.
Philadelphia Museum of Art: Bequest of Margaretta S. Hinchman.

Published simultaneously in Canada.

Printed in the United States of America.

International Standard Book Number: 0-669-20101-4

10   9   8   7   6   5   4   3   2   1

Preface

Teachers are the major influence on how well students read. Students don't learn to read assignments with a questioning mind if their teachers have deemphasized comprehension questions in classroom discussions and on tests. Nor do students develop their critical reading skills if their teachers have always favored factual and application (noncritical) questions in discussions and on readings.

Literal comprehension is the simplest level of comprehension and the one that makes the fewest demands on reasoning. Research indicates that questions calling for literal meaning are the most frequently asked by elementary- and secondary-school teachers. These questions depend for the most part on memory and recall of stated information.

In college reading, things change. College teachers often ask questions that call for critical reasoning, evaluation, explanation, or conjecture, but students have seldom had much experience—and rarely much training—in answering such questions. This fact is often demonstrated when students take tests covering assigned course readings or when they are required to take standardized tests such as the State of Florida CLAST, the State of Texas TASP exam, placement tests, entry exams, exit exams, proficiency tests, assessment tests, or even advanced tests such as state teacher-certification exams.

Acquire the Reading Edge

The primary goal of this book is to enable student readers to identify and acquire the specific reading skills that will enable them to become not only efficient, high-comprehension readers and test takers, but also successful college students. Unfortunately, not all college students are successful students; some students are marginal at best during their years in college and barely manage to graduate. Of course, this is not what they actually want. They would rather be successful students so that the time and money they spend in getting an education is well invested. They want to learn as much as possible as fast as possible, and to do this they must acquire some specific reading-comprehension skills if they are going to achieve the "edge" that will give them a learning advantage in their college education.

And that "edge" is not so tough to acquire.

This book, *The Reading Edge: Thirteen Ways to Build Reading Comprehension,* shows step by step, chapter by chapter, how to acquire that reading edge on tests as well as in reading textbooks. There are thirteen chapters, each one focusing on a specific way to increase comprehension of what students read in *any* college course, no matter what the subject area.

Learn a Basic Comprehension Skill in Each Chapter

In Chapter 1, students will focus on techniques for mastering and marking a chapter, page, or passage *as they are reading it* and in a way that will increase their speed of reading, flexibility, comprehension of what is read, and retention. They will learn to read with a pen or pencil in their hand, marking systematically.

In Chapters 2 through 4, students will learn practical ways to build their comprehension in the three specific *literal* comprehension areas commonly focused on in both classroom and standardized tests:

Chapter   2—Recognizing the Main Idea
Chapter   3—Identifying Supporting Details
Chapter   4—Determining the Meaning of Words from Context

In Chapters 5 through 13, students focus on nine additional ways to build their critical comprehension skills to handle reading assignments and critical thinking tests:

Chapter   5—Recognizing the Author's Purpose
Chapter   6—Identifying the Author's Overall Pattern of Organization
Chapter   7—Distinguishing Between Statements of Fact and Statements of Opinion
Chapter   8—Detecting Bias
Chapter   9—Recognizing the Author's Tone
Chapter 10—Recognizing Relations Within Sentences
Chapter 11—Recognizing Relations Between Sentences
Chapter 12—Recognizing Valid Arguments
Chapter 13—Drawing Logical Inferences and Conclusions

And that's it.

There are thirteen chapters and thirteen specific reading skills students need to improve if they are to achieve the "edge" in learning. Each chapter has several pages of clear, practical, how-to instruction in which that chapter's skill is explained and demonstrated. The demonstration is then analyzed to reinforce understanding. Each chapter's skill becomes second nature through practice required to complete the extensive exercises in each chapter.

Lots of Practice Develops Skill

The hundreds of reading selections and accompanying questions in this text are representative of the subjects and questions students will face in their college classes and on standardized exams of all types. Some of the passages (actually most of them) are of high interest and are entertaining —but some aren't. Some read like textbooks. Much of what students read in college will be interesting and entertaining, but much will appear to be slow, boring reading. But they will have to read it anyway. And like those diverse textbooks, this book includes a representative sampling from all subject areas and interest levels. Students will read about sex and sex roles, biting fish, baseball, movie critics, monsoons, robots, Sudden Infant Death Syndrome, a potato entrepreneur, computers, drugs, missiles, continental drift, suicide, toothpaste, Elvis, Indians, carbon 14 dating, scandal, horse races, juvenile gangs, and much more.

These reading passages were selected from current newspapers, magazines, and textbooks covering every area of study in college. Recent textbooks from such areas as economics, physical science, political science, and history are used as sources for the readings in the exercises in each chapter. Often students will create the questions for a particular reading selection, thus gaining skill in anticipating and analyzing test questions.

You will also find that the readings and practice questions have varying degrees of difficulty. Sometimes the questions are easily read, understood, and answered, while at other times the readings and passages appear to be difficult. That is the way the book is designed for several reasons.

1. College reading material has different levels of readability. One text may consist of a majority of short, clear, easily read and understood sentences. Another may be composed of long, convoluted sentences that are difficult to follow.
2. Some college texts by virtue of their subject matter are difficult to follow and understand, whereas other subjects seem to make the reading of the text much easier.
3. Some college texts from areas outside the student's particular interest are difficult to plow through. Even though students know they must read such texts, they have difficulty maintaining interest and understanding.

Individual students already may have developed high competency with a particular comprehension skill, such as determining the main idea, so that Chapter 2 (Recognizing the Main Idea) may seem easy to them. On the other hand, they may not have developed *any* competency in another skill, such as detecting bias, so they may feel the need to review and rework the exercises in Chapter 8 (Detecting Bias) more than once. But it doesn't matter that some college reading assignments may be difficult and others relatively easy; students still have to read diverse assignments—and they are expected to achieve high comprehension on all of them. Thus, in this book, as students learn new skills they will practice them on a range of different levels of difficulty and they will improve their reading comprehension in all areas. They will begin to develop *The Reading Edge.*

Diagnostic Tests Will Assist You

One last point. This book contains three diagnostic tests and a skill analysis guide designed to enable students to determine where their weaknesses and strengths are.

The Pre Test and Post Test each have 50 questions, and the Mid Test has 25 questions. The skill analysis guide allows students to diagnose weaknesses from the pattern of incorrect answers in the tests. The Pre Test enables students to identify their weak areas before they begin reading the text. Once students have identified their comprehension levels, they will be able to move quickly through chapters in which they are strong, and slowly, carefully, through chapters about comprehension skills in which they need to improve. The Mid Test and the Post Test will reveal where students are improving and where they still need work.

It's Time to Begin

And now it is time to begin. This book has been carefully designed to lead its readers into developing valuable reading-comprehension skills. All students need to do is faithfully work their way through the chapters and the results will speak for themselves. Their comprehension and critical reasoning skills will be developed, their ability to successfully answer test questions will improve, and their chances of successfully learning in classes will be increased. Students will have *The Reading Edge,* and that edge will make the difference for them in college and in life.

With Thanks

My thanks to the many colleagues who offered helpful observations and suggestions: Mary Ellman, Long Beach City College; Karen Haas, Manatee

Community College; Eric Hibbison, J. Sargeant Reynolds Community College; Sue Kahn, Miami-Dade Community College; and Mary Thrash, Brookhaven College. Many other colleagues gave me the benefit of their insights, research, and teaching experience. I thank you all. If this book helps students the way I believe it will, we can all take pride in that accomplishment.

A final special thanks goes to Laura Link for having the patience to decode my more than messy handwriting, and the skill with a word processor to create a manuscript that an editor, and then ultimately students, could read.

Ben E. Johnson

Contents

Part One
Literal Comprehension Skills

Chapter 2
Recognizing the Main Idea *51*

Chapter 3
Identifying Supporting Details *81*

Chapter 4
Determining the Meaning of Words from Context *109*

Part Two
Critical Comprehension Skills

Chapter 5
Recognizing the Author's Purpose   *129*

Chapter 6
Identifying the Author's Overall Pattern of Organization   *151*

Contents

Mid Test
Mid-Course Review and Diagnostic Test   *175*

Chapter 7
Distinguishing Between Statements of Fact and Statements of Opinion   *185*

Chapter 8
Detecting Bias   *205*

Chapter 9
Recognizing the Author's Tone   *219*

Chapter 10
Recognizing Relations Within Sentences   *241*

Chapter 11
Recognizing Relations Between Sentences   *255*

Contents

This test has a time limit; your instructor will inform you how many minutes you have. Your primary goal is to correctly answer as many questions as you can during the time allotted. When your test is graded, your instructor's comments and the Skill Analysis Guide at the end of the book will help you determine where your strengths and weaknesses in reading skills are. You don't need to finish the entire test to be able to determine your strengths and weaknesses. Knowing these qualities you will be able to pay special attention to the instructions and exercises in the chapters on topics where you lack strength. Results from this test and from the other tests in this book will help you gain "the reading edge."

INSTRUCTIONS

Read carefully but quickly the passages and the questions that follow each passage. Circle the letter for the correct answer to each question.

PASSAGE 1

1 Several centuries ago, before the Industrial Revolution, men
2 and women shared the provider role. Men were responsible
3 for providing food, either by hunting or by farming, and shel-

1

4 ter, perhaps by building it themselves. But women, too, were
5 expected to be providers. They provided food, in such activi-
6 ties as growing a garden, milling flour, and cooking. They
7 were responsible for other kinds of providing as well, such as
8 producing clothing by spinning, weaving, and sewing it. In
9 short, men and women shared the provider role. In an agri-
10 cultural society, they shared time and space as well, for men
11 were not off in factories while women remained at home.
12   Then came the Industrial Revolution. Men went out to
13 work in factories, and women stayed home. Thus their roles
14 became far more divided. The work men did became less
15 intrinsically satisfying—for example, forging a particular
16 part for a particular machine is likely to be less satisfying
17 than growing and harvesting one's own grain to become food
18 on the table. Often the only good thing about the work was
19 the money that was earned. Simultaneously, there was a shift
20 for men from the provider role to the *good provider role.* That
21 is, with the shift to an emphasis on earning money, the man
22 was expected to be a good provider for his family—to earn a
23 lot of money. The more money he earned, the more successful
24 and manly he was.
25   It is an understatement to say that the good provider role
26 is a high-pressure one. Once again, the sex-role strain
27 paradigm is applicable: the good provider role for men is a
28 source of strain. There is the pressure of being the sole
29 provider, with a great deal of money needed to support the
30 modern family and the wife not earning any. Further, the
31 good provider role is a highly competitive role; a man is in
32 competition with other men to provide for his family better
33 than those other men provide for theirs. Finally, it is a role
34 that is destroyed by unemployment, which may occur
35 through no fault of one's own but rather as a result of eco-
36 nomic conditions. It is no wonder that the Great Depression
37 shook the foundations of manhood. Nor is it a wonder that
38 one of the slogans of the men's liberation movement is "We're
39 not just success objects."

> —From *Half the Human Experience: The Psychology of Women,* 3d edition, by Janet Shibley Hyde. Copyright © 1985 by D. C. Heath and Company. Reprinted by permission of the publisher.

1.   The main idea in this passage is that
    a. the Industrial Revolution changed the roles of men and women.
    b. a good provider is a man who earns lots of money.

    c. the Great Depression shook the foundations of manhood.

    d. the male role has changed from provider to good provider.

2.   In line 27, the word paradigm means

    a. disease   b. model

    c. activity   d. influence

3.   In the sentence, "But women, too, were expected to be providers" (line 4) the author indicates that his or her purpose is

    a. to state a problem   b. to analyze something

    c. to evaluate   d. to inform

4.   In developing this passage, the pattern of organization the author uses can be described as

    a. contrast   b. time order

    c. simple listing   d. summary

5.   What does the sentence beginning in line 5 ("They provided food ...") do in relation to the sentence beginning in line 4 ("But women, too ...")?

    a. It expresses the similarities between something and an idea stated in the sentence in the first part of line 5.

    b. It gives specific examples of the ideas stated in the sentence in the first part of line 5.

    c. It defines something referred to in the sentence in the first part of line 5.

    d. It alters the meaning of the sentence in the first part of line 5.

6.   Is the author's statement in lines 36–37 that "the Great Depression shook the foundations of manhood" logically valid or invalid?

    a. valid   b. invalid

7.   You could infer all these statements *except*

    a. Being a *good provider* is much better than being a provider.

    b. When men lose their jobs they may be thought less than "manly."

    c. It is better today to be a farmer than a factory worker.

    d. Work that is intrinsically satisfying is very hard to secure.

PASSAGE 2

1 Alert reader Charles W. Bostian sent me an article from the
2 Roanoke, Va., *Times and World News* concerning a decision
3 by the Virginia General Assembly that eliminated the fish-
4 shooting season in the western part of the state.
5   For those of you who do not keep up with sports, I should

6 explain that people in western Virginia have been climbing
7 up into trees and shooting down at fish—mostly carp and
8 sucker—since the turn of the century. I swear this is true.
9   I spoke to Gail McConnell of Fort Blackmore, Va., who has
10 been shooting fish in the Clinch River for more than 25 years.
11 He said the best spot to shoot from is a bough overhanging
12 the water, so you can see the fish.
13   "You need a high-powered rifle to kill a fish," McConnell
14 said. "As a rule, you don't necessarily hit the fish. You kill the
15 fish by the bullet striking the bottom, and the fish is killed by
16 the concussion."
17   McConnell said there are 300 to 500 regular fish shooters,
18 but they don't have tournaments or anything. Still, I bet it's
19 very exciting to be along the Clinch River during fish-shoot-
20 ing season, with the gentle spring breeze carrying the telltale
21 "blam" of high-powered ammunition being fired at a 90-
22 degree angle down into the river, followed by the familiar
23 gentle burbling sound of fatally concussed carp bobbing to the
24 surface.
25   Fortunately, the state fish and game commission, after
26 meeting with a group of alarmed fish-shooters, has agreed
27 that at its meeting this month it will consider reinstating the
28 season. But there will undoubtedly be dissenters. There will
29 be some ecology-nut, bleeding-heart, Sierra-Club-member-
30 ship-card-carrying, whale-saving, non-Indiana-National-
31 Guard-serving, New-Age-Whole-Earth-herbal-tea-drinking
32 weenies who are going to oppose fish-shooting on the grounds
33 that it is unsportsmanlike. Well, perhaps these people will
34 change their tune when they learn about the California
35 Attack Fish.
36   I found out about these fish thanks to Maggie Weather-
37 stone, who alertly sent me an Associated Press article that
38 appeared with the headline: BIOLOGIST SHOCKED AS
39 FISH TAKE BIG BITES OUT OF PEOPLE. The story states
40 that some people were attacked this summer by fish while
41 wading in Lake Mendocino.
42   So I called up the state fisheries biologist who investigat-
43 ed the fish attacks, Weldon Jones. "It was kind of scary," he
44 reported. "We had bites that left blood running down the
45 legs."
46   Jones said his investigation indicated that the attacks
47 were caused by the fish being "cranky" from: (a) not having
48 enough food and; (b) protecting their nests during spawning.
49 He also said that the attacks have stopped.

4

50   But that does not mean we should not be alarmed. Let's
51 examine the sequence of events:
52   1. Virginia cancels the fish-shooting season.
53   2. Within months, fish as far away as California are
54 chomping on people.
55   It does not take a rocket scientist to see the connection
56 here. The question is: What should we, the citizenry, do about
57 it? Should we arm ourselves?

—From *The Bradenton Herald*, Bradenton, Florida, October 9, 1988. Copyright
© Dave Barry. Reprinted from *The Miami Herald*.

8.   The sentence beginning in line 13 of this passage ("You need a ...") is a statement of

    a. fact   b. opinion

9.   In this passage the author show bias against

    a. fish shooting   b. the Sierra Club membership
    c. fish shooting season   d. guns

10.   If the author were delivering this passage orally, his or her tone of voice would probably be

    a. playful   b. earnest
    c. ghoulish   d. hard

11.   The word or phrase that identifies the relation within the sentence beginning in line 18 ("Still, I bet it's ...") is

    a. time order   b. cause and effect
    c. simple listing   d. definition

12.   The statement in line 47 that "the attacks were caused by the fish being 'cranky'" is

    a. valid   b. invalid

PASSAGE 3

1 The Los Angeles Dodgers baseball team is one of the best and
2 most profitable franchises in professional sports.Of course,
3 some of the reasons for its enviable position are winning
4 teams (the Dodgers won more games than they lost for twen-
5 ty-one out of twenty-five seasons in Los Angeles), nonstop
6 sunny weather, and a market area of over 10 million people
7 to draw on for fans. But none of these would count for much
8 without the organizing abilities of the owners, Walter O'Mal-
9 ley and his son Peter, who follow sound management princi-
10 ples. According to former baseball commissioner Bowie Kuhn,

5

11 "They're just good businessmen. They could make money on
12 widgets."
13   The O'Malleys run the team using fundamental organiza-
14 tional principles. First, they pour all their business energies
15 into operating the team and don't have outside interests to
16 distract them, as some other owners do. They're usually
17 among the first to arrive at the stadium every day.
18   Second, they have a top-down, integrated system. They
19 own their own stadium and have a maintenance crew
20 keeping it spotless year round. So there are no conflicts in
21 scheduling, and the natural turf isn't damaged by teams from
22 other sports. They also promote each game as if it were a
23 special event, have plenty of parking space, and keep ticket
24 prices low.
25   Third, they try to keep stable, loyal personnel by taking
26 care of them with generous salaries and benefits, including a
27 profit-sharing plan. Loyalty is rewarded; disloyalty is pun-
28 ished. Former manager Walt Alston operated for twenty-
29 three years under a one-year contract; the vice-president of
30 personnel has been with the team forty-three years; and the
31 present manager, ebullient Tommy Lasorda, has been player,
32 scout, coach, and manager for thirty-four years. On the other
33 hand, one manager who had the nerve to demand a two-year
34 contract was fired, and a player who sang in a night club
35 after begging off from an exhibition tour was traded—in both
36 cases the O'Malleys were reacting to disloyalty to the team.
37 For loyal team members, though, the organization is one big,
38 supportive family. The team has its own private jet, which is
39 very convenient for the players and managers, as it lets them
40 be home more.
41   Fourth, the organization is departmentalized for the most
42 efficient possible operation. For example, while most teams
43 have only one publicity manager, the Dodgers have separate
44 managers for ticket sales, marketing, and concession sales,
45 and the owners keep hands off the operations of the depart-
46 ments to which they've delegated authority.
47   Finally, operations are standardized and applied to both
48 the main team and its minor league farm teams. The 1954
49 book *The Dodger Way to Play Baseball,* which tells how every
50 player at every level should play his position, ensures stan-
51 dardized operations in all the Dodgers' teams. Last, but not
52 least, the team has developed top-notch players through
53 training and promotion within.

—From *Business* by Leon C. Megginson et al. Copyright © 1985 by D. C. Heath
and Company. Reprinted by permission of the publisher.

13. The first sentence in the second paragraph ("The O'Malleys run ...")
indicates that the author's purpose is
a. to criticize   b. to inform
c. to tell a story   d. to state a problem

14. In developing this passage, the pattern of organization used by the author
can be described as
a. simple listing   b. generalization and example
c. cause and effect   d. statement and clarification

15. In this passage the author shows bias in favor of
a. two-year contracts   b. organizational principles
c. outside interests   d. small towns

16. The word or phrase that identifies the relationship within the sentence that
begins in line 32 ("On the other hand ...") is
a. cause and effect   b. statement and clarification
c. summary   d. contrast

17. What does the sentence beginning in line 25 ("Third, they try ...") do in relation to the sentence beginning in line 18 ("Second, they have ...")?
a. It is analyzed as to where it fits in with similar things mentioned in the
sentence beginning in line 18.
b. It contradicts something that is stated in the sentence beginning in line
18.
c. It gives a specific example of the idea stated in the sentence beginning in
line 18.
d. It indicates that a fact has been added to the ideas expressed in the sentence beginning in line 18.

18. Which one of these statements would the author of this passage support?
a. The Dodgers are a profitable franchise because of a combination of luck
and circumstances.
b. The Dodgers will continue to be a profitable franchise.
c. Any person with substantial money could run a profitable franchise.
d. Running a profitable baseball franchise is a simple matter.

PASSAGE 4

1 When Professor Wiley decided it was time to get a locked
2 home office for his consulting, it seemed a simple enough
3 matter to call in professionals to design and construct one in
4 his attic. He had no idea of the steps involved and just want-
5 ed the thing done efficiently and well. He rang up Paul Par-
6 due, president of Gulf Coast Construction Company, a small

7 new firm that had advertised in a local newspaper. Pardue
8 estimated the job at $2,000 (allowing for $700 gross profit)
9 and said it would be finished in five days. No problem!
10   Bob and Joe were assigned to the job. They arrived at
11 Professor Wiley's home bright and early, ready to go. All they
12 needed was an extension cord for their electric saw. "No prob-
13 lem," said Joe, who returned to the firm's office for the cord
14 while Bob waited. Checking in early that afternoon, the pro-
15 fessor was thrilled with the progress. The subflooring was
16 already in place. Being curious, he asked what type of insula-
17 tion they'd used under the subflooring. "Insulation? You
18 wanted insulation? Well, no problem," they drawled. After a
19 phone call to Mr. Pardue, Bob and Joe took up the subflooring
20 and left for the day.
21   Early the next afternoon, after installing the insulation
22 and putting back the subflooring, they began paneling the
23 inside of the office. Up to a point. They ran out of paneling; so
24 both went to a building supply store to buy more and then
25 quit early.
26   The next day, with an edge of justifiable homicide in his
27 voice, Professor Wiley inquired about *wall* insulation. No
28 problem. The panels came down, and Bob went out to buy
29 insulation and more paneling to install. The air conditioning
30 ducts were the next item to pose no problem for the intrepid
31 builders. Another phone call, another trip to buy insulation.
32   And it was no real problem that the door was installed the
33 wrong way, with the wrong doorknob (without a lock). Bob
34 and Joe just removed them, bought new ones, and reinstalled
35 them.
36   Three weeks later, the door still wouldn't lock, the office
37 wasn't finished, the costs had risen to $2,300, and Paul Par-
38 due couldn't understand what the problem was. Two months
39 later he declared bankruptcy.

    —From Megginson et al., *Business.*

19. The phrase in this passage that best illustrates the main idea in the passage, that lack of planning brings disaster, is which of these?

a. "no problem"   b. estimated the job

c. a simple enough matter   d. efficiently and well

20. In developing this passage, the pattern of organization used by the author can be described as

a. comparison   b. classification

c. statement and clarification   d. definition

21. The sentence beginning in line 32 of this passage ("And it was no ...") is a statement of

a. fact   b. opinion

22. The author of this passage has created a feeling that could be described as

a. prayerful   b. loving

c. excited   d. cynical

23. From this passage you could infer that Professor Wiley

a. will do his own remodeling from now on

b. will never again do any home remodeling

c. will not be willing to hire Gulf Coast Construction Company again

d. will be willing to hire Gulf Coast Construction Company again

PASSAGE 5

1 At night the land loses its heat more quickly than the water
2 and the air over the water is warmer. The convection cycle is
3 then reversed and at night a land breeze blows. Sea and land
4 breezes are sometimes referred to respectively as onshore
5 and offshore winds.
6   This local heating effect is also experienced in mountain
7 valleys. During the day the air in contact with the mountain
8 slopes heats up and rises, producing a valley breeze. At night
9 the slopes cool faster than the air at the same elevation over
10 the valley, and the cool air descends the slopes, giving rise to
11 a mountain breeze.
12   The heating effect that produces thermal circulation also
13 applies on a large scale. Seasonal heating and cooling of large
14 continental land masses initiate convection cycles. In the
15 summer the air over the heated continents rises, creating
16 low-pressure areas into which air flows. In winter, high-pres-
17 sure areas exist over the continents and air flows outward
18 toward the warmer low-pressure areas over the oceans.
19   The winds of these cycles are most pronounced on the
20 Asian continent and are called monsoons (Arabic *mausin,*
21 season). During the summer, sea air moves toward the heated
22 continent and is called the summer monsoon. As the moist
23 sea air travels inland toward the mountains, precipitation
24 occurs. The sea wind or summer monsoon is associated with
25 the wet season in southern and eastern Asia. In the winter
26 the cycle is reversed, and then a cold dry wind blows from the

27 mountains toward the sea. This prevailing land wind is called
28 the winter monsoon.
29   Other local winds depend on the local geography and
30 acquire names particular to that area. An example of such a
31 wind is the chinook, or "snow-eater," experienced on the east-
32 ward slopes of the Rocky Mountains. Similar winds are called
33 föhns in the Alps. The winds from the Pacific Ocean blow
34 toward and up the westward slopes of the Rockies. Since the
35 temperature decreases with altitude, much of the moisture is
36 lost as rain or snow on the westward slopes and near the top
37 of the mountains. As a result, dry air descends the eastern
38 slopes, becoming warm with descent. This chinook wind of
39 warm, dry air may cause a rapid rise in temperature and a
40 quick melting of the winter snow, hence the name "snow-
41 eater."

> —From *An Introduction to Physical Science,* 5th edition, by James T. Shipman
> et al. Copyright © 1987 by D. C. Heath and Company. Reprinted by permission
> of the publisher.

24. In this passage all these are names given for winds *except*

    a. chinook   b. "snow-eater"

    c. thermals   d. monsoons

25. The sentence beginning in line 25 of this passage ("In the winter the ...") is a statement of

    a. fact   b. opinion

26. The author of this passage creates a tone that can be described as

    a. frustrated   b. uneasy

    c. professional   d. indignant

27. The word or phrase that identifies the relationship within the sentence beginning in line 19 ("The winds of ...") is

    a. contrast   b. definition

    c. generalization and example   d. comparison

28. What does the sentence beginning in line 19 ("The winds of ...") do in relation to the sentence beginning in line 16 ("In winter ...")?

    a. It alters the meaning of something stated in the sentence beginning in line 16.

    b. It contradicts something stated in the sentence beginning in line 16.

    c. It summarizes something stated in the sentence beginning in line 16.

    d. It specifies clearly the meaning of something mentioned in the sentence beginning in line 16.

PASSAGE 6

1 General Electric has found robots far more productive in
2 some work than human workers. In one case, a robot saved
3 enough to pay for itself in ten months. At Ford Motor Compa-
4 ny, about fifty small robots are deftly fitting lightbulbs into
5 dashboards and speakers into car radios.
6   The next phase of the computer revolution may well turn
7 out to be the robot revolution. Robots have been fixtures in
8 comedy and science fiction for a long time, but the first indus-
9 trial robot wasn't used in the United States until 1961.
10 Industrial robots scarcely resemble the stereotyped
11 humanoid with flashing eyes and a control-panel chest.
12 They're basically just combinations of a computer with very
13 deft and efficient producing machines. What's really new, of
14 course, is the extent to which these electronic wonders are
15 transforming the way people work and the composition of the
16 work force, especially in Japan. There are about 36,000
17 robots working in Japan and approximately 6,500 in the
18 United States. In early 1982, Raymond Donovan, U.S. Secre-
19 tary of Labor, predicted that by 1990 half the workers in U.S.
20 factories would be specialists trained to service and repair
21 robots.
22   It's easy to see why these "steel-collar workers" can be
23 preferable to their human counterparts. They cause fewer
24 personnel problems: they're never absent, and they never ask
25 for more holidays, take vacations, or file grievances. They
26 also give more consistent attention to quality control, are
27 more efficient and effective performers, and are definitely
28 cheaper to keep. Robots, which cost about $30,000 to
29 $150,000 each, usually work two shifts a day. The displaced
30 workers would draw salaries and benefits of about $790,000 a
31 year. However, robots still cannot replace all facets of the
32 human worker. The automated factory is feasible, but when it
33 comes to reason and informed decisions, robots are still in the
34 same league with machines, at least for now.

—From Megginson et al., *Business*.

29. The subject in this passage is
    a. the automated factory   b. robot workers
    c. the computer revolution   d. robot vs. human being

30. The details given in lines 16–18 ("There are about ...") do which of these?

    a. Illustrate the technical superiority of Japanese technology over American technology.

    b. Show the growth in acceptance of robot workers worldwide.

    c. Demonstrate the need to catch up with Japanese technology.

    d. Warn against the possibility that robot workers will displace human workers.

31.   In line 4 the word *deftly* means

    a. slowly   b. correctly

    c. skillfully   d. expensively

32.   The first sentence in this passage ("General Electric has ...") indicates that the author's purpose is

    a. to compare   b. to defend an idea

    c. to evaluate   d. to criticize

33.   In this passage the author shows bias in favor of

    a. General Electric   b. Ford Motor Company

    c. steel-collar workers   d. more factory personnel

34.   The sentence beginning in line 7, "Robots have been fixtures in comedy and science fiction for a long time, but the first industrial robot wasn't used in the United States until 1961" is

    a. valid   b. invalid

35.   The writer of this passage probably

    a. feels threatened by robots

    b. believes robots make manufacturing much easier

    c. wants to see more robots employed in factories

    d. sees a role for both robot and human factory workers

PASSAGE 7

1 Each year approximately 8,000 infants in the United States
2 die, apparently the victims of Sudden Infant Death Syndrome
3 (SIDS), or crib death (so-called because it often occurs during
4 sleep). SIDS is the most common cause of death for infants
5 between 1 week and 1 year of age. More infants die of SIDS
6 than of cystic fibrosis, leukemia, cancer, heart disease, and
7 child abuse combined. Not only in the United States but
8 worldwide, statistics reveal that 1 out of 350 infants dies of
9 this condition.
10   SIDS has probably occurred since biblical times, although
11 our awareness and understanding of the extent of this fatal

12 condition is only recent. Researchers now know that the peak
13 incidence is among infants 2 to 3 months of age and that
14 SIDS is more likely to occur during the winter months. Near-
15 ly all SIDS deaths occur while the infant is quietly asleep. No
16 crying or noisy struggle precedes the death, which can hap-
17 pen unnoticed even if the parents are sleeping in the same
18 room.
19   Male infants are at greater risk for crib death than
20 females. And, although crib death can strike any child, and
21 most victims are well-cared-for and well-nourished infants,
22 the incidence of SIDS is higher among poor families. It is also
23 higher among babies born prematurely or who are of low
24 birth weight and among babies born to women who smoked
25 heavily or were seriously anemic during pregnancy. In addi-
26 tion, SIDS is more likely to occur in infants who have a cold
27 or a runny nose and to infants who are bottle fed rather than
28 breastfed. These characteristics, which have been found to be
29 common among infants who have succumbed to SIDS, enable
30 us to identify infants who are at high risk for SIDS so that
31 special attention can be given to them for its prevention.
32   The prevention of SIDS, while not yet entirely possible, is
33 dependent on researchers' attempts to isolate its causes.
34 Numerous theories have been advanced to explain the condi-
35 tion. For example, botulism (acute food poisoning) appears to
36 be the cause of some cases of SIDS, and there may also be a
37 genetic explanation, as a baby born in a family where an
38 infant has died of SIDS may wake up from sleep less often
39 than do most other babies, suggesting that he maybe vulner-
40 able to SIDS.
41   Some researchers also note that SIDS could be related to
42 a subtle damage to the body's respiratory control center,
43 which is located in the brainstem. This damage usually
44 occurs during the prenatal period due to a drop in maternal
45 blood pressure, maternal anemia, or cigarette smoking by the
46 mother during pregnancy, and it is suspected to be a problem
47 in babies who are born prematurely.
48   Researchers are also investigating the possibility that
49 *apnea,* the temporary cessation of breathing common in pre-
50 mature infants, is the cause of SIDS. Researchers believe
51 that brief apneic pauses during sleep are predictive of longer,
52 potentially fatal pauses. An apnea monitor is used to prevent
53 SIDS in infants with apnea. The monitor is attached to the
54 infant's thorax during sleep and records respiratory activity.
55 If no respiration occurs for 20 seconds, an alarm is set off,

56 and the person responding must initiate respiration, usually
57 by gently shaking the infant.

—From *Children: Development and Social Issues* by Edward F. Zigler and Matia
Finn-Stevenson. Copyright © 1987 by D. C. Heath and Company. Reprinted
by permission of the publisher.

36.   The main idea in this passage is that
   a. Male infants are at greater risk of SIDS than females.
   b. The causes of sudden infant death syndrome are still unknown.
   c. More infants die of SIDS than of cystic fibrosis, leukemia, cancer, heart
      disease, and child abuse combined.
   d. Premature babies are prone to SIDS.

37.   As used in the last paragraph in this passage, the word *apnea* means
   a. irregular waking and falling asleep again
   b. inability to stay asleep for long periods
   c. taking deep breaths while sleeping
   d. temporary cessation of breathing

38.   In developing this passage, the pattern of organization used by the author
   can be described as
   a. time order   b. comparison
   c. summary   d. statement and clarification

39.   The word or phrase that identifies the relationship within the sentence
   beginning in line 5 ("More infants die ...") is
   a. comparison   b. classification
   c. definition   d. cause and effect

40.   What does the sentence beginning in line 25 ("In addition ...") do in relation
   to the sentence beginning in line 22 ("It is also ...")?
   a. It indicates a subsequent effect of something discussed in the sentence
      beginning in line 22.
   b. It indicates the order of something referred to in the sentence beginning
      in line 22.
   c. It contradicts a statement made in the sentence beginning in line 22.
   d. It indicates a fact that has been added to the sentence beginning in line
      22.

PASSAGE 8

1 At age thirteen, J. R. Simplot had a fight with his father,
2 quit the eighth grade, and moved into a boardinghouse. He
3 then worked on canals and sorted potatoes until he'd saved

4 enough money to buy 700 hogs, which he traded in to buy
5 some potato fields and machinery. Next came a newfangled
6 electric potato sorter, which was to be the foundation of his
7 business, the J. R. Simplot Company.
8   The family-owned business, which he controls, is now run
9 by a management team that includes his four children and a
10 son-in-law. The firm sells frozen french fries and other potato
11 products to fast-food chains, and expected annual sales to top
12 $1 billion.
13   According to Simplot, his success comes from guts, hustle,
14 rugged individualism, and hanging on when things were
15 tough. He still lives in what he calls a "comfortable old
16 shack," although he has a posh high-rise office near Boise,
17 Idaho. And his red Continental sports a license plate that
18 reads "MR SPUD." This whole empire was founded on his
19 personal motto, "When the time is right you got to *do* it."
20 Simplot has a dashing style; he scorns formalities and
21 embraces quick, decisive action. He avoids red tape and
22 group decisions as if they were potato blight. (He says he
23 never held a staff meeting when he was president of the firm,
24 which was until 1973.) His first food-processing contract "was
25 written on the back of an envelope with a guy I met while
26 waiting to collect a debt in California." He used the same
27 approach in the early 1960s to get a contract to sell frozen
28 french fries, on which he held the patent, to Ray Kroc, who
29 was just starting a hamburger chain. After spending the
30 night at Kroc's California home, they shook hands and the
31 deal was set—for Simplot to supply the first string of McDon-
32 ald's restaurants.

—From Megginson et al., *Business*.

41. The subject in this passage is
    a. family owned businesses   b. a potato empire
    c. the success of J. R. Simplot   d. McDonald's restaurants

42. The details given in lines 10–12 ("The firm sells …") do which of these?
    a. provide evidence in support of a conclusion
    b. show the money that can be made from potatoes
    c. assist readers searching for potential employment
    d. define the ideas that have been stated

43. The sentence beginning in line 13 of this passage ("According to Simplot, his …") is a statement of
    a. fact   b. opinion

44. The author of this passage creates a tone that can be described as
   a. pessimistic
   b. prayerful
   c. optimistic
   d. incredulous

PASSAGE 9

1 From the beginning of the world until 1980 or so, there were
2 maybe a million computers. Since then, more than that have
3 been sold every year—some 20,000 Apple units alone have
4 been delivered each month. By the end of this decade, com-
5 puters may be selling at the rate of nearly 11 million a year.
6 According to a 1984 study by the U.S. Commerce Depart-
7 ment, worldwide sales of software alone could reach $55 bil-
8 lion by 1987—representing a 30% *annual* increase since
9 1983. International Data Corporation estimates that there
10 will be 400 million computers in the United States by the
11 turn of the century. Despite periodic setbacks (in a single
12 week early in 1985, IBM ended production of the failed PCjr,
13 Apple temporarily closed down its Macintosh production
14 facilities due to massive overstocks, and Wang also declared a
15 one-month halt in production), growing sales and expanding
16 markets seem inevitable.
17   That optimistic view is a matter of simple economics: as
18 the price of something desirable gets lower, the volume of its
19 sales increases as the number of people who can afford it
20 becomes larger. The computer industry's costs are dropping
21 rapidly: in 1982, a 64K chip wholesaled for $10; by 1985, its
22 price was less than $2. And the savings are, as they say,
23 passed on to the consumer.
24   A hand-held computer cost over $150 in 1980, about $75
25 in 1985, and will cost about $20 in 1990. By then, a tiny but
26 powerful programmable computer, costing less than a clock-
27 radio, could be connected to equally inexpensive peripherals
28 to form the core of a home computer system. With such a sys-
29 tem, less expensive than the average stereo-television console
30 of today, cable TV subscribers could access their bank's elec-
31 tronic banking service to pay bills, make rent or mortgage
32 payments, make deposits and withdrawals, or secure loans.
33 Users could "thumb through" store catalogs on their video
34 monitor, order items and arrange deliveries, even "window
35 shop" whole malls to make price comparisons, to search out
36 special sales, or to look for gift ideas. Newspapers,

37 magazines, sports scores, and financial news could all be
38 accessed directly from the average middle-class living room.

—From *Computers and Applications* by Daniel Slotnick et al. Copyright © 1986
by D. C. Heath and Company. Reprinted by permission of the publisher.

45. The main idea in this passage can be stated as
a. The price of computers is continuing to decrease.
b. Uses of computers continue to expand.
c. The computer industry's costs are dropping rapidly.
d. The expanding market for computers is inevitable.

46. This passage suggests that all these are factors in the continued increase in computer sales *except*
a. declining cost of computers
b. declining cost of chips
c. increase in uses for computers
d. increase in trained computer users

47. In line 38 the word *accessed* means
a. approached   b. desired
c. counted   d. destroyed

48. The third sentence in this passage (line 4, "By the end ...") indicates that the author's purpose is
a. to classify   b. to offer a solution
c. to present new information d. to persuade

49. In this passage the author shows bias against
a. lower prices for computers   b. higher prices for computers
c. computer "window shopping"   d. computers

50. The statement in lines 24 and 25 that "a hand-held computer cost over $150 in 1980, about $75 in 1985, and ... about $20 in 1990" is
a. valid   b. invalid

17

Chapter 1

Quick Tips for Mastering Reading and Reading Tests

'Tis the good reader that makes the good book.
> —Ralph Waldo Emerson

What does it matter if we have a new book or an old book, if we open neither?
> —Jesse Jackson

Reading without thinking gives one a disorderly mind, and thinking without reading makes one unbalanced.
> —Confucius

This chapter will help you to:

1. know how *not* to read and mark textbooks and study material.
2. read with a pen in your hand.
3. pace yourself for efficient reading.
4. mark the margins as you read without losing comprehension.
5. anticipate and prepare for reading-test questions.
6. benefit from the techniques called skimming, scanning, and glancing.

How Do You Feel about Reading?

We often don't give the subject of reading much thought. It is just something that we do. Answer these questions quickly and without giving your answers much thought until you have answered all the questions.

19

1. Do you like some things about reading?

    Yes   No

    What are they? ....

    ....

2. Do you not like some things about reading?

    Yes   No

    What are they? ....

    ....

3. Are you a good reader?

    Yes   No

    Why do you think so? ....

    ....

4. Can you read if you don't have a book?

    Yes   No

    Why? ....

    Why not? ....

5. What things do we have to learn how to do to be good readers? ....

    ....

6. What is reading? ....

    ....

7. Why do you read? ....

    ....

8. Would you read if you didn't have to? ....

    ....

9. What is a "good" reader? ....

    ....

10. Do you want to be a good reader?

    Yes   No

    Why or why not? ....

    ....

Look over your answers carefully. Do your answers give you any idea about your attitude toward reading? What is your attitude? How would you describe it? How will your attitude affect your attempts to improve your skill in reading comprehension in this course?

....

....

....

....

....

Students fail to do well in reading college textbooks and on tests of reading comprehension for many reasons. The cause may be failure to decode or understand words used, inability to explain or remember, inability to follow directions, insufficient vocabulary, lack of interest in the material, complexity of syntax, complexity in ideas and their relations. Perhaps failure to do well on a test is a fault built into the test.

Most tests of reading comprehension follow an outline of specific skills that can be measured with some objectivity, such as the skills you will study in this book.

In the twelve chapters that follow you will learn and practice twelve specific skills in reading comprehension, skills that will enable you to become a much more efficient reader and also to score higher on tests you take in college.

In addition to these twelve specific reading skills, you are about to develop several general techniques for reading which will also improve your efficiency in reading and which are especially useful in *taking tests* and *mastering textbooks* in any subject. These general skills apply equally to everything you read in your day-to-day college studies and assignments. The best students—the "super students"—know and successfully use these techniques for everything they read. If you follow these tips and practices as you use this book, you will find that your reading skills improve dramatically.

Prereading Activities in This Textbook

Did you know that one very serviceable function of writing is to clarify your thinking? Writing helps pull out of our background our experience and embedded knowledge about a subject, our *schema*, creating a framework to which we can attach new information and experiences. Writing about material we are learning, even before we have fully learned it, makes us more sensitive to information and experiences that we will later confront. We are thus better able to deal with subjects and their influence on our lives.

21

Writing to comprehend also is a powerful way of comprehending and retaining useful ideas. Writing about our reading develops in us *active* reading skills and enables us to better understand and interact with writers and the ideas they write about. Each chapter in this text employs writing-to-comprehend activities, usually near the beginning of the chapter.

We want you to feel how useful the prereading, writing, and discussion activities in each chapter can be, and to see that participating fully in them can be helpful. Anything you think about, you can talk about; anything you say, you can write; anything you can write, you can read; and anything you can read can be meaningful.

Any ideas that you read that are meaningful to you increase your "reading edge."

Writing to Comprehend

Write a brief response to these questions. Because we ask for your impressions, no response is right or wrong.

1. What qualities (of any kind) have you noticed that seem to describe your friends or acquaintances who are efficient readers? Are these efficient readers always superior students? Why or why not? What things might cause an efficient reader to be a poor student at times?

   ....
   ....
   ....
   ....
   ....

2. What reading shortcuts, tricks, or techniques have you seen employed, or have you used yourself, which seem to help people read faster, understand more fully, or remember longer? Describe them and tell how they seemed to work.

   ....
   ....
   ....

3. How do you think *glancing* at the reading passages to locate words and their contexts will affect your comprehension later as you read the passages and answer the questions? How does *anticipating* the topics in the reading passages affect your comprehension and retention?

....

....

....

....

....

How Not to Read in College

Before you learn improved ways of reading, understand that no longer will you be reading in the way you probably always have. For most of us, our old reading pattern is just too inefficient. It may be comfortable; it may be familiar; it may be *easy;* but it is no longer useful if you are going to make the most of your reading time in college.

The way in which you no longer want to read is to simply begin on the first page of the assignment and read through to the last page, using a felt-tip pen to underline the things that strike you as worth remembering. That may be the way in which you have always read your assignments, but you will no longer use it. Now you will have a better way. Try the following tips immediately. Put them into practice as you learn them and while you are reading this book.

How You Should Read Everything

These efficient reading techniques can be applied to everything you read from now on, including any tests or examinations that require you to read a passage and answer questions about it.

Tip 1: Always Read with a Pen in Your Hand

Trust me on this one for now. Just grab a pen—preferably one with a narrow, felt-tip point—and hold it as if you were planning to write. In the next several paragraphs you will see how having the pen in your hand as you read will increase both your speed and comprehension in reading. If you haven't yet grabbed the pen, do so now, and then read the next efficiency tip.

Tip 2: As You Read, Pace Yourself

The world's most efficient readers know it helps to pace themselves as they read, adjusting their pace so that they can increase their speed, their concentration, and their comprehension of the material they are reading.

Pacing while you read may be done in several ways, but probably this way is the easiest and the best. In pacing you simply make a left-to-right movement with the pen you hold in your hand across the page, along each line you are reading and from line to line. This pacing movement directs and "pulls" your eyes along each line at a steady speed (or *pace*) without the jerky, regressive eye movements that we all adopt as we are learning to read. You are not marking or underlining with your pen. It is simply acting as a pointer for your eyes, a moving target to follow. Your eyes will follow the pacer's motion at a faster than normal (but still comfortable and efficient) speed. In reading acceleration (speed-reading) classes, expensive reading machines and other devices are often employed as pacers to get you to move your eyes faster and more *steadily* across the lines, but you really don't need these machines to accomplish the same thing. You can just as effectively—and probably much more efficiently—use the pen in your hand to accomplish the same acceleration.

TRY IT NOW

Pacing is really very simple, and perhaps you are already doing it. If not, try it now as you are reading this book. Simply hold the pen as if you were going to write, but instead of writing use the pen as a pointer when you read. Don't touch the page with the pen, but move its tip slightly ahead of your eyes. This steady left-to-right motion will pull your eyes along the line to keep up with the moving pen point.

Keep in mind, though, that you aren't just moving your hand and your eyes; you are *reading*. Don't pace yourself any faster than your ability to comprehend the ideas you are reading. If you find that you are zipping along but don't know what you're reading, you are going too fast. Slow down. Let your comprehension determine how fast you should pace yourself.

As you reach the end of a line, simply flick the pen back to the beginning of the next line and start moving along that line. This mechanical trick will very quickly develop into a rhythmic pattern of reading that does a lot to eliminate the choppy, start–stop, unthinking, regressive backtracking pattern that most of us employ. You may stop, back up, and reread, however, if you do not understand what you are reading. That's not regression; it is recognizing that you don't understand, and you want to keep doing so whenever necessary. It is a sign that you are aware of when you are comprehending and when you are not. After a few weeks of practicing with pacing on everything you read, you will find that your rate of reading has increased and your comprehension has significantly improved.

An increase in comprehension should not surprise you. Reading without a pacer is a *mental* exercise subject to many distractions. Reading with a pacer becomes a *mental and physical* act. When you are physically involved (pacing yourself with eye–hand coordination) you will find that you are concentrating much more on the material you are reading.

And you'll find it much easier to stay awake while you are reading.

Tip 3: Don't Underline as You Read—Mark the Margins

Now that you are pacing with your pen as you read, you can add yet another high-efficiency reading technique to your growing repertoire of reading skills. You can *mark the passage as you read it*. Should you? Yes and no. Yes, you should get in the habit of selectively marking everything as you read it. *If done correctly,* marking a book while you read it helps comprehension and, at the same time, helps if you have to refer back to the passage later—and you will frequently have to look back at a passage when you take reading tests. But, *no,* you should not mark the passage as you read it if you are simply *underlining* as you read (as you may be doing right now), because underlining can hinder efficient reading, especially on a test that times your performance. Also, you are often not permitted to make marks of *any* kind on a standardized test.

DON'T DO THIS

In high school you probably got in the habit of dragging a felt-tip pen or "highlighter" along the lines as you read. You may have gone halfway through a sentence (you always had to read halfway through a sentence to get some idea of what the sentence was about) and then decided that it might be an important sentence, and so you stopped reading to go back to the beginning of the sentence to underline what you had just read. This procedure interrupts your concentration on the passage you are reading as you stop to do something else, slows you down, and greatly reduces your comprehension and retention. You may even be one of those "neat" underliners who uses a straightedge to make certain that the underlining is neat. Talk about messing up your reading comprehension! You end up doing so many things all at once as you are reading that you may retain very little when you finish. When you are done you have a passage with lots of ink on it, and probably feel you know more about what you just read than you really do. With all that activity, you may have taken much longer to read the material than it deserved.

But you can read faster and mark at the same time without losing comprehension.

Don't underline while you are reading, but instead mark the whereabouts of useful information, or of something that strikes you as potentially worthwhile in a passage by putting a mark or symbol in the *margin* at the end of the line where the information lies. You can do so easily, especially because you are now pacing yourself with a moving hand holding a pen. The technique takes very little effort, and you lose no reading comprehension, for you simply dot or otherwise mark in the margins as you read. You read faster, you avoid ruining your comprehension, and later you can locate information at a glance simply by fanning through the pages as you look at your symbols in the margins. One word of caution: Library books or other books not belonging to you should never be marked. Mark only books that belong to you.

Tip 4: Use Margin Marks

Marking the margins as you read is a very good idea, but with just a little effort you can create specific margin marks that *represent specific things* in the lines opposite the marks. If you create symbols that always represent the same things (those you feel need to be identified in each passage), and then always use those same symbols to mark the margins, you will be able to "read" the margins at a glance to find specific kinds of information without searching haphazardly. This quick reading is especially helpful when you take reading tests, or when you review a text.

You may wish to create your own symbols for the kinds of distinctive information that you need to be able to find, but for now just associate (and memorize) the eleven symbols in the table on page 27. These eleven symbols go with the specific comprehension skills you will cover in this book.

After you have memorized these margin marks and have related each to the competency being tested, start using this system of margin marking. Now, while you are reading this book, make certain that you read with pen in hand, pace yourself, and start marking the margins with the symbols. All eleven symbols can be employed on the material you are reading now, and the more you use this system, the easier it gets. You will soon be able to mark an assigned reading passage or a reading test without consciously thinking about each symbol.

Margin Marks

Competency	Suggested Margin Mark
Literal Comprehension Skills	
1. Main idea	——— (solid line)
2. Details (may be many)	– – – – (broken line)
3. Word meanings (circle new or unusual words)	◯ (circle)
Critical Comprehension Skills	
4. Author's purpose ("the goal is," and so on)	✱ (asterisk)
5. Pattern of organization (cause and effect and so on)	P (the letter P)
6. Fact or opinion (mark only opinion)	O (the letter O)
7. Bias (when obvious)	B (the letter B)
8. Tone (words that indicate attitude)	T (the letter T)
9. Relations *within* sentences	( ) (parentheses)
10. Relations *between* sentences	△ (triangle)
11. Valid or invalid argument (mark only invalid)	∧ (inverted V)
12. Logical inference (if inferred, it is not written, and so no mark)	

This marked passage shows how to employ some of these margin marks.

P✱ One helpful way of building comprehension is to *question before reading.* You must always be conscious of comprehension as you read, and you can best accomplish this understanding by reading with a questioning mind. You've been in situations in which you've been asked to read specific pages in preparing for a class. And you did the reading. But in class, when you were questioned about the content on those pages, it may have seemed that you didn't know much. Has this happened to you? Sure.

△   But how different it was when the teacher asked you to read specific pages and also indicated what it was that you should look for: "Discover the route that Marco Polo took on his journey." "What were the major cities he visited?" "What were the bodies of water he had to cross?" And so on. What a tremendous difference it made when you were questioned on the material. You knew three times as much as you ordinarily knew after reading an assignment.   ○
     ○

     What was the difference? You were reading with a questioning mind. You were reading with a purpose, and not just ○ passively passing your eyes over pages. You must raise questions about your reading material *before* you begin reading. What do you want to get from your reading? What is the thesis or problem in the passage? What is the sequence of ideas? By <u>raising questions</u> like these before you read, you will <u>recognize the answers</u> when you come across them, and you will   —
remember them.

The eleven specific symbols represent the reading comprehension competencies

Examples of Personal Symbols

Item	Margin Mark
Things in a series, in order	① ② and so on
Good quotation	" "
Questionable, puzzling	?
Summary (first one, second one, and so on)	[1] [2] and so on
Strongly agree or disagree	A /D
Check with the professor on this point.	✓
Example, illustration	E
Definition	def
Good exam question	X
Reread later	RR

you are studying in this book, but you may want to memorize and use several other margin marks as you are reading. We encourage you to create your own symbols and use them regularly. A few suggestions for additional margin marks appear in the table on page 28.

Tip 5: Anticipate and Prepare for Reading Test Questions

These successful reading practices are used by the world's best students whenever they read and mark their textbooks and when they take reading tests. Always employ them whenever you take a reading test. If, however, the test booklet is reusable, be certain not to make any marks on it. Check with your professor before beginning a test.

First: Write down the time you are allowed for taking the test. Then, allot your time for each of the reading questions so that you don't spend too much time on any one passage or question.

Second: Often it is a good idea to read the *questions* for each passage *before* you read the passage. *Don't read the answer choices for each question*—the options will only confuse you. By reading the several questions asked about each passage *before* you read it, you will *actively* read (with a questioning mind), looking for specific answers to questions rather than passively plodding through a passage in which everything seems of equal importance.

When you read the questions first, your mind *actively* processes what you read—and you remember it longer. Add your new margin-marking skill to your active processing and you have a highly effective test-taking ability.

Third: Skim, scan, and glance as you read the test passages. If you have a reading passage of more than one paragraph, begin by skimming it.

Skimming is a very simple but effective way of identifying the main idea in a passage. *You read only the first sentence in each paragraph* (often the first sentence is the topic sentence) to get the main idea in the passage. Skimming takes only a few seconds but provides an overview of material you are about to read and often identifies the main idea (usually one of the test questions you are asked to identify), and gives you a framework within which the details make sense as you read the passage. This overview also helps you read faster because the passage seems familiar so that you naturally speed up. Also, by skimming you can later locate information you need to recheck to answer a question without reading the entire passage.

Scanning is another very effective technique that allows you to look for a word, a number, or another *detail* (unlike skimming, with which you look for a main idea). To scan, you must know what you are looking for. You then move your pacer pen in a steady zigzag from the beginning of the pattern down through the paragraph. At the same time, silently repeat to yourself the word or phrase you are looking for. This repetition will heighten your visual perception, and as you pass near the word, it will seem to jump out at you. You will be *passing* words (not reading) at very high speed. Usually several test questions will require you to scan the reading passage in this way to identify specific words.

Glancing is a third skill that will be useful as you read and take tests. Flick your eyes over a passage with no definite movement pattern to get an impression of the passage's internal structure. Glancing is useful when you are asked to determine whether a passage is ordered by time, by cause and effect, or by some other pattern of organization. Often a glance will enable you to spot words such as *first, second, third* or *Monday, Wednesday, Friday,* which indicate patterned organization (in this case, time order).

Fourth: Eliminate immediately any choices that seem unreasonable, irrelevant, or contradictory. Often the test questions include answer choices that are too extreme or give themselves away as illogical or impossible. By removing these at once (and crossing off their letters on your test sheet), you are more likely to pick the correct answer. A guess between two choices stands a better chance of being correct than a guess among four choices. If you are left with two choices, you can approach them as true-false answers, asking, "For this question, would this answer be true or false?" This approach often makes the correct answer clear. Always make sure that you read *all* the answer choices before you pick one, even if you feel strongly that the *first* answer you read is correct. You are looking for the *best* answer, not simply a possible one.

Fifth: Answer all the questions for each reading selection before you move on to the next selection. If you don't know the answer, waste no time struggling with it. Make an educated guess and select one of the answers. At the same time, however, put a question mark in the margin next to the question. If you have extra time, you can easily spot it and come back to it. Remember that you are usually not penalized for guessing—answer all the questions.

What Are Your Thoughts?

1. How can improved skill in reading comprehension be used in your college courses, and what difference should it make?

....

....

....

2. Pacing yourself seems awkward when you first try it, but can you imagine a time in the future when you might be able to pace yourself without even thinking about it? When will that be? What will you have to do to get to that stage?

....

....

....

3. What benefits may come from learning to read more efficiently while you learn to mark the margins in the material you are reading with a symbol system that identifies the location of useful information?

....

....

....

4. How can these marked margins in your textbooks help you later? At the end of the semester?

....

....

....

5. Can you think of any margin-mark symbols that may be appropriate for your courses in art, music, mathematics, biology, literature, business, chemistry, and so on?

....

....

....

6. Can you think of any way to "mark" the margins in books that don't belong to you (library books, borrowed books, and so on) without actually marking them? How about marking on a sheet of paper placed next to the book? Why not mark on those little yellow self-adhesive slips of paper that can be stuck on the page temporarily?

....

....

....

7. What is the relation between knowing good reading and test-taking strategies, and being well prepared on the material on which you are being tested?

....

....

....

8. Just what are the differences among skimming, scanning, and skipping? Can you think of useful applications for each of these techniques?

....

....

....

Words to Read by

By scanning the reading passages that follow, locate the words listed below on the pages indicated. Suggest a definition for each word as it was used in the passage and write it on the lines provided. If you cannot come up with a definition from the context and use of a word, look it up in the dictionary and write the dictionary definition on the lines. Be ready to discuss how you arrived at your definition for each word.

Even though you have not yet read the passages, what information do you think will be in these readings? Next to each word you define, jot down a topic or two that you think may be touched on in the reading.

adolescents (page 37) ....

....

thalidomide (page 37) ....

....

ironically (page 38) ....

....

invulnerable (page 38) ....

....

megaton (page 38) ....

dispersed (page 38) ....

deterrent (page 38) ....

payloads (page 38) ....

saturation (page 39) ....

butcher (page 40) ....

establishment (page 40) ....

bankrupt (page 40) ....

entrepreneurs (page 40) ....

theory (pages 35, 41) ....

serendipitous (page 41) ....

acquisitions (page 41) ....

renovation (page 42) ....

elaborate (page 42) ....

Compare your definitions with those at the end of this chapter.

Practice Exercises

EXERCISE 1

In these sentences, fill in the word or phrase that is missing. The first one is done for you.

1. In this book ..*12*.. skills in reading comprehension are taught that will enable you to become a more efficient reader.

2. You are encouraged always to read with a .... in your hand.

3. Creating a left-to-right movement across the page, along each line, and from line to line is called ....

4. As you read, you should let your .... determine how fast you pace yourself.

5. It is not uncommon for students to .... their reading speed and .... their comprehension after practicing pacing for a few weeks.

6. Underlining as you read can be a .... to efficient reading.

7. Highlighting or underlining as you read slows you down and reduces your ....

8. .... the margins is a good alternative to underlining as you read.

9. Margin marking as you read helps you quickly .... information at a glance on a later occasion.

10. Instead of .... you may wish to use symbols in the margins that go with specific kinds of information you are trying to locate.

EXERCISE 2

This short passage entitled "Origin" is from a science textbook. Without glancing at the reading passage, speculate about the information you think will be included in the reading. Identify at least four topics that you think may be the subject in this passage.

1. ....

2. ....

3. ....

4. ....

Now read the selection. When you are finished, answer these two questions.

5. Did you guess correctly for any of your four topics?

....

6. How did this speculating about ideas that would be covered affect your interest in what you read, your comprehension while you were reading, and your retention after you finished reading?

....

....

ORIGIN

The origin of the atmosphere is generally associated with the origin of the Earth, which is some four to five billion years old. There are several theories of cosmogony that attempt to explain the origin of the universe. Without speculating on the validity of any one theory, it is generally agreed that at the time of the creation of our solar system, the planets were extremely hot masses, since their creation by any means would require enormous amounts of energy.

In the beginning, then, the Earth was a molten mass surrounded by hot gases, probably methane, ammonia, and hydrogen compounds. Because of their high temperatures and inherent kinetic energy, large amounts of these gases escaped into space. As the Earth cooled, gases that were dissolved in the molten mass were released, giving rise to H_2O, N_2, and CO_2 in our atmosphere. The water vapor condensed and reevaporated, causing cooling and solidification of the Earth's crust with subsequent erosion and formation of bodies of water. The gases cooled along with the planet and, being then less energetic, were retained by gravitational attraction. At this time, life began to appear.

How life occurred is still a mystery. However, scientists have shown that the fundamental building blocks of life, the amino acids, can be constructed from combinations of methane, hydrogen, ammonia, and water, all of which were available on the cooling Earth. (See the Miller-Urey experiment.) In any event, the appearance of plant life allowed the formation of oxygen and the evolution of animal life. Plants produce oxygen by photosynthesis, the process by which CO_2 and H_2O are converted into sugars (carbohydrates) and O_2, using the energy from the Sun.

The key to photosynthesis is the ability of chlorophyll, the green pigment in plants, to convert sunlight into chemical energy. In chemical notation, the photosynthesis process may be expressed

$$(n)\ CO_2 + (n)\ H_2O \xrightarrow[\text{chlorophyll}]{\text{sunlight}} (CH_2O)_n + (n)\ O_2$$

where the n's indicate the numbers that balance the chemical equation. Photosynthesis accounts for the liberation of approximately 130 billion tons of oxygen into the air annually, with some 2000 billion tons of CO_2 being involved in the process. Over one-half of the photosynthesis takes place in the oceans, which contain many forms of green plants. Originally, oxygen may also have come from the dissociation of water.

—From *Reading Comprehension*, 2d edition, by John D. McNeil. Copyright © 1987, 1984 by Scott, Foresman and Company. Reprinted by permission.

EXERCISE 3

Place each margin-mark symbol next to the skill it represents. Remember, one of the comprehension skills doesn't have a symbol. Do you remember why? The first one is done for you.

Skills	Margin Marks
——— **1.** main idea	$\wedge$
……… **2.** details	G
……… **3.** word meanings	T
……… **4.** author's purpose	———
……… **5.** pattern of organization	– – – –
……… **6.** fact or opinion	$*$
……… **7.** bias	( )
……… **8.** tone	B
……… **9.** relationship *within* sentence	$\triangle$
……… **10.** relationship *between* sentences	O
……… **11.** valid or invalid arguments	P
……… **12.** logical inference	

EXERCISE 4

On these reading selections use the suggested symbols and mark the margins *as you read*. Don't stop and reread, just read through once, marking as you go.

Then, compare your marking with the marked passage at the end of the chapter. Is your passage marked in the same way as the passage in the answers at the end of the chapter? If you have trouble with any comprehension skill, don't worry about it. With practice you will soon thoroughly understand the skills and how to employ them efficiently as you read. In the mean time, this margin marking can be a very useful skill, especially when you are being tested on material that you read.

Do you remember what these margin-marking symbols represent? Remind yourself by looking back at page 27 if you don't remember.

1. RUNAWAY YOUTHS

The problem of runaway youths has become a major national concern. About 500,000 adolescents run away from home each year. They are ill-equipped to fend for themselves adequately, and in many cases they are only 12 to 14 years old, which means they cannot legally hold a job. Even if they were capable of holding their own in the world, their opportunity to do so is slim since pimps and hustlers await them in the bus stations of cities they are running to. They lure the unsuspecting teens by promising them food, shelter, and money, but they then torture them physically and emotionally, forcing them into submission and putting them to work as prostitutes or in pornographic movies. This is true for both girls and boys, but it is especially prevalent among boys, who become prostitutes for homosexuals. These adolescents suffer untold damage to their minds and bodies and cannot escape the terrible situation they are in as they are constantly watched and, in effect, held hostage by those who took them off the streets.

> —From Zigler and Finn-Stevenson, *Children: Development and Social Issues.*

2. THE FAILURE TO TEST

There are about 8,000 young adults who are living testimony to the importance of checking for the potential side effects of a scientific breakthrough— their mothers were given the sedative thalidomide during the first 3 months of pregnancy. The German inventor of thalidomide, Chemie Grunenthal, did not test the effect of the drug on pregnant animals prior to distributing it. Nonetheless, some distributors claimed—in the absence of supportive evidence—that thalidomide could be given with complete safety to pregnant women with no negative side effects on the mother or the child. Women who took thalidomide produced severely deformed or retarded children.

The detective work involved in the discovery of the link between these birth defects and thalidomide is described in a fascinating book, *Suffer the Children: The Story of Thalidomide.* The Food and Drug Administration (FDA), often accused of being overly conservative, refused to permit the sale of thalidomide in the United States. Ironically, the American distributor for Grunenthal threatened to bring a libel suit against Dr. Francis Kelsey, the FDA medical officer most responsible for blocking the sale. Eventually, Grunenthal administered thalidomide to pregnant mice and found that it crossed the placenta. Unfortunately for the thousands of thalidomide babies, this testing was not done until a month *after* thalidomide was withdrawn from the market.

> —From *Sexual Interactions,* 2d edition, by Albert R. Allgeier and Elizabeth R. Allgeier. Copyright © 1986 by D. C. Heath and Company. Reprinted by permission of the publisher.

3.

WEAPONS STOCKPILES

Quite often statistics fail to convey the full meaning intended, but we think the following figures demonstrate clearly why each side has an invulnerable second-strike capability.

The United States had 1,034 solid-fueled Minuteman missiles in 1984. These intercontinental ballistic missiles (ICBMs) travel at speeds in excess of 17,000 miles per hour. This means they can reach any target in the Soviet Union in about thirty minutes. The carry 1.2–9.0 megaton warheads. One megaton is equivalent to the destructive capacity of one million tons of TNT. The atomic bombs dropped on Hiroshima and Nagasaki in World War II were only the equivalent of 20,000 tons of TNT (20 kilotons).

The Minuteman missiles are placed in deep underground silos and encased in reinforced concrete in order to survive any nuclear attack. The solid fuel permits launching within 32 seconds. Most of them are dispersed throughout the western and midwestern United States, making it very difficult to destroy all of them in a surprise attack.

In addition, the United States has 37 Polaris submarines with 16 launching pads each, for a total of 592 missiles. These have one-half to one megaton warheads. The current generation of Poseidon missiles has a range of 3,000 miles. The subs are nuclear powered and can remain submerged for long periods of time (months). Their swiftness, mobility, and concealability make them excellent second-strike forces. They fire their missiles without surfacing, thereby making it very difficult to eliminate them in a surprise attack. They are widely dispersed and follow irregular travel patterns. The primitive state of antisubmarine warfare (ASW) increases their deterrent value.

The United States also has 324 long-range bombers that can fly nonstop to the Soviet Union, drop their nuclear payloads (between 20 and 40 megatons each), and return to their home bases without landing to refuel. About 30 percent of them are kept in a constant state of alert.

Given this quantity, quality, and diversity of weapons and weapons delivery systems, it is highly unlikely that anyone would deliberately launch a nuclear attack against the United States. Even if 90 percent of our strike force were destroyed, the remaining 10 percent is sufficient to inflict horrendous damage on the attacker. The amount of saturation bombing needed to overcome our second-strike force is so great that the attacker would probably be killed by his own fallout.

—From *Systems of Society: An Introduction to Social Sciences*, 4th edition, by Manuel G. Mendoza and Vince Napoli. Copyright © 1986 by D. C. Heath and Company. Reprinted by permission of the publisher.

EXERCISE 5

Place these margin-mark symbols next to the statements they represent. The first one is done for you.

	Statements	Margin Marks
①②	1. things in a series	X
....	2. good quotation	① ②
....	3. questionable, puzzling	[!]
....	4. summary	?
....	5. strongly agree or disagree	RR
....	6. check with the professor	def
....	7. example, illustration	A/D
....	8. definition	E
....	9. good exam question	" "
....	10. reread later	✓

EXERCISE 6

On these reading selections, use the suggested margin symbols *as you read* to identify important information in the readings. Use all the margin symbols you have learned. When you finish, compare your marked passages with the marked passages at the end of the chapter.

1. *The American Dream.* Ben Chase was employed as a butcher in a grocery chain store for ten years. He knew his trade well, worked hard, saved whatever he could, and dreamed of starting a business of his own. His wife, Gertrude, also had a job and added her savings to her husband's. In 1970 they heard of a small slaughtering and meat-packing establishment that was for sale in a rural area. With their own savings, a loan from a relative, and a loan from a bank, they bought their own business.

   Ben and Gertrude worked hard, sometimes more than 65 hours a week. They were good managers, and they knew how to deal with the farmers and the meat distributors. Their business grew. They had made enough contacts with farmers to ensure a continuing supply, and they had no difficulty in selling everything they could produce. Now semiretired, they own a business worth a million dollars. They have lived the American dream.

   A Different Story. When George Morris returned from military service, he got a job in a men's clothing store. He worked for two years learning many aspects of the business. At the end of that time he made the decision to go into business for himself. For $20,000, he bought a rundown store in a poor business location. His own savings and a loan from his parents covered $10,000 of the cost; he borrowed the additional $10,000 from a bank.

   George knew that the price of the business was low because much of the merchandise was out of style. However, he believed that as he sold these outdated goods (he had no capital to buy new merchandise and had not established a credit rating yet), he would be able to replace them with the stylish clothing people wanted. He hoped that by marking down the prices on what he had, he could soon clear out his old stock. He also counted on patronage from his many friends.

   Two months after George opened his store, a new men's clothing store, part of a chain, opened three blocks away. Now George's stock of suits that had but a short time ago been in style could not be sold for even a third of its original cost. George did not take in even enough money to pay his rent and his note at the bank. Most of his merchandise was valueless. By the end of one year, George Morris was bankrupt, his store just another among the statistics of business failures.

   In 1984 there were 700,000 new businesses. What new entrepreneurs fail to realize, or choose to ignore, is that the average life expectancy of a business is less than five years, that about 40 percent of all retail businesses last less than two years, and that many businesses that do survive pay their owners less than they could earn by working for someone else. If we define small businesses as those firms employing fewer than 50 persons, then 96 percent of all businesses are small. Yet the importance of small businesses in the nation's economy, together with the uncertainty of operations of many small firms, raises a question as to whether small businesses will continue to be important in our economy.

   —From *Introductory Economics,* 6th edition, by Sanford D. Gordon and

2.   Perhaps the most important advance in our understanding of the geology of the Earth during the twentieth century has been the development of the theory of continental drift and plate tectonics. Alfred Wegener, German meteorologist, in a publication in 1915, presented the concept that about 200 million years ago the present continents were one huge land mass or super-continent, which he called Pangaea. This land mass broke up and drifted apart, leading to present day positions of the continents, which still are slowly moving. Earth scientists have long regarded the Earth as a rigid body, but the discoveries that the Earth's interior may be slowly deformable led to the conclusion that the surface is mobile. The results of geological research in the last 20 years support Wegener's theory. But how could the large separation of the plates take place?

In 1960 Harvey Hess, of Princeton University, proposed that the sea-floor cracks open along the crest of the mid-ocean ridges and that new sea floor forms there and spreads apart. The process is known as sea-floor spreading. Today most geologists support the theory of plate tectonics, which includes continental drift, sea-floor spreading, and subduction.

—From Shipman et al., *An Introduction to Physical Science.*

3.   The main card catalog at the Library of Congress—the rows and rows of massive wooden cabinets that hold 23 million well-thumbed index cards—is gradually becoming obsolete as the library moves toward automation.

Traditionalists worry that they are losing a cherished national institution, a place where scholars can make serendipitous discoveries among the cards and where more than a few romances have started from chance encounters.

Library officials, on the other hand, assert that the evolving computerized catalog is a physical necessity at the world's largest library, which has to add two million index cards each year. The general collection's card catalog, which dates back to 1800, occupies several rooms—about the size of half a city block—and has 22 trays of cards on Shakespeare alone.

Even with increasing automation, the old card catalog will not be abandoned for at least four more years, according to library spokesman Craig D'Ooge, mostly because the cards are being microfilmed. "And it's for certain that as long as there's a need for it, it will be accessible [to] scholars," he said. But it is obvious that the card catalog's days are numbered. In 1981, the catalog was "frozen" so that books obtained after January 2, 1981, were recorded only in the computerized files. And by the end of 1984, virtually all of the library's English-language books were cataloged in the automated system and available to researchers through 40 terminals in the library's reading rooms, according to John W. Kimball, head of the automation and reference collections section in the general reading rooms.

The automation has proceeded on two fronts. Since 1968, the library has cataloged new acquisitions in its machine-readable cataloging (Marc) computer system, and recently the library converted its 1979 list of 5.5 million books into computer format to cover pre-1968 items, in what is called the pre-Marc system.

Consequently, a researcher looking for English-language books on Shakespeare, for example, now could use a computer terminal to find at least 90% of the library's books on the subject, Kimball said ....

The library has about 71 million items now that could be cataloged. "We're talking now about having only cataloged about 7.5 million books in machine-readable form, so we've got a long way to go," Kimball said.

To handle the huge data base, he added, the library will replace its two IBM 3033 mainframes in the next few months "with whatever is equivalent to IBM's best computer now," because the data files simply require faster and more powerful processors ....

The automation projects will continue as the library undergoes a major renovation, to be completed by 1992. By January 1987, Kimball explained, the number of computer terminals will increase to between 75 and 100. The wood cabinets, with their elaborate and historic carvings, will survive as part of the high-tech catalog, Kimball said, by way of some artful carpentry work.

—From Slotnick et al., *Computers and Applications.*

EXERCISE 7

In your own words, and from memory, write brief definitions for these necessary functions. Afterward, check your work by flipping back to the page in this chapter on which the function was defined and see how close your definition is to the original definition. Write the page number on which the definition is given next to your definition. This notation will be helpful to you in class discussions. The first function is defined for you.

1. pacing *moving your finger or pen left to right along each line as you read* .... (page 24)

2. margin mark ....
   .... (page   )

3. skimming ....
   .... (page   )

4. scanning ....
   .... (page   )

5. glancing ....

.... (page   )

Answers to Selected Exercises

WORDS TO READ BY

You will find variation in definitions but they should be similar to these.

adolescents: youth
thalidomide: a drug
ironically: incongruity between that which is expected and that which happens
invulnerable: incapable of being damaged
megaton: explosive force equal to 1 million tons of TNT
dispersed: spread widely
deterrent: something that prevents or discourages
payload: that which is being carried
saturation: completely filled or covered
butcher: a person who cuts up meat as a profession
establishment: the group who control or run society or government
bankrupt: without material assets; legal term
entrepreneurs: people who take chances by starting businesses
theory: statement designed to explain a phenomenon
serendipitous: making valuable discoveries by accident
acquisitions: things acquired
renovation: something restored to an earlier condition
elaborate: go into detail

EXERCISE 3

1. ▬▬   2. – – –   3. ◯   4. ✳

5. P   6. O   7. B   8. T

9. ( )   10. △   11. ∧   12. none

EXERCISE 5

1. ① ②   2. " "   3. ?   4. [ı]

5. A|D   6. ✓   7. E   8. def

9. X   10. RR

EXERCISE 6

1. *The American Dream.* Ben Chase was employed as a butcher in a grocery chain store for ten years. He knew his trade well, worked hard, saved whatever he could, and dreamed of starting a business of his own. His wife, Gertrude, also had a job and added her savings to her husband's. In 1970 they heard of a small slaughtering and meat-packing establishment that was — — — for sale in a rural area. With their own savings, a loan from a relative, and a loan from a bank, they bought their own business.

    Ben and Gertrude worked hard, sometimes more than 65 hours a week. They were good managers, and they knew how to deal with the farmers and △ the meat distributors. Their business grew. They had made enough contacts with farmers to ensure a continuing supply, and they had no difficulty in selling everything they could produce. Now semiretired, they own a business worth a million dollars. They have lived the American dream.

    △ *A Different Story.* When George Morris returned from military service, he got a job in a men's clothing store. He worked for two years learning many aspects of the business. At the end of that time he made the decision to go — — — into business for himself. For $20,000, he bought a rundown store in a poor business location. His own savings and a loan from his parents covered $10,000 of the cost; he borrowed the additional $10,000 from a bank.

    George knew that the price of the business was low because much of the — — — merchandise was out of style. However, he believed that as he sold these outdated goods (he had no capital to buy new merchandise and had not △ established a credit rating yet), he would be able to replace them with the stylish clothing people wanted. He hoped that by marking down the prices on what he had, he could soon clear out his old stock. He also counted on patronage from his many friends.

    Two months after George opened his store, a new men's clothing store, — — — part of a chain, opened three blocks away. Now George's stock of suits that had but a short time ago been in style could not be sold for even a third of its original cost. George did not take in even enough money to pay his rent and his note at the bank. Most of his merchandise was valueless. By the end of one year, George Morris was bankrupt, his store just another among the statistics of business failures.

    — — — In 1984 there were 700,000 new businesses. What new entrepreneurs fail to realize, or choose to ignore, is that the average life expectancy of a business is less than five years, that about 40 percent of all retail businesses last less than two years, and that many businesses that do survive pay their owners less than they could earn by working for someone else. If we define small businesses as those firms employing fewer than 50 persons, then 96 percent of all businesses are small. Yet the importance of small businesses in the nation's economy, together with the uncertainty of operations of many

✳ small firms, raises a question as to whether small businesses will continue to be important in our economy.

—From Gordon and Dawson, *Introductory Economics.*

Notice especially two things about this marked passage.

1. Not everything that could be marked is marked. Your marking depends on what you consider important in your reading of the passage.
2. The last paragraph is packed with good stuff (can you remember what the symbols represent?) and shows how margin marking can bring to your attention sections of your reading that are very important. Rereading and studying this last paragraph is a must before an exam on this passage.

2. Perhaps the most important advance in our understanding of the geology of the Earth during the twentieth century has been the development of the theory of continental drift and plate tectonics. Alfred Wegener, German meteorologist, in a publication in 1915, presented the concept that about 200 million years ago the present continents were one huge land mass or supercontinent, which he called Pangaea. This land mass broke up and drifted apart, leading to present day positions of the continents, which still are slowly moving. Earth scientists have long regarded the Earth as a rigid body, but the discoveries that the Earth's interior may be slowly deformable led to the conclusion that the surface is mobile. The results of geological research in the last 20 years support Wegener's theory. But how could the large separation of the plates take place?

In 1960 Harvey Hess, of Princeton University, proposed that the sea floor cracks open along the crest of the mid-ocean ridges and that new sea floor forms there and spreads apart. The process is known as sea floor spreading. Today most geologists support the theory of plate tectonics which includes continental drift, sea floor spreading, and subduction.

—From Shipman et al., *An Introduction to Physical Science.*

Notice that in this passage are four terms which need to be learned and which probably will show up on a test sometime in the future.

3. The main card catalog at the Library of Congress—the rows and rows of massive wooden cabinets that hold 23 million well-thumbed index cards— is gradually becoming obsolete as the library moves toward automation.

Traditionalists worry that they are losing a cherished national institution, a place where scholars can make serendipitous discoveries among the cards and where more than a few romances have started from chance encounters.

Library officials, on the other hand, assert that the evolving computerized catalog is a physical necessity at the world's largest library, which has to add

▬▬▬ two million index cards each year. The general collection's card catalog, which dates back to 1800, occupies several rooms—about the size of half a city block—and has 22 trays of cards on Shakespeare alone.

Even with increasing automation, the old card catalog will not be abandoned for at least four more years, according to library spokesman Craig D'Ooge, mostly because the cards are being microfilmed. "And it's for certain that as long as there's a need for it, it will be accessible [to] scholars," he said. But it is obvious that the card catalog's days are numbered. In 1981, the catalog was "frozen" so that books obtained after January 2, 1981, were recorded only in the computerized files. And by the end of 1984, virtually all of the library's English-language books were cataloged in the automated system and available to researchers through 40 terminals in the library's reading rooms, according to John W. Kimball, head of the automation and reference collections section in the general reading rooms.

The automation has proceeded on two fronts. Since 1968, the library has ① cataloged new acquisitions in its machine-readable cataloging (Marc) computer system, and recently the library converted its 1979 list of 5.5 million ② books into computer format to cover pre-1968 items, in what is called the pre-Marc system.

△ Consequently, a researcher looking for English-language books on Shakespeare, for example, now could use a computer terminal to find at least 90% of the library's books on the subject, Kimball said ....

▬▬▬ The library has about 71 million items now that could be cataloged. "We're talking now about having only cataloged about 7.5 million books in machine-readable form, so we've got a long way to go," Kimball said.

To handle the huge data base, he added, the library will replace its two IBM 3033 mainframes in the next few months "with whatever is equivalent to IBM's best computer now," because the data files simply require faster and more powerful processors ....

▬▬▬ The automation projects will continue as the library undergoes a major renovation, to be completed by 1992. By January 1987, Kimball explained, the number of computer terminals will increase to between 75 and 100. The wood cabinets, with their elaborate and historic carvings, will survive as part of the high-tech catalog, Kimball said, by way of some artful carpentry work.

—From Slotnick et al., *Computers and Applications.*

This passage lends itself to marking for details in each paragraph. It is up to the reader to determine just which details to margin mark.

EXERCISE 7

1. moving your finger or pen left to right along each line as you read (page 24)
2. putting a mark or symbol in the margin as you read to identify significant information (page 26)

3. reading the first sentence in each paragraph to discover the main idea (page 29)
4. rapidly passing through paragraphs looking for details (page 29)
5. getting an impression of the internal structure in a passage before you start reading; flicking your eyes quickly over it (page 30)

Part One

Literal Comprehension Skills

In the next three chapters—Chapters 2, 3, and 4—we discuss the three literal comprehension skills that are crucial to your understanding of passages that you read. These are usually the easiest skills to learn because they depend on simple awareness and understanding of the ideas that are stated. You are not required to do such things as evaluate written material, question statements, determine validity, or infer results. The literal comprehension skills merely require attention to the ideas the author has stated.

The three basic comprehension skills you will study are:

1. recognizing the main idea (Chapter 2);
2. identifying supporting details (Chapter 3);
3. determining word meanings from context (Chapter 4).

Skill in these three types of comprehension will enable you to determine accurately *what* was stated.

Chapter 2

Recognizing the Main Idea

One can live in the shadow of an idea without grasping it.

—Elizabeth Bowen

Hang ideas! They are tramps, vagabonds, knocking at the back-door of your mind....

—Joseph Conrad

This chapter will help you to:

1. quickly recognize the main idea in reading materials.
2. differentiate among the topic, the topic sentence, and the main idea.
3. recognize the value of making up mental headlines to summarize the passage.
4. raise three key questions that pinpoint the main idea.
5. spot misleading answer choices that may confuse you on tests.

Probably the most useful skill you can develop that will improve both your reading comprehension and your performance on tests in class and later on standardized national exams is recognizing main ideas. In nearly all tests covering reading materials assigned in class you are expected to demonstrate that you can identify the subject that a reading selection is about, whether it is a paragraph, an essay, a chapter, or a book, without being misled by supporting details or ideas. The *main idea, controlling idea,* or *central idea* all mean the same thing. It is simply the main point the author is trying to get across to the reader.

How to Recognize the Main Idea

You may recognize the main idea in a paragraph or a passage in several ways.

1. The significance of its content or the force with which it is expressed.

> No event has had greater influence on this nation than the tragic death of John F. Kennedy.

2. Summation of the passage's content.

> These statements all prove that use of the death penalty is not a deterrent in any way to crimes of violence.

3. An idea expressed as a well-said, formal-sounding statement and a complete thought.

> Air pollution in our big cities has become the number one urban health problem.

4. If the passage seems to have only one general point, it includes the main idea. If it has two or more seemingly equal general points, the relation between them includes the main idea. First general point:

> We have a major shortage of large-denomination paper currency in this country.

Second general point:

> Drug dealers are hoarding large-denomination bills.

Main idea:

> Because drug dealers are hoarding large-denomination bills, we have a shortage of these bills in circulation in the United States.

The Topic, the Topic Sentence, and the Main Idea

Sometimes we confuse the *topic* and the *topic sentence* with the *main idea*. To avoid this confusion, keep these ideas in mind.

1. The *topic* is the subject that the passage is about in the most general sense. It may be expressed in a *word* or a *phrase*. War, abortion, civil rights, water safety, pain: these are all *topics*, not main ideas.
2. The *topic sentence* in a paragraph (or the *thesis statement* in a long passage) *includes* the main idea. It is the sentence in the passage that best expresses

the subject that the entire passage is about. The topic sentence always mentions the topic and then makes a strong statement or a claim about the topic. Generally, the topic sentence is easily identified because it sticks out by summing up the main idea in the passage. It is a mistake, however, to assume that one of the answer choices on a test will be a word-for-word duplication of a topic sentence.

Also remember that unfortunately, and contrary to what we used to be taught, the topic sentence is not always the first sentence in the paragraph. It may be the first sentence, but it could be anywhere. It may not even be stated—it may be *implied*.

3. The *main idea* is always expressed as a complete thought. This primary idea of the passage, the main idea, may also be stated in different words and in many locations. The main *idea* is the important one, no matter how it is expressed.

The Importance of Summarizing

The very useful skill of summarizing is often helpful in determining the topic, the topic sentence, or the main idea in a reading selection. Summarizing is a tool for understanding because it focuses on the *necessary* and eliminates the *unnecessary* in a passage. These are the six steps in creating a good summary of anything you read.

1. Eliminate unnecessary material. Anything that is trivial should be deleted.
2. Eliminate material which is important but which is redundant. It may be important, but don't keep including it. Once is enough.
3. Use a summary word instead of a list of items. If a writer discusses a series of related things, such as cars, trucks, and buses, substitute the word *vehicles*.
4. Use an encompassing word for a series of actions or events. For example, "Alice went to work" summarizes: "Alice got up and took a shower. She got dressed. She got in the car and drove downtown ...."
5. Select a topic sentence for each paragraph. If you find a topic sentence, it is usually the author's summary. But less than a third of all expository paragraphs have topic sentences. Fiction seldom includes topic sentences because narrative moves in a time-order sequence and writers feel that topic sentences slow down the narrative.
6. If the passage has no topic sentence, create your own.

Practice applying the summarizing steps to this passage on reading comprehension. First, read the essay. Then write a summary sentence for each paragraph, applying as many summary-writing steps as apply. Finally, combine your summary statements into a summary of summaries; use the format suggested at the end of the passage. You should find that the procedure positively affects your understanding of main ideas in material that you read.

What is meant by *finding the main idea?* How should we teach pupils to do it? Let's start by looking at how comprehension tests define *finding the main idea.* Some require that the pupil choose the best title for a passage. Others ask that pupils identify the most general statement of three—for example: *The husky pulls the sled. Dogs work. The sheep dog watches the herd.* In some tests a brief story is presented along with several moral pronouncements, one of which might be inferred from the story. Other tests present a paragraph from which the pupil must select the factual generalization most consistent with the information in the paragraph. Occasionally, the pupil must identify or propose a theme that subsumes the ideas expressed in a number of paragraphs. Obviously, these tests are not measuring the same things. Identifying a topic sentence is much easier than inferring an unstated theme or generalization for a work.

Similar differences regarding the meaning of main ideas are found in writings on the subject. One writer says that any text can be divided into two, often unequal, parts. The first is the *theme,* or topic, of the text—the part that deals with what is already known. The second part, the *rheme,* is composed of new information about this subject. By this definition, topics are not main ideas, for they simply prepare the reader for what is to come. On the other hand, drawing conclusions from the new information is a main idea.

In contrast, another writer defines a theme as the main idea of a book, article, or chapter in a text. The theme may be implied or directly stated. If implied, the reader has to infer what the content of the text suggests about an aspect of the human condition or world knowledge. Still other writers say that the main idea of any piece is related to its location in the hierarchy of superordinate, coordinate, and subordinate terms. In a passage giving an example, a concept, and a generalization, the generalization must be the main idea.

Importance has something to do with main ideas. In fact, one author has proposed (facetiously) a test to rate the importance of main ideas. He calls it the *aha!—so what!* test.* If

*P. David Pearson and Dale D. Johnson, *Teaching Reading Comprehension* (New York: Holt, Rinehart and Winston, 1978).

the main idea elicits an *aha!* reaction, it's probably a meaningful conclusion. If it elicits a *so what!* reaction, it is probably a relatively vacuous summary label. The problem is, there is not always general agreement among readers of all ages and places as to what is important. When readers are asked to read from given perspectives, they show greater agreement as to which ideas are important than when they read from their own perspectives.

Identifying main ideas in expository pieces is more difficult than in narrative. In narratives, importance means centrality to the story; character, goals, and setting are high in the hierarchy, and particular events are low. In expository texts, importance usually means how superordinate the idea is in a hierarchy leading from specific to general statements.

—From McNeil, *Reading Comprehension*.

RULES APPLIED

Place a check mark in the blank if you applied the rules to each paragraph.

1. Eliminated unnecessary material   ....
2. Eliminated redundancies   ....
3. Substituted summary word for list   ....
4. Used encompassing word for series of events   ....
5. Selected a topic sentence   ....
6. Created a topic sentence   ....

SUMMARY SENTENCES FOR PARAGRAPHS

1. ....
....

2. ....
....

3. ....
....

4. ....
   ....

5. ....
   ....

SUMMARY OF SUMMARIES

....

....

....

....

The Reinforced Idea

To be certain that you have identified the main idea, check to make sure that that idea is backed up, supported, restated, *reinforced* by the rest of the passage. If it is not, or if it is contradicted in some way, it is not the main idea no matter how effective it sounds.

Sometimes writing a *mental headline* as if to summarize the passage and the most important thing being said helps you focus on the main idea. Is your mental headline close to one of the test answer choices? Chances are, that's the correct response.

Three Key Questions

When you are not sure which is the main idea, it always helps to ask yourself three key questions.

1. What is this passage about? (What is the *topic?*) For example, you might conclude that the topic in a reading selection is *cars*.
2. What is the purpose in discussing this subject (cars)? You may determine that the purpose is to *describe* owning a specific model and year—a *1964 Corvette*.
3. What is the main idea that the author wants you to know about this specific subject (1964 Corvettes)? "The 1964 Corvettes provide their owners with pride of ownership unmatched by any other car." (The main idea.)

On paper, raising these three questions after you read seems cumbersome and time consuming, and maybe at first it is—but only at first. Very quickly, raising these questions as you read becomes second nature for you. This practice turns recognizing main ideas into an efficient experience.

Be Aware of Answers That May Confuse You

Very often, the examination answer choices themselves may trip you up. Misleading answer choices (often intentional) like these are often included.

1. A *partial* statement of the main idea.
2. A *reference* to the main idea, but *not* the main idea.
3. A *reference* to an idea in the passage that is expanded in the answer with information *not* in the passage.
4. A misinterpretation (often slight) of main-idea information in the passage, giving the *feel* of truth.

More Than One Main Idea

Sometimes it is very difficult to identify the main idea in a reading passage because two or more ideas may appear to be of equal weight. On standardized tests you will be permitted only one choice of a main idea as *the* correct answer, but in this book and in this class you are encouraged to make your choice—and then you must be ready to give reasons for your selection. Perhaps the main idea you suggest is wild and far from correct because you missed something significant or misinterpreted the ideas you read—but maybe not. Once you explain the reasoning behind your choice, you may find agreement among your classmates and the instructor. Remember, it's not vital for you to be correct; you do need to *comprehend* what you are reading, and often the material you read is shaped and understood according to your schema, which may differ from everyone else's, changing its meaning for you. First, be certain that you comprehend, then pick the main idea that fits your understanding, and last, be ready with your reasons. If you do these things, you are developing the "reading edge."

Main-Idea Margin Mark ———

The margin mark for main ideas is a straight line (———). Practice finding and marking in the margins the main ideas in the longer readings that follow. You will find that you quickly acquire skill in identifying main ideas.

Also, don't forget to preview the reading selections and test questions (where appropriate) before you begin reading.

Anticipate the Topics

These topics are the subjects in some of the reading selections in the exercises coming up in this chapter. As a way of heightening your interest in the passages you are about to read and as a way to start you considering all you know on these topics, jot down the first several words or phrases that enter your mind as you read each word. In class, we'll share our words with other class members. All this reading will heighten your awareness as you read.

high population ....

when life began ....

military service ....

ancient hunters ....

Victorians ....

suicidal personalities ....

freshmen ....

advertising ....

occupational safety ....

the opposite sex ....

Freudian theory ....

Indian warrior ....

computers ....

love ....

sex ....

carbon 14 dating ....

children ....

Galileo ....

horse race ....

economist ....

early man ....

nuclear power plants ....

entrepreneurs ....

delinquents ....

family violence ....

moon ....

What Are Your Thoughts?

1. For most college students, recognizing the main idea is the reading skill most highly developed by the time they get to college. Why is that?

....

....

....

2. What are some ways of recognizing the main idea that may not have been mentioned in this chapter but that you use when you read?

....

....

....

3. What things may confuse you as you try to identify the topic sentence in a paragraph?

....

....

....

4. Which parts of the explanation in this chapter about locating the main idea seemed inadequate or confusing to you?

....

....

....

5. What does *schema* mean when it applies to understanding the passage you are reading?

....

....

....

6. Can you think of a reason for a reading selection's having two main ideas?

....

....

....

Writing to Comprehend

1. Explain as clearly as you can the difference among topic, topic sentence, and main idea.

....

....

....

....

....

2. What is a "reinforced idea" and how is it "reinforced"?

....

....

....

....

....

3. What is the most interesting thing (newspaper, book, magazine article, menu, road map, and so on) that you have read during the past few days? Tell us about it. What made it interesting?

....

....

....

....

....

4. Why is it so important to have a reason for selecting the "correct" answer that you choose?

....

....

....

....

....

Words to Read by

The words in the left column are used in reading exercises in this chapter. Match as many as you can with the definitions in the right column by putting the letter of the appropriate definition on the line at left. When you finish, turn to the page and passage where the word is used and check to see that your match is correct. Be ready to discuss the reasons for your selections. What were your clues to meanings?

.... consequences (page 65)   a. front

.... windfall (65)   b. established firmly

.... façade (66)   c. sexual

.... ambivalent (66)   d. between people

.... glut (66)   e. a person who studies or practices theology

.... well-entrenched (67)   f. a person who studies or practices physics

.... innovations (67)   g. results

.... erogenous (68)   h. social position

.... interpersonal (69)   i. a person who studies the economy

.... theologian (69)   j. conflicting feelings

.... conjecture (71)   k. speculation

.... physicist (72)   l. oversupply

.... economist (74)   m. something new

.... status (76)   n. length of time

.... duration (76)   o. unexpected good fortune

Correct answers are at the end of the chapter.

Practice Exercises

EXERCISE 1

Each group of words is made up of a topic and five idea words that would help develop that topic. Circle the topic word in each line. The first one is done for you.

1.   fishing, long walks, (vacation,) picnics, campfires, ants

2.   Patton, da Vinci, Einstein, Kennedy, leadership, Caesar

3.   education, college, elementary school, high school, graduate school, vocational school

4.   hockey, golf, baseball, tennis, football, sports

5.   diamonds, gems, rubies, sapphires, topazes, emeralds

6.   earthquake, fire, disaster, hurricane, tornado, drought

7.   clothes, shirts, dresses, slacks, socks, jackets

8.   square dance, foxtrot, waltz, ballroom dancing, jitterbug

9.   rose, pansy, carnation, daffodil, iris, flowers

EXERCISE 2

These groups of words include specific words that are part of a general topic. Write the topic that best describes all the words in each group. The first one is done for you.

1. Apache
Cherokee
Cheyenne
Mohawk
Topic *Indians*

2. blue
beige
lavender
gray
Topic ....

3. lasagna
fried chicken
pancakes
onion soup
Topic ....

4. surgeon
accountant
attorney
flight controller
Topic ....

5. triangle
cube
circle
rectangle
Topic ....

6. aerobics
weight lifting
jogging
swimming
Topic ....

7. France
India
Morocco
Afghanistan
Topic ....

8. calculus
composition
psychology
history
Topic ....

9. *Casablanca*
E.T.
Friday the 13th
Rambo
Topic ....

10. clap
hum
whistle
scream
Topic ....

EXERCISE 3

In these exercises, pick the topic (and label it T), the topic sentence (TS), and the sentences that serve as illustrations or examples for the main idea (EX). The first one is done for you.

Group A

EX **1.** Platters of chicken or spareribs, bowls of potato salad or pasta salad all had their admirers standing nearby.

T **2.** The church picnic.

EX. **3.** Chocolate cakes, sponge cakes, and fragrant brownies were lined up three deep.

T.S. **4.** The church picnic gave the parishioners a chance to show off their skill at cooking and baking.

Group B

.... **1.** Sugar often replaces nourishing food in a diet.

.... **2.** Sugar contributes no protein, fat, vitamins, or minerals.

.... **3.** Eating sugar can be worse than eating nothing.

.... **4.** Sugar as an "antinutrient."

Group C

.... **1.** Country square dancing.

.... **2.** Every Saturday night the town hall fills up with scores of square dancers, all having a good time.

.... **3.** The women's bright dresses compete for attention.

.... **4.** Even the children are included in the stomping and twirling.

Group D

.... **1.** Problems in America.

.... **2.** Use of illegal drugs has increased.

.... **3.** A high percentage of inner-city children never finish elementary school.

.... **4.** America today has profound problems with drugs, poverty, and illiteracy.

Group E

.... **1.** Today's technology.

.... **2.** One of every two homes has a videocassette recorder (VCR) and a microwave oven.

.... **3.** The highly developed technology of the 1980s has resulted in many discoveries that can make life more enjoyable.

.... **4.** Electronic alarm systems make our homes safe.

EXERCISE 4

Underline the word or phrase that best identifies the topic in each of these paragraphs. The first one is done for you.

1. Crowding human beings and motor vehicles into small geographic areas can have serious economic consequences. New York City has a population density of 77,000 per square mile in one of its boroughs. High population density often results in high crime rates, overcrowded housing, serious traffic problems, and high disease rates.
    —From Gordon and Dawson, *Introductory Economics*.

    a. New York City   b. high population density
    c. motor vehicles   d. disease

2. We do not know how life began, but the fact that we exist proves that the right ingredients, in the right amounts, and arranged in the correct way, did come together at some time in the past. The best approximation is that it happened at least 2.5 to 3 billion years ago.
    —From Shipman et al., *An Introduction to Physical Science*.

    a. the past   b. evolution
    c. time   d. origin of life

3. What is the result of the military experience for the individual male? It makes a man out of him, of course. Slogans such as "The Army will make a man out of you" and "The Marines take only a few good men" provide ample testimony to the cultural notion that the military experience turns boys into men.
    —From Hyde, *Half the Human Experience: The Psychology of Women*.

    a. military experience   b. the army
    c. the Marines   d. turning men into boys

4. Search for food occupied most of the ancient hunter's day. If hunters bagged small animals, the family or band would feast for a day, then move on; killing a mammoth or a mastodon was a windfall for the hunting band because it provided food for several days.
    —From *The American Indian* by Arrell Morgan Gibson. Copyright © 1980 by D. C. Heath and Company. Reprinted by permission of the publisher.

    a. the search for food   b. hunting
    c. the ancient hunter's day   d. mammoth hunting

5. While proper Victorian men and women maintained a façade of public morality, pornography, prostitution, and extramarital sex flourished behind the scenes. Officially the harlot (prostitute) was the worst of all women and a social outcast, but she was tolerated because she provided an outlet through which the proper Victorian husband could satisfy his burdensome passion.

—From Allgeier and Allgeier, *Sexual Interactions*.

a. public morality
c. passion

b. Victorian husbands
d. Victorian sexual attitudes

EXERCISE 5

Remember that topic sentences may appear anywhere in the paragraph. In these paragraphs, identify the number of the sentence that acts as the topic sentence. Note: Sometimes a topic sentence provides the main idea for more than one paragraph. The first one is done for you.

1. [1] It is known today that most suicidal personalities have some common psychosocial characteristics. [2] The main one is difficulty in relating satisfactorily with others on a sustained emotional basis. [3] This seems to result from their frequent tendency to be overly sensitive to loss and rejection, to poor self-esteem, and, often, to excessive expectations for themselves and others. [4] As a result, they can accumulate anger, and, in turn, become loners and alienate themselves from society. [5] However, they generally remain ambivalent in their suicidal propensities, and, while many reject help by professionals, they still desperately wish they could make it, wish that someone would be accepting and nice to them.

—From *Sociology: Social Science and Social Concern* by Richie P. Lowry and Robert P. Rankin. Copyright © 1977 by D. C. Heath and Company. Reprinted by permission of the publisher.

Topic sentence ......**1**..........

2. [1] A survey by the Council of Education in 1980 found that freshman students are becoming much more materialistic. [2] "Being well off financially" was considered an "important" or "essential" goal by 28 percent more men and 77 percent more women than in 1970. [3] Over 15 percent of the women and 18 percent of the men planned business careers, as compared to 4 percent and 17 percent in 1970. [4] Although a glut of business graduates is hitting the job market, career opportunities are still great for students with business education and training. [5] One out of every ten employees is a manager. [6] Also, firms hire business graduates as trainees for management and related positions.

—From Megginson et al., *Business*.

Topic sentence ....

3. [1] When Aim toothpaste was developed to take on Crest, what did management need to know in order to position its gel toothpaste appropriately against such a well-entrenched leader? [2] In order for Burger King to attack McDonald's, it needed to know what consumers felt they were not getting. [3] Miller Lite Beer took a discarded product (low-calorie beer) and built a new product category using advertising and positioning. [4] What was in their situation analysis that allowed them to see what no other firm had seen? ... [5] As the first step in developing a campaign, the situation analysis is vital. [6] If it is done poorly, the entire campaign can easily go astray.

> —From *Advertising* by Michael Rothschild. Copyright © 1987 by D. C. Heath and Company. Reprinted by permission of the publisher.

Topic sentence ....

4. [1] Small firms produce two-and-a-half times as many innovations as large firms relative to the number of people employed. [2] The first automobile, airplane, jet engine, helicopter, office copying machine, instant camera, and air conditioner were among the breakthroughs that sprang from the workshops of small businesses. [3] Other important innovations include the aerosol can, foam fire extinguishers, heart pacemakers, quick-frozen foods, the safety razor, the vacuum tube, and the zipper.

> —From Megginson et al., *Business*.

Topic sentence ....

5. [1] During the average work day in the United States, one worker is injured every fourteen seconds, and one worker is killed every thirty-seven minutes. [2] Each year, over 14,000 workers are killed in job-related activities, and 2.4 million workers are seriously injured, at a cost of over $12 billion in lost wages, reduced output, and other losses.

[3] While business is doing much to improve this situation, the Occupational Safety and Health Act of 1970 (OSHAct) has speeded up these activities by establishing a regulatory agency, the Occupational Safety and Health Administration (OSHA) to enforce safety standards. [4] OSHA inspectors are concentrating on those industries with the highest accident rates.

> —From Megginson et al., *Business*.

Topic sentence ....

EXERCISE 6

For these passages, write an acceptable topic sentence that captures the content of the passage. The first one is done for you.

1. The first thing that strikes the careless observer is that women are unlike men. They are "the opposite sex"—(though why "opposite" I do not know; what is the "neighboring sex"?). But the fundamental thing is that women are more like men than anything else in the world.

    —From Dorothy L. Sayers, "The Human Not-Quite Human" in *Unpopular Opinions* (Victor Gollancz, 1946), p. 116.

    Topic sentence *The phrase "the opposite sex" is an inappropriate label for women because men and women are fundamentally the same.*

2. One of Freud's greatest contributions was to view human personality as being the result of *development*. That is, he saw the personality of an adult as the result of previous experiences, and he believed that early childhood experiences were most critical. He proposed a stage theory of psychosexual development, each stage being characterized by a focus on one of the erogenous zones. According to his view, all humans pass through the stages in a fixed, chronological sequence—first the oral, then the anal, and then the phallic stage—during the first five or six years of life.

    —From Hyde, *Half the Human Experience: The Psychology of Women.*

    Topic sentence ....

    ....

    ....

3. In the warrior society, "warfare became as ritualized as medieval knighthood." The ritual and pageantry of Plains warriorhood included a hierarchy of honors centering on the coup, or strike. The coup count, the record of the warrior's feats of daring, skill, and bravery, was most important in gaining public esteem. Each warrior member of the sodality sought to exceed all others in daring, reckless exposure to the greatest hazard, and thus gain the greatest public recognition. There was special merit for coup count when the enemy was not slain but only touched by the daring warrior with special wand or baton called the coup stick. Accumulated brave deeds or coups yielded political power and was the avenue to band and tribal leadership.

    —From Gibson, *The American Indian.*

    Topic sentence ....

    ....

    ....

4. On a cloudy November afternoon, a visitor sat before a blank computer

screen in an IBM laboratory preparing to dictate a message that the computer would try to transcribe. The IBM scientists demonstrating the system handed him a list of suggested sentences to read aloud. Instead he made up his own, pausing between words as they had instructed him: "I ... am ... really ... surprised ... that ... this ... computer ... can ... understand ... what I ... say ... period." As he spoke, each word popped up instantly in blue letters on an adjacent screen that monitored the inner workings of the computer as it tried to decide what it was hearing. As the sentence grew longer, words began to change from blue to a rich green—in IBM's system, the color is certainty. A fraction of a second after the visitor shut his mouth, the complete sentence was delivered to the screen in front of him.

—From Slotnick et al., *Computers and Applications.*

Topic sentence ....

....

....

5.   Among Senator William Proxmire's attacks on research is that directed at a University of Minnesota study of interpersonal relations designed "to find out why or how or if or how long people fall in love." The Wisconsin Democrat labeled this study "My choice for the biggest waste of the taxpayer's money for the month of March. Even if they spend $84 million or $84 billion, they couldn't get an answer anyone would believe. I'm against it because I don't want the answer. I believe that 200 million other Americans want to leave some things in life a mystery, and right at the top of things we don't want to know is why a man falls in love with a woman and vice versa." Mr. Proxmire consequently told the National Science Foundation to "get out of the love racket. Leave that to Elizabeth Barrett Browning and Irving Berlin."

—From "Love and Senator Proxmire," *Chronicle of Higher Education,* 1975, p. 5.

Topic sentence ....

....

....

EXERCISE 7

The main idea in a passage may be stated in a topic sentence or it *may* be unstated. In these passages, use the questions that follow to determine the main idea. The first one is done for you.

1.   Early in 1975, Dr. Henry P. Van Dusen, well-known Protestant theologian and former President of Union Theological Seminary, and his wife died. At first, it was believed that their deaths were from natural causes. Some months later, however, it became known that they had left a letter explaining their plan to take their own lives with an overdose of pills. Dr. and Mrs. Van Dusen explained that they had lived full lives, were ill and at an advanced age, and were afraid to die without dignity of some crippling disease. Furthermore, they were morally concerned about taking up space in a world with too many mouths and too little food, when the beauty and meaning of life had disappeared for them. As religious people, they were not afraid of death.

—From Norman Cousins, "The Right to Die," *Saturday Review,* 2 (14 June 1975), p. 4.

a. What is the subject in this paragraph?

Suicide

b. What is the author's purpose in discussing the subject?

to give a reason for some people's suicide

c. What is the main idea you should understand about the subject in relation to the purpose?

For some people under some conditions, suicide is seen as a reasonable alternative to continuing to live.

2. In contemporary North American culture, it is commonly believed that males are more sexual than females—that males have stronger and more frequent sexual appetites, and that they enjoy sex more than do females. Earlier in this century it was believed that females were passive and uninterested in sex, but during the latter half of the century females have come to be perceived as willing to engage in sexual relations under certain conditions and —given a skillful partner—able to enjoy sexual stimulation. The general belief about differences in male and female sexuality is reflected in the old phrase "Men give love to get sex; women give sex to get love."

—From Allgeier and Allgeier, *Sexual Interactions.*

a. What is the subject in this paragraph?

b. What is the author's purpose in discussing the subject?

c. What is the main idea you should understand about the subject in relation to the purpose?

....

....

....

3.   This isn't just idle conjecture. New York's Citibank plans to have more than half its 2.5 million account-holders on-line by 1995. Major retail chains like J. C. Penney's are experimenting with at-home shopping systems, and computer-based news, sports, and entertainment services such as QUBE and Teletext are already available. A shopping mall near Washington, D.C., offers shoppers a "window shopping" service accessible through a modem. The service lists sales and specials in a store-by-store index. Users can call up price comparisons of particular items, place orders, and request gift sugges-tions for women, men, children, pets, older relatives, secretaries, or a variety of other recipient categories.

The wide availability of inexpensive computers could have a dramatic impact on our society.

—From Slotnick et al., *Computers and Applications.*

a. What is the subject in this paragraph?

....

b. What is the author's purpose in discussing the subject?

....

c. What is the main idea you should understand about the subject in rela-tion to the purpose?

....

....

....

4.   Carbon 14 dating is a widely used method for determining the age of Paleo-Indian material. Carbon 14, a radioactive element or isotope, is present in all living plants and animals. When a plant or animal dies, carbon 14 decay begins and continues at a fixed rate that can be measured. Analysis of bone, wood (including charred wood in ancient campfires), horn, hair, and shell objects by the carbon 14 test measures the amount of carbon 14 isotope present and yields an approximate age with a possible error of two hundred years either way. The limit for measuring carbon 14 loss is 50,000 years; beyond that age, carbon 14 loss in an object is complete.

—From Gibson, *The American Indian.*

a. What is the subject in this paragraph?

....

    b. What is the author's purpose in discussing the subject?

    ....

    c. What is the main idea you should understand about the subject in relation to the purpose?

    ....

    ....

    ....

5. Yesterday my daughter Margaret, age four and a half (the half is very important to her), was telling me about the games she had been playing at her preschool. She played with her boy friend, Dimitrios. He says he's going to marry her when they grow up. They played "Superfriends." She told me that Dimitrios chose a character he wanted to be, such as Superman, and then she played the female counterpart, Supergirl. Or they played "Dukes of Hazzard," and she was Daisy. I had to sit down for a minute while processing the significance of all she was saying. She hasn't even started kindergarten yet, and her femaleness and its requirements are so clear to her. She understands that the male chooses what he wants to be and then she follows, picking up the female counterpart role. She has learned that he is Super*man* while she is Super*girl*. I tried to talk her out of it. I said if he is Superman, she could be Super*woman*. She said there is no Superwoman. I asked her why Dimitrios always got to choose what they played. Why couldn't she pick Wonderwoman and he could be Wonderman? or Wonderboy? She said it couldn't be played that way. I asked why. She said it just couldn't. After a while I gave up.

    —From Hyde, *Half the Human Experience: The Psychology of Women.*

    a. What is the subject in this paragraph?

    ....

    b. What is the author's purpose in discussing the subject?

    ....

    c. What is the main idea you should understand about the subject in relation to the purpose?

    ....

    ....

    ....

6. The great Italian physicist Galileo Galilei (1564–1642) was the first scientist to assert that all objects fall downward with the same acceleration. Of course, this assumes that frictional effects are negligible. We can state this assertion of Galileo as follows:

> If frictional effects can be disregarded, every freely falling object near the Earth's surface accelerates downward at the same rate, regardless of the mass of the object.

The correctness of Galileo's assertion can be seen by dropping a small mass, such as a coin, and a large mass, such as a book, at the same time. The two objects will hit at the same time. It is believed that Galileo himself performed such experiments.

—From Shipman et al., *An Introduction to Physical Science.*

a. What is the subject in this paragraph?

....

b. What is the author's purpose in discussing the subject?

....

c. What is the main idea you should understand about the subject in relation to the purpose?

....

....

....

7.   Your common sense tells you to bet on Rambling Ralph.
     You do.
     The race begins and Rambling Ralph, running free and easy, settles into a comfortable third position. As they enter the back stretch, he eases into second place. By this time you're getting very excited. At the top of the home stretch, he is challenging for the lead. You close your eyes, clasp your hands and say a short prayer. You hear a tremendous roar from the crowd; you open your eyes in time to see the horses cross the finish line; the winner—Cunning Clyde. Cunning Clyde? Damn!!

—From Mendoza and Napoli, *Systems of Society: An Introduction to Social Sciences.*

a. What is the subject in this paragraph?

....

b. What is the author's purpose in discussing the subject?

....

c. What is the main idea you should understand about the subject in relation to the purpose?

....

....

....

8. "An economist is someone who doesn't know what he's talking about, but makes you think it's *your* fault." "An economist is a person who has no idea what's happening in the present but predicts what will happen in the future." "If you made all economists lie down end to end, they'd never reach a conclusion." These are some of the many humorous comments that suggest that professional economists are far from omniscient.

—From Gordon and Dawson, *Introductory Economics.*

a. What is the subject in this paragraph?

....

b. What is the author's purpose in discussing the subject?

....

c. What is the main idea you should understand about the subject in relation to the purpose?

....

....

....

9. The appearance of human beings is fairly recent with respect to the geological time scale. The earliest evidence indicates they have been in existence at least one million years. It has been suggested that human beings' ability to reason was first put to use during an ice age, when they were forced from the trees into a cold environment and reasoned that to survive they must hunt in groups. Possessing intelligence, they invented stone tools and developed a crude language in order to live together and to fight their enemies better. Early people fought not only the wild beasts and the forces of nature, but made war against their neighbors as well. They discovered fire and learned to control it. The need for refuge from the fear of certain natural phenomena gave rise to religious rites and the worship of gods. As the climate became warmer, the hunters became shepherds who, with the passing of time, became farmers. Through necessity the plow was invented, animals were domesticated, the use of clay was developed, and weaving wool and flax was learned. Copper was discovered and then tin, which when it was combined with copper made bronze. Iron and other metals were discovered and used in numerous ways.

—From Shipman et al., *An Introduction to Physical Science.*

a. What is the subject in this paragraph?

....

b. What is the author's purpose in discussing the subject?

....

c. What is the main idea you should understand about the subject in rela-tion to the purpose?

....

....

....

10. Long Island, New York, has a growing population and strong industrial development, both of which are creating the need for more electric power. The Long Island Lighting Company insists that its Shoreham nuclear power plant (built at a cost of $4.5 billion) should be allowed to operate at full capacity to meet this need. Some experts say that the plant is safe and that all we need to do is "turn on the switch." Many Island residents, however, fear that an accident at Shoreham would endanger their lives and that it would not be possible to evacuate people from the area. Some business executives, noting that Long Island electricity rates are already among the highest in the nation, are threatening to move their firms elsewhere if adequate power is not made available at reasonable rates. Of course, this would mean the loss of many jobs. What should be done in this situation? If Shoreham is not allowed to operate, who will pay the cost of the $4.5 billion plant?

—From Gordon and Dawson, *Introductory Economics.*

a. What is the subject in this paragraph?

....

b. What is the author's purpose in discussing the subject?

....

c. What is the main idea you should understand about the subject in rela-tion to the purpose?

....

....

....

EXERCISE 8

In a brief statement, identify the main idea in these passages. Remember that the main idea is the most important one the author is trying to express about the topic. The first one is done for you.

1. Of course, things don't just happen by themselves in any economic endeavor, especially in the world of free enterprise and profit. Someone has to make them happen. Entrepreneurs are the innovative owner-managers who create some new product or service or suggest a better way of using existing products or services. They are the first risk takers to see that the public wants a new product or service and to try to provide it. Entrepreneurs think up ways to satisfy people's needs. They invest money, time, and effort in organizing and managing a firm; run the risk of failure; and reap the rewards of success.

    —From Megginson et al., *Business.*

    Main idea *Entrepreneurs are leading players in the world of free enterprise.*

    ....

2. Some boys became delinquent because they were more highly exposed to the risk of becoming illegitimate fathers, having to fight, or having to use a knife or a gun. For example, constant sexual intercourse was the norm among lower-class boys, and it was a form of behavior that received much support from adults in the subculture. A boy who was successful with girls often emerged as a gang leader. Sexual activity was one way to maintain status, and this reward outweighed the risk of parenthood and punishment by society when illegitimacy resulted. In addition, since most of the gangs studied were conflict gangs, the importance of fighting was evident. Fighting, too, was related to status management within the gang and between the gang and the larger society. Analysis of a gang fight that broke out one night at an athletic event led to the conclusion that it all started when a 21-year-old gang leader was reprimanded by a detached worker for wanting to buy beer at an event sponsored by the YMCA. The leader lost face in the eyes of his peers. The worker ordered the whole gang to leave the scene, and this was a status threat to the group as well as to the leader. As a result, the shamed gang started a fight with other gangs.

    —From Lowry and Rankin, *Sociology: Social Science and Social Concern.*

Main idea ....

....

....

3.   Although the family in America is romanticized as a haven of peace and safety, current estimates are that the incidence of family violence is high. In the largest and best study on the topic, sociologist Murray Straus (1980) analyzed a probability sample of over 2,000 families. The data indicated that 16 percent of the couples experienced some violence between themselves (ranging from slapping to actual beating) within the last year. Over the duration of a marriage, that would mean that about 28 percent would be involved in violence between spouses. Straus estimates that in about 5 percent of marriages the wife is actually beaten at some time during the marriage. The average frequency of beating is 2.4 times per year.

—From Hyde, *Half the Human Experience: The Psychology of Women.*

Main idea ....

....

....

4.   The Earth's moon at its brightest is a wondrous sight as it reflects the Sun's light back to Earth. The moon appears quite large to Earth observers. In fact, our moon is the largest moon of any inner planet. Mercury and Venus have no moons and the moons of Mars are quite small. Our moon is the fifth largest in the solar system. A unique feature of the Earth and the moon is that they are nearer in size than any other planet and its satellite.

—From Shipman et al., *An Introduction to Physical Science.*

Main idea ....

....

....

5.   My daughter loves to look at the family photography albums. She begs to see the pictures of herself as a baby or a two-year-old and to hear the stories of the funny things she did or said at that age. She nags to see the pictures of me dressed in my cowgirl outfit at age five and to hear how I wanted to be Dale Evans (Roy Rogers' other half) when I grew up. Then she triumphantly announces, "But you didn't, you're a professor."

—From Hyde, *Half the Human Experience: The Psychology of Women.*

Main idea ....

....

....

EXERCISE 9

Identify the topic sentence for each of the paragraphs in this passage on "Spiny Delicacies."

SPINY DELICACIES

The south Texas jetties are also the home of the sea urchin *Arbacia punctulata*. This purple urchin is also a herbivore who enjoys large, leafy seaweeds. Its long spines protect it from many potential predators, but it is still vulnerable to the crushing force of waves breaking against the jetties and to the strong jaws of some aggressive fishes. Hence it prefers to stay in the crevices and on the leeward side of the jetty. The sea urchin's gonads are eaten as a delicacy in many parts of the world. The shell of a sea urchin is called a test and the bumps represent the points where the spines were attached. The test is composed of fused calcareous plates, fitted together in a sturdy zigzag pattern.

The rows of tiny holes in the *Arbacia* test are openings for tube feet. These tube feet have a hollow core filled with seawater and a sucker at the tip. The urchin extends its feet by forcing more seawater into them until the sucker touches and attaches to the substrate. By contracting muscles in the tube feet, the urchin shortens them and pulls itself toward the point where the sucker is attached. By coordinating the movements of its tube feet, and with some help from the spines, the urchin is able to move quite easily across either horizontal or vertical surfaces. The spines on the top and bottom of the urchin are shorter than those around its equator, making it easier for the tube feet to reach the ground.

The two larger openings in the test are for the mouth and anus. The anus is located on the top side of the urchin, the mouth on the side nearest the substrate. The mouth contains an unusual chewing apparatus called the Aristotle's lantern. It consists of the housing and musculature for five long teeth, which meet at their tips to form a five-sided bite.

Arbacia is easily confused with another jetty urchin, *Echinometra lucunter*. Both species are approximately the same size and same color and are nearly equally abundant on South Texas jetties. However, they can be distinguished by close inspection of the plates surrounding the anal opening on the upper surface. In *Arbacia* these plates are four in number (sometimes three or five) and are sculptured with fine grooves in a reticulate pattern. In

Echinometra there are numerous plates of various sizes with assorted bumps similar to those on which the spines pivot. Moreover, the spines around *Echinometra's* mouth have sharp tips, as opposed to the flattened tips of the oral spines in *Arbacia.*

—From *The Beachcomber's Guide to Gulf Coast Marine Life* by Nick Fotheringham. Copyright © 1980 by Lone Star Books, Houston (a Division of Gulf Publishing Co.). Reprinted by permission of the publisher.

Paragraph 1 ....

....

Paragraph 2 ....

....

Paragraph 3 ....

....

Paragraph 4 ....

....

Now, identify the main idea in this selection. Write it in your own words.

Main idea ....

....

....

Answers to Selected Exercises

WORDS TO READ BY

g. consequences   l. glut   d. interpersonal   i. economist
o. windfall   b. well intentioned   e. theologian   h. status
a. façade   m. innovations   k. conjecture   n. duration
j. ambivalent   c. erogenous   f. physicist

EXERCISE 1

1. vacation   2. leadership   3. education
4. sports   5. gems   6. disasters
7. clothes   8. dancing   9. flowers

EXERCISE 3

Group A	Group B	Group C	Group D	Group E
1. EX	1. EX	1. T	1. T	1. T
2. T	2. EX	2. TS	2. EX	2. EX
3. EX	3. TS	3. EX	3. EX	3. TS
4. TS	4. T	4. EX	4. TS	4. EX

EXERCISE 5

1. 1   2. 4   3. 5   4. 1   5. 3

EXERCISE 7

Correct answers may be stated in many different ways.

1a. suicide
  b. to give a reason for some people's suicides
  c. For some people under some conditions, suicide is seen as a reasonable alternative to continuing to live.
2a. sexuality
  b. to show that beliefs in male or female sexuality are changing
  c. Beliefs about differences in male or female sexuality are changing.
3a. computers
  b. to show the increasing uses of computers
  c. The availability of computers could dramatically affect our society.
4a. carbon 14 dating
  b. to identify carbon 14 dating as a reliable method for determining age
  c. Carbon 14 dating is a widely used method for determining age.
5a. the female role
  b. to show that femaleness and its requirements are learned early
  c. Female roles are learned early and are difficult to change.
6a. Galileo's assertion about falling objects
  b. Galileo's assertion about falling objects was correct.
  c. The correctness of Galileo's assertion about falling objects can be tested.
7a. a race
  b. to tell how Rambling Ralph ran in a race
  c. Common sense was wrong about Rambling Ralph and the race.
8a. economists
  b. to show that economists are not always correct
  c. Economists are not always viewed as omniscient.
9a. the development of man and his skill
  b. to show the relations between necessity and man's development
  c. Through necessity, man and his civilization developed.
10a. nuclear power plants
  b. to show the controversy surrounding nuclear power plants
  c. Nuclear power plants provide both electricity and controversy.

Chapter 3

Identifying Supporting Details

Merely corroborative detail, intended to give
artistic verisimilitude to an otherwise bald
and unconvincing narrative.

—*The Mikado*

This chapter will help you to:

1. identify which details are important and which are not.
2. understand why some details acquire importance.
3. know which questions to ask to determine important details.
4. avoid being fooled by a paraphrase.
5. recognize difficulties in correctly answering questions about details.

All reading material is made up of main ideas and supporting details. These details are composed of all the facts and secondary ideas that an author uses to develop and support the main idea or ideas. Authors need such details to explain thoroughly the idea they intend to get across. Generally, though, these supporting details are important *only* as they relate to and support the main idea. Usually, the more complex the idea the more details you need to clarify or develop a point, but they have little value in themselves unless they support the main idea.

Writing to Comprehend

1. Find examples illustrating these kinds of detail questions. Make up a question or two to fit each category.

   specific-answer questions ....

   ....

   sequence-of-events questions ....

   ....

   following-directions questions ....

   ....

   inference questions ....

   ....

   Put a plus mark (+) next to the questions you consider to be "fair" detail questions. Put a minus mark (–) next to those you feel may not be "fair." Unsure which are which? Put a question mark (?) next to the questions. Now, in just a brief paragraph, and using your questions as examples, discuss just what it is that makes a question "fair" or "unfair."

   ....

   ....

   ....

   ....

   ....

2. How do you feel about your ability to correctly answer detail questions? Are they generally easy to answer, or do you often have trouble with them and find other types of questions easier to answer? If so, discuss the type of questions you prefer to answer, and why. Perhaps the title of this paragraph should be "All Tests Should Have Only One Kind of Question—And Why."

   ....

   ....

```
..................................................................................
..................................................................................
..................................................................................
```

Not All Details Are Important

No one can remember all the details in some kinds of reading, even though the details may be easy to recognize while you are reading. You may in fact attempt to underline, list, or in some other way keep track of *all* details when you read. Usually you will work against yourself, for you do not need all the details to understand and remember the *main idea*. All details are not equally important.

What Are Your Thoughts?

1. To demonstrate that not all details are important, describe what occurred on a recent television program or in a recent movie that the other members of the class may be familiar with. Describe as much of the detail as you can remember and then discuss the purpose for including those details. Could some details (a few, many) have been left out, still keeping the story line effective? Which details were absolutely necessary to the story? Why do you think so?

```
..................................................................................
..................................................................................
..................................................................................
```

2. Are you ever aware that you are understanding, or not understanding, as you are reading? If you are aware that you are not understanding, what do you do?

```
..................................................................................
..................................................................................
..................................................................................
```

3. What are some reasons for being aware of details when we are reading or studying?

....

....

....

4. Why are inference questions often so difficult to answer?

....

....

....

Sometimes We Find Too Much Emphasis on Details

We have all had the unfortunate experience of taking a test on an assigned reading for which we have been asked to recall or identify details that were so trivial or so isolated from the main idea or topic that we cannot recall having run into them in our reading. We guessed, therefore, and we may or may not have answered the question correctly. Usually we end up feeling such questions are unfair, and we wonder what the teacher hopes to accomplish by focusing test questions on the minutiae in the reading assignment. This is both a fair question to raise and a fair criticism.

But not all details are unimportant. Next to being able to quickly and easily recognize the main idea in a reading, recognizing and recalling *important* details as you read is the most useful skill in reading comprehension you will use both in college and outside of college.

Details May Be Very Important

Often the details matter as much to us as the main ideas, especially in the exercise we know as *study* reading. These details

1. help us understand the main idea.
2. provide evidence to support a conclusion.
3. provide concrete illustrations.
4. define that which has been said.
5. explain or give examples of the main idea.
6. provide interest.

Questions That Help Determine Important Details

An *important* detail supports the main idea in a passage; we can identify it by asking these questions. If it is an important detail, you should be able to answer these questions with a "yes."

1. Is this a detail the author uses to support or prove the main idea?
2. If this detail were omitted, would the main idea be incomplete, or would the meaning change?
3. Does this detail add to the main idea, or does it change it?
4. Does this detail relate to the other details in a significant way?

Remember, minor details may be interesting but they don't change the author's message.

Answering Test Questions on Supporting Details

When being tested on an assigned reading, you should expect to be asked questions that test your recall of supporting details. Here are some common types of questions.

1. Specific-answer questions.

   How many soldiers died in Vietnam?

2. Sequence-of-events questions.

   What happened to the car after it went through the red light?

3. Following-directions questions.

   Was Alfred to turn left or right at the stop sign?

4. Inference questions ("reading between the lines").

   The example about shooting the wild mustangs is used for what purpose?

Inference Questions Are a Little Tricky

Inference questions are quite common on tests in college. You are expected to conclude correctly statements that aren't directly stated. You are expected to use the information the writer provides, plus facts you already have, to make an educated guess or prediction. You combine experience, knowledge, and common sense with the author's words to lead to an unstated conclusion. Here increased education, experience, and age benefit you.

Don't Be Fooled by a Paraphrase

A test question may not *quote* specifically from the passage read, but instead may restate or paraphrase a supporting detail. Don't be tricked into making the wrong choice because the question paraphrases part of the reading, or because the correct answer may also be a paraphrase. Often, correctly answering a detail question simply requires *general* recall of the passage you have read.

What to Look Out for

Often, selecting a correct response when you have detail questions is complicated by three things.

1. The detail, which in fact may be in the reading passage, is not related to the question being asked.
2. You may *know* a detail is true but it does *not* appear in the passage.
3. Negatively stated questions (such as, "All these *except...*") confuse us. The correct response is the option that is *not* a supporting detail given in the passage.

Often we are so eager to answer the question quickly that we select the first answer we see that we recall was in the passage, forgetting that we are looking for an answer *not* mentioned.

Supporting-Details Margin Mark – – – –

The margin mark for identifying supporting details in a reading selection is a broken (or dotted) line. As you read these selections, practice identifying and marking supporting details. Also, just to keep your newly acquired skills from getting rusty, locate and mark the *main ideas* as well.

Words to Read by

Answer these questions by looking up the key word in each sentence in your dictionary. The pages in parentheses locate the passage that includes the key word. You may wish to read that key word in its context. Write the answer on the lines provided. How do you determine which word(s) to look up?

---

1. What is a *regent*? (91) ....

   ....

2. Is *mozzarella* from Greece or Italy? (91) ....

   ....

3. What is a synonym for *havoc?* (92) ....

   ....

4. What does the *feasibility* of something mean? (93) ....

   ....

5. Why is *colour* spelled in this way? (95) ....

   ....

6. Can a person be a *phenomenon?* (96) ....

   ....

7. Can you have a *paucity* of things you can count? (96) ....

   ....

8. How can you be *aggressively apologetic?* (97) ....

   ....

9. Besides a small fish, what does *throwback* mean? (97) ....

   ....

10. Does *bazaar* or *bizarre* mean being odd or strikingly unconvention-

    al? (99) ....

11. How many years in a *millennium?* (100) ....

    ....

12. Does *pharmacology* or *pharmacopoeia* mean the science of drugs, in-

    cluding their effects? (101) ....

13. How old are your *peers?* (102) ....

    ....

14. How does a person who runs *fastidiously* do so? (102) ....

    ....

15. What does *permeates* mean? (103) ....

....

Answers are at the end of the chapter.

Anticipate the Topics

These are the subjects in some of the reading exercises coming up in this chapter. On the line next to each one, jot down the first few words or phrases that you associate with the topic when you think of it.

birth control ....

Nutrasweet ....

spelling ....

study ....

Greek system ....

art ....

lies ....

music magazine ....

writing ....

drug users ....

Indians ....

bystanders ....

Benjamin Franklin ....

Nixon ....

gang members ....

violence ....

dolphin ....

kissing ....

drug dependency ....

height ....

style ....

Practice Exercises

EXERCISE 1

In each of these exercises a main idea is stated, followed by a list of details. Read the details and indicate on the lines provided whether each detail is important (I) or unimportant (U). The first one is partially completed.

1. Washington, D.C., is an exciting city to visit.

..U... a. It often gets quite warm in the city.

.... b. The Kennedy Center for the Performing Arts offers many plays and concerts.

..I.... c. You often catch glimpses of famous politicians.

..U.... d. The Potomac River is there.

.... e. The Smithsonian Institution is there.

.... f. The world-famous National Gallery is in the city.

.... g. Washington has a fairly high rate of illiteracy.

.... h. The famed statues and monuments are all within easy reach.

2. Florida is a great place for a vacation.

.... a. Several major entertainment parks are in that state.

.... b. Once in a while the temperature drops into the 30s.

.... c. The climate is ideal all year.

.... d. Most beaches are beautiful and not too crowded.

.... e. Seeing exotic birds and animals in parks and in natural places is very common.

.... f. Accommodation rates are very reasonable.

.... g. Orange trees grow in many people's yards.

.... h. The majority of Floridians appear to be retired and elderly.

3.   My older brother seems to have a confused double standard about morality.

.... a. He is always telling his young son not to lie, but he lies himself.

.... b. He borrowed his neighbor's electric drill and kept it for months but yells at me if I don't return his things quickly.

.... c. His wife is really nice.

.... d. He lives in Detroit, Michigan.

.... e. He brags about overcharging customers and getting away with it.

.... f. He is constantly looking for ways of "beating" the IRS.

.... g. He loves to drive high-powered sports cars.

.... h. He gets upset if a cashier makes a mistake that shortchanges him.

4.   Many species of great birds live in the local marshlands.

.... a. Birds thrive there because people don't.

.... b. Marshlands are protected by the federal government.

.... c. Several kinds of herons may be seen any day.

.... d. Oystercatchers, black skimmers, and egrets are commonly seen.

.... e. Marshlands have few natural enemies for birds.

.... f. Marshlands often breed mosquitos.

.... g. Marshlands often attract both salt-water and fresh-water birds.

.... h. Marshlands make excellent nesting areas for birds.

5.   Flying is rapidly becoming the most efficient way to travel around the country.

.... a. For significant distances, air travel is faster than any other form of transportation.

.... b. Per mile traveled, flying is also cheaper.

.... c. Trains are more comfortable than planes.

.... d. Unlike buses and trains, airplanes are scheduled around the clock.

.... e. Air-travel regulation strictly watches to prevent breakdowns.

.... f. A trip from Denver to New York costs $212.

.... g. Flying through the clouds is fun.

.... h. Delays at airports have been significantly reduced in recent years.

EXERCISE 2

In these paragraphs from campus newspapers, the sentences have been numbered. Identify the primary function of the detail in the sentence indicated. Because one detail may serve more than one purpose in a paragraph, be ready to justify your choice. The first one has been completed for you.

1. *Birth Control Ban.* [1] Contradicting national efforts to control birthrate and sexually transmitted diseases, four member schools of the Texas State U. system recently abolished the sale and/or distribution of contraceptive devices from the schools' health clinics. [2] The ruling will affect Angelo State U., Sul Ross U., Southwest Texas State U. (STSU) and Sam Houston U. [3] John Noone, director of the STSU Health Clinic, said although there was "considerable student involvement and opposition," the Board of Regents quickly "handed down their decision." [4] Noone said that aside from the distribution of contraceptives "things won't change that much." [5] He then confirmed, "We will comply with the [Board of Regents'] decision."

   —Bill Morrison, *The Pine Log,* Stephen F. Austin State University, Texas.

   The details in sentence 2 do which of these?

   a. Help readers understand the main idea.
   (b.) Provide concrete illustrations.
   c. Provide the topic with interest.
   d. Provide evidence supporting a conclusion.

2. *Nutrasweet Safe for Healthy People.* [1] It's safe for most healthy people to guzzle diet soda sweetened with aspartame, also known as Nutrasweet, U. of Minnesota researchers say. [2] In a study of 108 people, scientists could find no significant differences between those who consumed aspartame with meals for 24 weeks and those who took a placebo. [3] They concluded that aspartame does not cause headaches or other problems in healthy people, but the sweetener is hazardous for people born with the metabolism problem called phenylketonuria. [4] Those people can suffer brain damage if they consume too much phenylalanine, one of the amino acids in aspartame.

   —Dolores Lotz, *The Minnesota Daily,* University of Minnesota, Twin Cities.

   The details in sentence 2 do which of these?

   a. Define the statements made.
   b. Provide evidence supporting a conclusion.
   c. Provide interest.
   d. Give an example of the main idea.

3. *Spelling Checks by Phone.* [1] Need to know how to spell "mozzarella"? [2] Or maybe you need to know the difference between "lay" and "lie." [3] Call the Grammar Crisis Line at Ball State U. and your problems may be solved.

[4] The hotline, which operates Monday through Friday, employs 18 to 25 students. [5] It began four years ago for students who need to know a quick answer and a simple explanation from a trained tutor.

—Pat Hughes, *The Ball State Daily News*, Ball State University, Indiana.

The details in sentence 5 do which of these?

a. Provide evidence supporting a conclusion.
b. Give an example of the main idea.
c. Define the statements made.
d. Help readers understand the main idea.

4. *Student Stranded in Germany.* [1] Mohsen Zakeri, an Iranian-born graduate student at the U. of Utah, has been stranded in Germany for more than nine months. [2] Zakeri, a doctoral candidate in the history department, returned to Iran last summer to complete research for his dissertation. [3] When he attempted to pick up his renewed student visa in Frankfurt, Germany, he was told that questions about his application would delay his return to the University. [4] His visit to East Berlin was considered "adverse information" to renew his visa.

—Shauna Bona, *The Daily Utah Chronicle*, University of Utah.

The details in sentence 3 do which of these?

a. Provide a concrete illustration.
b. Define the statements made.
c. Help readers understand the main idea.
d. Provide evidence supporting a conclusion.

5. *Who Ya Gonna Call?* [1] Armed with toy guns, games, food and a radio, a team of four students invades rooms of diligent students to relieve the stress caused by the pursuit of a higher education. [2] They're "Study Busters," and for a fee, they can provide students with an entertaining study break. [3] Buster Jim Rogan said a typical bust consists of closing the student's books, gathering neighbors, dancing, eating and playing a game of Twister. [4] "Their first reaction is always shock," Rogan said. [5] "How often do people come into your room and cause a general havoc?"

—Gina La Vecchia, *Marquette Tribune*, Marquette University, Wisconsin.

The details in sentence 5 do which of these?

a. Provide interest.
b. Define a word or an idea.
c. Give an example of the main idea.
d. Help readers understand the main idea.

6. [1] The Board of Trustees of Franklin and Marshall College, Pa., have voted to "derecognize" the Greek system because it promotes underage drinking. [2] This reflects a nationwide trend, as many colleges have voted to derecognize or reform their present Greek systems. [3] The colleges are reacting to problems including discrimination, rapes and college liability for damage caused by fraternities and sororities.

> —Jennifer Mezey, *The Oberlin Review*, Oberlin College, Ohio.

The details in sentence 3 do which of these?

   a. Provide evidence supporting a conclusion.

   b. Help readers understand the main idea.

   c. Give an example of the main idea.

   d. Provide interest.

7. *Hanging Art in People's Ears.* [1] Two Stanford Graduate School of Business students, Ed Earl and Norton Rappaport, are developing The San Francisco Rock and Roll Museum. [2] They have their work cut out for them—they need to raise $20 million to fund the non-profit museum, which should open in three to five years. [3] Determined to find the feasibility of the project, the pair oversaw a research study done by a consulting company. [4] The research predicts the museum will draw between 300,000 and 500,000 people annually. [5] "I think of this museum as a way to hang art in people's ears." Earl said.

> —Michelle Finkel, *The Stanford Daily*, Stanford University, California.

The details in sentence 5 do which of these?

   a. Provide a concrete illustration.

   b. Define statements made.

   c. Provide evidence supporting a conclusion.

   d. Provide interest.

8. *Lies, Lies, Lies.* [1] Caroline and Michelle Enterprises, a company aptly named for Texas Tech U. students Caroline O'Neal and Michelle Phillips, markets T-shirts with the "Top 10 Lies Heard at Texas Tech" printed on the back. [2] After consulting an attorney, locating a screen printer and obtaining permission from the dean of students, the pair was in business. [3] The women, who have sold about 250 shirts, will donate between 15 and 25 percent of their profits to an outreach group for drug and alcohol abusers. [4] The students say they have actually heard all of the "lies" they print. [5] And the No. 1 lie, according to Caroline and Michelle? "Texas Tech was my first choice …"

> —Troy Hattaway, *The University Daily*, Texas Tech University.

The details in sentence 5 do which of these?

    a. Provide evidence supporting a conclusion.

    b. Define statements made.

    c. Provide a concrete illustration.

    d. Provide interest.

9. *A David Letterman Scholarship?* [1] For students interested in finding out about the plethora of private scholarships available, a computer firm has the answer. [2] For $69, Financial Guidance Services will provide you with a list of scholarships, ranging from awards benefiting descendants of Confederate soldiers to grants given to grocery store clerks only. [3] Even *Late Night* talk show host David Letterman has endowed a scholarship for "C" students at his alma mater, Ball State U., Ind. [4] To qualify, students must have never achieved a grade point average higher than 2.0.

      —Tim Lubina, *The Pioneer*, California State University, Hayward.

The details in sentence 3 do which of these?

    a. Provide evidence supporting a conclusion.

    b. Provide a concrete illustration.

    c. Define statements made.

    d. Help readers understand the main idea.

10. *Magazine Covers Flexible Music.* [1] When he was 13, Richard Shupe decided he was fed up with commercial music and threw away his record collection. [2] "I knew there had to be more out there," he said. [3] So Shupe started an alternative music newsletter which he sent to music promoters and record companies. [4] His "low-quality" newsletter turned into *Reflex*, a magazine dedicated to alternative music. [5] Shupe has distributed *Reflex* throughout the world. [6] One of the magazine's unique features is the Flexidisk, a vinyl record inserted in each issue that looks suspiciously like the disks of the Jackson 5 found on the backs of Frosted Flakes boxes 15 years ago.

      —Mary Pagnotta, *The Brown & White*, Lehigh University, Pennsylvania.

The details in sentence 6 do which of these?

    a. Provide interest.

    b. Provide evidence supporting a conclusion.

    c. Define statements made.

    d. Give an example of the main idea.

EXERCISE 3

For these passages, a question about the main idea is asked. The answer to each question will be the major supporting details in each passage. Read the passages carefully, using your margin mark for details: – – – –. This marking will be especially helpful to you in the more difficult passages. The first one has been completed for you.

1. Writing imaginatively cannot be taught. It can be studied in examples—the writings of Defoe, Shakespeare, La Fontaine and Jules Verne show what can be done, but not how to do it. In this, writing is on a par with art and the product of an artisan's hands. The painter can no more convey the secret of his imaginative handling of colour than the plumber can teach that little extra touch he gives a wiped joint. All three, writer, artist, artisan, have secrets springing from within. After learning the principles, they go on to produce their works inspired by the dignity of accomplishment due to their gifts.

> —From *Communicating in Business Today* by Ruth G. Newman. Copyright © 1987 by D. C. Heath and Company. Reprinted by permission of the publisher.

Like imaginative writing, what two things cannot be taught?

a. *imaginative handling of color by a painter*

b. *the extra touch of the plumber (or artisan)*

2. Kenniston (1968) describes three groups of drug users on college campuses: tasters, seekers, and heads. By far the largest group are those he calls *tasters*. Tasters' use of drugs is usually casual or experimental. The second group are called *seekers*. Their use of drugs is occasional but regular. They try to achieve heightened awareness, relief from boredom or depression, or just plain "an experience." Finally, the most regular users of drugs are the *heads*. They are a small but highly visible minority who use drugs with frequent regularity. As Keniston says, however, even heads are not necessarily drug addicted, although addicted youths would fall into this category. The important point is that, even with the general upswing in drug use, the percent of regular drug users among the college population is relatively small and varies with the type of college campus and the section of the country.

> —From *Adolescents* by Gary M. Ingersoll. Copyright © 1982 by D. C. Heath and Company. Reprinted by permission of the publisher.

How are the three groups of drug users on college campuses described?

a. ....

b. ....

c. ....

3. Almost since the time of Columbus, the native Americans have suffered

cruelly at the whim of the invaders. That is simply a very terrible, shameful fact. There has been everything from early germ warfare (Lord Jeffrey Amherst gave Indians disease-infested blankets that killed them and made old Lord Jeff even more wealthy), to broken treaties and promises, to forced marches from swamps to dust bowls, to simple murder.

To understate, Liberal America has not done itself proud in its dealings with the natives of this land.

> —From *A Preface to Politics*, 4th edition, by David F. Scherman with Bob Waterman. Copyright © 1986 by D. C. Heath and Company. Reprinted by permission of the publisher.

What four things illustrate our cruel treatment of native Americans?

a. ....

b. ....

c. ....

d. ....

4. The issue of not assisting someone in distress is by no means a modern phenomenon; it was a matter of concern even in biblical times. Social psychologists have carried out many experiments in both field and laboratory to determine the factors influencing bystanders' responses to people who appear to be in distress. These studies reveal that if there are many bystanders, if someone else is perceived as more expert or as having more responsibility, if the situation is ambiguous, or if the person in distress is considered responsible for his or her own plight, then the observer is less likely to intervene. All these conditions diminish personal responsibility.

> —From Scherman, *A Preface to Politics*.

What two factors influence bystanders' responses to people who appear to be in distress?

a. ....

....

b. ....

....

5. Benjamin Franklin once blamed the wilderness for the paucity of American literature. Americans, he explained, were so busy taming a continent that they lacked time for plays and poetry. The explanation was plausible but not sufficient. Another factor was the shortage of type, ink, and paper, all of which had to be imported from Europe in the early days. As a result,

American printers preferred timely periodicals, such as newspapers and almanacs, which did not tie up their machinery for long periods of time.

—From *Representative Americans: The Revolutionary Generation* by Norman K. Risjord. Copyright © 1986 by D. C. Heath and Company. Reprinted by permission of the publisher.

A major reason for early scarcity of American literature was shortages in what three things?

a. ....

b. ....

c. ....

6. Richard Nixon may well be the most controversial political personality in recent American history. He built his career on the most inflammatory issues of the day, from red-chasing in the 1940s to the Vietnam War in the 1960s, and the Watergate episode ended his public life with the most explosive constitutional crisis in over a century. Ever combative and resourceful, he antagonized his enemies and cultivated his followers with unremitting energy and skill. Hence, there are few "objective" accounts of the Nixon years; passion still guides the pens of most writers (including Nixon himself), producing assessments that are either bitterly critical or aggressively apologetic. Thus it may be some time before historians can make a balanced appraisal of Nixon's role. The stain of Watergate, for example, has almost blotted from the record Nixon's initiatives in foreign policy, especially toward China. Whatever the final judgment, it seems that historians will be unforgiving of the wounds that Watergate inflicted on the American body politic. Trust in elected leaders is an essential but fragile ingredient in a democracy, and that trust was badly undermined by the Watergate revelations.

—From *The American Pageant* by Thomas Bailey and David M. Kennedy. Copyright © 1986 by D. C. Heath and Company. Reprinted by permission of the publisher.

Why was Watergate such a disaster for Richard Nixon and the American public?

a. ....

....

b. ....

....

7. Unfortunately, too many business writers act as though they are being paid by the word. Some of this long-windedness is a throwback to their junior high school days when a strict teacher ordered up a specific number of pages, and students met that requirement no matter how little they had to say. In other cases, wordiness arises from a mistaken belief that business writing ought to sound and look a certain way, that it requires a bit of pomp and circumstance to pass muster. Perhaps more forgivably, some writers are too wordy because they believe that by eliminating words they will also eliminate needed information. This is not true. The conciseness that is appropriate to business writing does not require that you deplete the substance of your documents.

—From Newman, *Communicating in Business Today.*

What are the reasons for wordiness in business writing?

a. ....

....

b. ....

....

c. ....

....

8. The stereotyped model of juvenile crime is built around the concept of the street gang. That stereotype has been nurtured by the media even in the face of evidence that most delinquent acts are not done by gangs. However, street gangs do constitute a major problem, because the crimes they do commit may become excessively violent. In spite of the interest and attention devoted to street gangs, little can be stated with any certainty about their structure. Gang members are typically not willing to be interviewed, and when they are interviewed, one suspects they are telling the interviewer what he or she wants to hear.

—From Ingersoll, *Adolescents.*

Why do people hold a stereotype about juvenile crime?

a. ....

b. ....

c. ....

9. Violence haunted America in the mid-1960s, and it stalked grotesquely onto center stage on November 22, 1963. While riding in an open limousine in downtown Dallas, Texas, President Kennedy was shot in the brain by a concealed rifleman and died within seconds. As a stunned nation nursed its grief, the tragedy grew still more unbelievable. The alleged assassin, a furtive figure named Lee Harvey Oswald, was himself shot to death in front of the television cameras by a self-appointed avenger, Jack Ruby. So bizarre were the events surrounding the two murders that even an elaborate official investigation conducted by Chief Justice Warren could not quiet all doubts and theories about what had really happened.

—From Bailey and Kennedy, *The American Pageant.*

What are the names of the three people closest to our understanding in the assassination of John F. Kennedy?

a. ....

b. ....

c. ....

10. A school of approximately 50 *Delphinus delphis* was sighted. As soon as the Zodiac (our boat) approached, they increased speed, dived, and changed direction under water. The school reassembled behind the Zodiac. The yacht took over the chase and an animal was wounded by the harpoon. We saw quite clearly how other dolphins came immediately to the help of the wounded animal on the starboard side of the yacht. They supported the wounded dolphin with their flippers and bodies and carried it to the surface. It blew 2–3 times and then dived. The whole incident lasted about 30 seconds and was repeated twice when the animal appeared unable to surface alone. All the animals including the wounded dolphin then dived and swam quickly out of sight.

—From *Personality,* 2d edition, by Seymour Feshbach and Bernard Weiner. Copyright © 1986 by D. C. Heath and Company. Reprinted by permission of the publisher.

How many boats were involved in the dolphin-wounding episode?

a. ....

EXERCISE 4

These exercises test your ability to read longer passages and then determine important details when detail or inference questions are asked in varied ways. Put a check mark next to the answer that best completes the question. The first one has been done for you.

The Lima Beans of Romance. [1] There are two types of people who go on blind dates: We're one type and they're the other.

[2] If it weren't for blind dates, they'd have no dates at all. [3] For this reason, they actually look forward to blind dates. [4] We regard blind dates as as insult to our own ability to get a date.

[5] Does this mean we shouldn't go on blind dates? [6] Of course. [7] But it

doesn't mean that we won't. [8] And if you do, be sure to take precautionary steps.

[9] For starters, nearly all blind dates originate through a friend or a roommate, the two people who are most likely to know that recently you've been spending more time alone than the Maytag repairman.

[10] They tell you it's for your own good—the same line your mom would use to get you to eat your lima beans. [11] Blind dates are the lima beans of romance.

[12] Listen for euphemisms. [13] If they say, "She has a nice personality," it probably just means that she hasn't taken an ax to anyone lately.

[14] If you agree to the date, immediately go someplace where you don't need to talk, since conversation will initially be somewhat stilted. [15] Movies were created with this in mind.

[16] If the chemistry is poisonous—and you didn't abort the date at midmovie—you must deal with the kiss-off. [17] When the time comes, say something like: "I'm not feeling well, and I could very well throw up at anytime. [18] How about a good night kiss?"

[19] Another method is more subtle. [20] If she doesn't want to tell the guy he's a gutter germ but still wants him to know that she won't kiss him now or at any other time in this millennium, she just says, "I'm sorry, but I don't kiss a guy on the last date."

[21] Given the horror stories we've all heard and indeed lived through, why do so many of us continue to go on blind dates? [22] Simply because blind dates pique our most basic romantic desire: to meet Mr. or Ms. Right and live happily ever after. [23] Because it's not someone we already know, it must be someone we don't know. [24] This hope keeps us betting on a long shot.

—Chris Lamb, *The Daily Iowan*, University of Iowa.

1. The example in sentence 13, "taken an axe to anyone lately," is used to illustrate

.... a. that blind dates can be dangerous.

.... b. that women are always capable of wild behavior.

...✔..... c. how friends deemphasize negative qualities of blind dates they introduce us to.

.... d. that nothing is ever the way it is supposed to be.

2. The sentence that best supports the main idea in the passage is

.... a. sentence 9: "For starters, nearly all blind dates ...."

.... b. sentence 14: "If you agree to the date ...."

.... c. sentence 17: "When the time comes, say ...."

.... d. sentence 22: "Simply because blind dates pique ...."

3. Sentence 11, "Blind dates are the lima beans of romance," compares blind dates to

.... a. vegetables rich in nourishment.

.... b. vegetables that many people find distasteful.

.... c. vegetables that we rarely eat.

.... d. vegetables that are often misunderstood.

[1] Dr. Joseph Zabik, a researcher in alcoholism and pharmacology at Purdue University, describes the progression toward drug dependence in the following manner (personal interview): Initially an individual may experiment with a drug out of curiosity or to be part of the crowd. [2] An adolescent who continues to use the drug regularly over an extended period of time develops a tolerance to the drug. [3] That is, at first a small dose creates the desired state of mind. [4] Gradually, however, larger and larger amounts of the drug are required to achieve the same impact. [5] Individuals who continue to use these increased dosages may develop a physical or psychological dependence on the drug. [6] Although some drugs have no known physically addictive characteristics, all may have psychologically addictive characteristics. [7] Dependence is most obvious when an adolescent goes through a period of withdrawal, in which the drug of dependence is no longer available. [8] Withdrawal symptoms may be mild—including minor physical discomfort and anxiety or irritability—or, in cases of strong dependence on certain drugs, it may be *very* stressful, with severe pain and paranoid hallucinations. [9] Although not all drug users develop a physical or psychological dependence, it is, nonetheless, a very real possibility. [10] The common notion that addicts were once "experimenters" has a good deal of truth in it.

—From Feshbach and Weiner, *Personality*.

4. Sentence 8, "Withdrawal symptoms may be mild ..." is used to illustrate

.... a. physical difficulties resulting from drug dependence.

.... b. that drug dependence isn't always a horrible experience.

.... c. that tolerance to drugs needs to be established and maintained.

.... d. that psychological addiction is always worse than physical addiction.

5. The reference in sentence 1 to Dr. Joseph Zabik, a Purdue University researcher, is intended to

.... a. point out the high quality of Purdue University research.

.... b. suggest that academia can always be trusted.

.... c. identify who is worried about drugs and where.

.... d. give scientific and academic credibility to statements that follow.

[1] Today's youths are taller than those in previous generations. [2] If you were to compare the average heights of youths in 1902 to current norms for children and youths, you would find that from ages six to fifteen today's boys range from 7.9 to 12.9 cm. (centimeters—about three to five inches) taller than their 1902 peers. [3] Girls are, on the average, between 4.7 and 12.4 cm. (about two to five inches) taller than their 1902 peers for the same age groups. [4] At ages seventeen and eighteen, or at approximately adult height, the differences level out and males are about 5.2 cm. (about two inches) taller and females 3.7 cm. (one and a half inches) taller than their 1902 counterparts. [5] In the 1890s, less than 5 percent of young men were over six feet tall. [6] Today more than that percentage of fifteen-year-olds and nearly 25 percent of eighteen-year-olds exceed six feet. [7] This trend toward ever-taller generations, however, seems to be tapering off.

—From Feshbach and Weiner, *Personality.*

6. Which sentence appears to best support the topic sentence (sentence 1), "Today's youths are taller ..."?

.... a. sentence 3: "Girls are ..."

.... b. sentence 7: "This trend ..."

.... c. sentence 6: "Today more than ..."

.... d. sentence 3: "At ages seventeen ..."

7. This passage compares heights of boys and girls in 1902 with those of youths today to show

.... a. that being taller is an advantage nowadays.

.... b. a trend toward taller youths.

.... c. improved diet is a cause of increased height.

.... d. that today's youths start growing taller earlier than in 1902.

WORD ORDER: STYLE IN THE MAKING

[1] Writers who are conscientious but inexperienced often write with a great deal of self-conscious effort. [2] Worrying constantly, they inch ahead word by word. [3] When they have finally reached the end of the piece, they breathe a sigh of relief. [4] They have done their best. [5] They are off the hook.

[6] Before they start to write, experienced writers generally think very hard about their audience and their purpose. [7] They devote time to sketching out the structure of the piece and perhaps to obsessing a bit about their first few sentences. [8] But once over these hurdles, these writers do not fastidiously choose their words like cherries from a tree. [9] Rather, they let them fall upon the page as if their order were predestined. [10] Such writers know well enough that nothing about this first rush of words has any

relationship to destiny. [11] Even though it frequently contains much worth retaining, this spontaneous outpouring represents only one of many possibilities for expressing the same thoughts.

[12] Most writers want and need the luxury of shaking the tree and letting the fruit fall as it will. [13] If we free our inner voice, it speaks to us rapidly and distinctly. [14] By recording the words we hear, we quickly give form and substance to our thoughts. [15] Half-formed ideas drifting through a writer's mind are, of course, nearly impossible to evaluate or revise. [16] And frequently they are lost before we even have the opportunity to try. [17] But an idea that has been made tangible and visible can be clarified and refined at will. [18] And writers *must* revise. [19] The more knowledgeable and particular the writer, the more complex or sensitive the purpose, the more time the revision may take, and the better the result is likely to be.

[20] Your "gut" reaction to your first draft can provide some insights, but it will only carry you a short distance. [21] To strengthen your phrasing and sentence structure, you again need to know precisely what you are trying to do and how you are going to do it. [22] As with word choice, revising word order with confidence requires some real knowledge of specific rules and techniques. [23] Although this knowledge permeates even your first drafts, you appreciate it the most when you revise. [24] It helps you to spot weaknesses immediately and to know exactly what remedies to apply.

—From Newman, *Communicating in Business Today.*

8. All these are often factors in writing done by inexperienced writers except

.... a. inching ahead word by word.

.... b. worrying constantly.

.... c. breathing a sigh of relief.

.... d. thinking hard about audience and purpose.

9. The example of cherries on a cherry tree is used to illustrate

.... a. the difficulty of selecting the best word among many.

.... b. the way in which words fall into place in writing.

.... c. the difficulty in getting the reader's attention and keeping it.

.... d. the technique of using images all readers recognize.

10. In sentence 20 ("Your gut reaction ...") the reader is encouraged to

.... a. recognize the need to be very logical.

.... b. trust your instinct for saying insightful things in your first draft.

.... c. identify the needs before you do the writing.

.... d. know that all truth is "felt" in the "gut."

EXERCISE 5

Read this passage on lightning and then do these three things.

—Identify the main idea in the passage.
—Identify the topic sentence in each of the four paragraphs.
—List the details (major and minor) in each paragraph.

Bolts of lightning have tremendous energies. It is estimated that the temperature in the vicinity of a lightning flash is of the order of 15,000–30,000°C. This is quite large compared to the Sun's surface temperature of 6000°C. The awesome electrical properties of lightning become clear when you compare it with ordinary household electricity, which has up to 240 volts and 100–200 amperes of current available at the main service panel. A typical lightning discharge has from 10–100 million volts and up to 300,000 amperes of current. It can leap up to a mile or more.

A lightning flash's sudden release of energy explosively heats the air, producing the compressions we hear as thunder. When heard at a distance of about 100 m (33 ft) or less from the discharge channel, thunder consists of one loud bang or "clap." When heard at a distance of 1 km (0.62 mi) from the discharge channel, thunder generally consists of a rumbling sound punctuated by several large claps. In general, thunder cannot be heard at distances of more than 25 km (16 mi) from the discharge channel. Presumably, the loud bang of thunder heard when one sees a nearby lightning flash is due to the strong sound wave from the channel base. For an observer at a distance of 1 km from the lightning channel, the initial loud bang is refracted overhead due to temperature variations in the air, and the discharge begins with a rumble. At distances greater than 25 km, the sound is refracted above the observer.

The association of thunder with lightning was postulated very early. In his famous treatise *Meteorologica,* Aristotle presented the general idea, but in a somewhat incorrect, reversed fashion. He thought that thunder resulted when heat condensed from clouds.

> ... moving violently and striking against the surrounding clouds delivers a blow, whose noise is called thunder. ... Besides, the pressed out wind is usually consumed by a delicate and gentle flame, and this is what we call lightning. ... It is produced after the blow and thus also after the thunder; but it seems to be produced before the thunder because seeing precedes hearing. We have clear proof that seeing precedes hearing when we observe the oarsmen of a trireme, for as they draw back their oars for a second stroke we hear the sound of their first stroke.

Taking the proper sequence of lightning and thunder, since lightning flashes generally occur near the storm center, the resultant thunder provides a method of easily approximating the distance to the storm. Light travels at approximately 186,000 mi/s, and the lightning flash is seen without any appreciable time lapse. Sound, however, travels at approximately 1/5 mi/s, and a time lapse occurs between seeing the lightning flash and hearing the thunder. This phenomenon is also observed when watching someone at a distance fire a gun at night or hit a baseball. The report of the gun or the "crack" of the bat is always heard after the flash of the gun is observed or the baseball is well on its way. Seeing does precede hearing, as Aristotle thought. By counting the seconds between seeing the lightning flash and hearing the thunder, an estimate of the distance of the storm center may be obtained. For example, if 5 s elapsed, then the storm center would be approximately 1 mi away, taking the velocity of sound as 1/5 mi/s; if 8 s elapsed, the storm would be 1-3/5 mi away.

—From Shipman et al., *An Introduction to Physical Science.*

Main idea ....

....

1. Topic sentence of paragraph 1: ....

....

Details: ....

....

....

2. Topic sentence of paragraph 2: ....

....

Details: ....

....

....

3. Topic sentence of paragraph 3: ....

....

Details: ....

....

....

4. Topic sentence of paragraph 4: ....

....

Details: ....

....

....

Answers to Selected Exercises

WORDS TO READ BY

You will find variation in definitions.
1. someone who serves on a governing board
2. Italy
3. destruction, ruin, confusion
4. its capability for being accomplished
5. a British variation
6. yes
7. yes
8. *Apologetic* also refers to a formal defense.
9. a reversion to an earlier stage
10. bizarre
11. 1,000
12. pharmacology
13. approximately the same age
14. carefully in all ways
15. Something spreads or flows throughout.

EXERCISE 1

1a. U	2a. I	3a. I	4a. I	5a. I
b. I	b. U	b. I	b. U	b. I
c. I	c. I	c. U	c. I	c. U
d. U	d. I	d. U	d. I	d. I
e. I	e. I	e. I	e. I	e. I
f. I	f. I	f. I	f. U	f. U
g. U	g. U	g. U	g. I	g. U
h. I	h. U	h. I	h. I	h. I

EXERCISE 3

1a. imaginative handling of color by a painter
 b. the extra touch of the plumber
2a. Tasters use drugs casually or experimentally.
 b. Seekers use drugs occasionally but regularly.
 c. Heads use drugs frequently and regularly.

3a. germ warfare
  b. broken treaties and promises
  c. forced marches
  d. murder
4a. If many bystanders are present, someone else is perceived as more responsible.
  b. If the situation is ambiguous, or if the person in distress is considered responsible for his or her own plight, the observer is less likely to intervene.
5a. type
  b. ink
  c. paper
6a. Watergate overshadows Nixon's initiatives in foreign policy, especially toward China.
  b. The trust in an elected leader was badly undermined.
7a. In junior high school, emphasis was on quantity of writing.
  b. The mistaken belief is that business writing requires "pomp and circumstance."
  c. Some writers don't eliminate words because they are afraid they will eliminate needed information.
8a. Media coverage is misleading.
  b. Gang members don't like to be interviewed.
  c. When interviewed, gang members tell the interviewer what he or she wants to hear.
9a. Lee Harvey Oswald
  b. Jack Ruby
  c. Chief Justice Warren
10a. two, the Zodiac and the yacht

```
┌─────────────────────────────┐
│                             │
│        Chapter 4            │
│                             │
├─────────────────────────────┤
│                             │
│      Determining the        │
│     Meaning of Words        │
│       from Context          │
│                             │
└─────────────────────────────┘
```

The chief virtue that language can have is
clearness, and nothing detracts from it so
much as the use of unfamiliar words.

—Galen

This chapter will help you to:

1. learn new words from their context, without stopping to look up their definitions.
2. use context to your advantage.
3. recognize context clues and the ways in which they define new words.
4. know what to look out for when you are tested on words in context.

To be an efficient reader—and thus a successful student—you will need to
know a lot of words. The English language has about 750,000 words, and
more new words are coming into use daily. A beginning college student may
know up to 25,000 of those words (not counting plurals and variants of those
words). As a result, the materials you read for college courses are likely to include
many words that you don't know. It is estimated that freshmen with a fifteen-
credit course load may encounter 3,000 to 6,000 new words each term. Also, words
are constantly being redefined. Each word takes on additional meanings as time
passes until it has many meanings.

Every time you read an assignment for a college course you are likely to come
across words that you do not know. What should you do? If a teacher were asking
you this question, you would give the expected answer: stop and look it up in

the dictionary. Even though you know that may be the response the teacher wants to hear—and it is a very good way to learn the meaning of a word—you also know that in practice it is the last resort, not the first choice. Usually, stopping to look up a word in a dictionary is inconvenient, and it is often impossible if you are doing a timed reading or testing passage.

Use the Context to Your Advantage

A much better way to learn word meanings, and the method most often used by adult readers, is to learn them as you read, by using context clues. The teacher should expect you to answer, "Omit the word, use the context to help you understand the word, and look it up later." In this way you identify the correct meaning belonging to a specific word by recognizing and interpreting other words in the surrounding context. This technique really is a lot easier than it sounds because most writers, realizing that readers often have trouble recognizing words, deliberately put in clues that will define or suggest the words' correct meaning. Even when the meanings of words are not *specifically* identified in the context, they may be implied—that is, suggested or hinted at so that you can accurately guess at the correct meaning.

Writing to Comprehend

1. Explain briefly in your own words just what context is. Is the context around something written, or said, limited to a specified number of sentences? Just how far does a context extend? Does a context consist of "layers," some applying more to the meaning of words than other "layers"?

   ....

   ....

   ....

   ....

   ....

2. Can you know and use too many words? Explain your thinking.

   ....

   ....

....

....

....

3. If someone didn't know how to read, what things would you tell him or her?

....

....

....

....

....

4. Do preconceptions and readers' attitudes affect ability to learn from the material read? In what ways?

....

....

....

....

....

Awareness of Context Is Crucial

The context is the part of the reading that immediately surrounds the word and makes it meaningful. Context may be a phrase, sentence, paragraph, or longer passage. Often a word standing by itself has little meaning, or has several possible meanings, and requires a context to give it a specific meaning. A frequently used word that illustrates this condition is *principal*. It could mean several things.

Mr. Gordon was the high school principal.

The stockbroker was a principal in the corporate merger.

The principal due upon sale of the property was $10,000.

As you can see, context is crucial to a word's meaning.

Context Clues Define New Words

The more you force yourself to be aware of context clues as you read, the sooner it will become second nature for you to learn new words in this way without their slowing you down or causing you to stumble as you read.

Seven clues will enable you to determine correct meanings from context.

1. *Synonyms:* A writer using a difficult word will often choose a more familiar word or words with the same meaning to make the difficult word understandable.

   > Ballet students appear so *lithe*; they are so limber and flexible.

   > The *cataract* was spectacular; the steep waterfall dropped abruptly eighty feet.

2. *Restatement:* Close to a synonym, a restatement differs in that a difficult word is usually restated in *simpler* form. The restatement is often set off by commas.

   > The poetry was *sublime,* lofty and moving, and brought me close to tears.

   > The village was *depopulated,* most of the residents dead or moved, but the livestock remained untouched.

3. *Contrast:* Sometimes a writer uses a contrast to clarify a word's meaning, and an antonym, a word of opposite meaning (Did you notice the restatement?), is used to accomplish the differentiation. Often, *contrast* clue words such as *but, however,* or *in contrast to* are used. These words are clues that contrast is being used.

   > This town has a *dearth* of restaurants but an abundance of bars.

   > She tried to *synthesize* everything she had read on the subject of twentieth-century art in contrast to separating each element she knew about nineteenth-century art.

4. *Definition:* Very often a writer will simply include a definition for a difficult word.

   > A *dialect* is a form of speech from a specific region.

   > A *jovial* person is good-humored and merry.

5. *Explanation:* An explanation is close to a definition. As an aid to the reader, the difficult word is explained, usually in simpler words, to make the meaning

clearer. The explanation is generally a bit longer than a definition and is usually found in one or more different sentences.

> The chrome is beginning to *corrode*. It shows signs of pitting and of being eaten away gradually.

> It was a *martial* parade: signs of the military were everywhere. Everyone was in uniform; guns, cannon, tanks were on display, and jet fighters flew overhead.

Note: Sometimes the explanation for a word is presented *before* the word is given:

> The puppy was a complete bother and an annoyance to all the neighbors. It was a continual *nuisance*.

6. *Examples:* A major section or the entire passage may act as a definition, example, or illustration of a word. This context clue is a little harder to spot initially and requires the reader to use more reasoning. Often *your* experiences provide common-sense clues to the meaning of an example and the meaning of a word.

> The movie was packed with *morbid* scenes such as the mother's death, the father's suicide, and the neighbor girl's crippling.

> His alibi was *substantiated* when John's friends offered personal testimony, letters of documentation, and three videotapes showing that he was present at the party.

7. *Mood or tone:* The *mood* or *tone* of a passage (discussed further in Chapter 6) often gives you clues to the meaning of a word used in the passage. People often refer to mood or tone as the "feeling" the words generate.

> The inmates' *demented* yelling and screaming seemed to penetrate the three-foot grey walls and the moss-covered roof of the institution.

> Her *obsequious* conduct soon had all the other groupies fawning around the band members, speaking shyly and taking every opportunity to convey how fortunate they felt to be in the presence of such a famous band.

What to Look Out for

Often when you are tested on words in context, things can be a little tricky. Watch out for:

- A definition for the word would be correct if it were used in a different context. (Remember *principal*?) Do not assume you know the word's meaning if you know *one* meaning; the context may require a different meaning.
- *Another* word or phrase, close in meaning, appearing in the passage may be mistaken for the definition.
- Other answer choices "look good" and lead to a snap decision.

Word-Meaning Margin Mark

A circle (as if you were circling a new word) in the margin indicates a new word in that line. You may even wish to circle the word itself in the line if you have the time. Get in the habit of identifying these new words in context as you read.

What Are Your Thoughts?

1. What is the best way for you to go about permanently learning words from their context clues? Should you write new words down? Should you attempt to use new words in your speaking and writing? What are the best ways you can think of for retaining the words you learn in context?

   ....

   ....

   ....

2. Of the seven clues discussed in this chapter that will enable you to determine correct meanings from context, which are the easiest to spot? Why? Which are the most difficult? Why?

   ....

   ....

   ....

3. Look over the exercises in this chapter and see if you can find a reading selection or a question or two that touch your emotions, either negatively or positively. Does the subject of the question ordinarily make you angry, sad, happy, sentimental, or irritated when you bump into it? If so, discuss how you think that heightened emotional response affects your understanding of the passage you are reading.

   ....

....

....

4. What must you understand to make sense of material you read? How important is it that reading be meaningful?

....

....

....

Anticipate the Topics

The subjects of the five long reading passages in this chapter are listed here. Without reading the passages, write a few sentences about each subject, addressing the topic and what you don't understand about the subject.

evolution ....

....

....

money ....

....

....

magnetism ....

....

....

Clovis man ....

....

....

computer applications ....

....

....

As you write, are you aware of how hard it is to write about subjects you are unfamiliar with? Why is that?

Practice Exercises

EXERCISE 1

Using context clues, circle the letter of the best definition for the italicized word in each sentence. Be ready to explain how you came to your decision. The first one has been done for you.

1. Some days I feel so *lethargic* that I just don't want to move.
   a. excited
   b. artistic
   c. sluggish
   d. hungry

2. She seems *averse* to all the suggested courses of action. She doesn't like any of them.
   a. opposed
   b. dedicated
   c. excited
   d. suspicious

3. The suggestions on how and where to invest were *dubious* at best. They were somewhat radical as well as harebrained.
   a. rewarding
   b. innovative
   c. tested
   d. suspect

4. I was in a *nostalgic* mood, longing for the "good old days" when things were simpler.
   a. drunken
   b. bad-tempered
   c. unthinking
   d. yearning

5. The businessman practiced calming meditation in an attempt to *alleviate* the stress he felt.
   a. lighten
   b. increase
   c. enjoy
   d. understand

6. Western cultures have a strong *taboo* about the practice of incest. In fact, most societies have laws against incest.
   a. fascination
   b. misunderstanding
   c. prohibition
   d. appreciation

7. A *discordant* tone hurt the discussions on nuclear disarmament. An occasional disagreement was to be expected.
   a. musical
   b. humorous
   c. lacking accord
   d. scary

8. To study whether or not a behavior is *innate*, one must isolate the subject at birth so that behavior will not be influenced by surroundings and family members.

a. learned   b. inborn

c. correct   d. disrespectful

9. The *curettage,* or surgical scraping of a body cavity, is done in an operating room.

    a. medical cart   b. medical specialist

    c. medical procedure   d. medical equipment

10. *Dire* predictions about hurricane Helena led everyone to leave the island.

    a. disastrous   b. enjoyable

    c. necessary   d. unrealistic

EXERCISE 2

Use context clues to figure out the meanings of the italicized words in these sentences, and write your definition on the lines provided. The first one is done for you.

1. The *ghostwriter* never gets credit for the writing and never gets his or her name on the cover of the book.

   ghostwriter: *a writer who receives no credit or recognition for the writing*

2. The action was *incongruous,* not consistent with logical, customary, or appropriate behavior.

   incongruous: ....

   ....

3. The *landlubber* was so unfamiliar with the sea that he was seasick within five minutes of getting on the ship.

   landlubber: ....

   ....

4. The *magenta* dress could be seen a block away. Its bright, purplish red stood out dramatically.

   magenta: ....

   ....

5. The courts ordered the unions to delay any action. This *moratorium* enabled the produce to be shipped before it spoiled.

moratorium: ....
....

6. Only a notary public can *notarize* the document. The notary must witness and authenticate the signature.

notarize: ....
....

7. In the fourth century the Macedonians developed the *phalanx,* an infantry formation with overlapping shields and long spears.

phalanx: ....
....

8. The *plaintive* weeping of the children was heard for several days after their father died.

plaintive: ....
....

9. It was a *plash,* not even big enough or loud enough to be considered a splash.

plash: ....
....

10. The *Shoshones* occupied large areas in the western United States before the white man arrived.

Shoshones: ....
....

EXERCISE 3

Read these passages and then answer the questions that follow. Use context clues to select the best answers. The first question is done for you.

[1] Like all other life forms, *Homo sapiens* is a product of evolution. [2] Although all the specific facts of evolution are not known and may never be fully known, we can make some educated guesses as to how it is that human beings have evolved. [3] It is most important, however, to note that while there is widespread agreement concerning some aspects of human evolution, there is also widespread disagreement concerning others. [4] We have attempted to

limit the following discussion to areas of widespread agreement. [5] We believe, therefore, that most of the social scientists who are directly concerned with human evolution would agree with what is presented.

[6] Life on this planet began at least a billion years ago, but there were no signs of human beings then. [7] Not until 70 million years ago did the first traces of "humanness" appear—in the form of small, squirrellike, tree-dwelling prosimians (premonkeys) that lived in the tropical forest: the animals had a tendency to hold objects in their claws and a tendency to rely on their eyes rather than their noses for hunting. [8] Both of these traits were adaptations to arboreal life (tree-living), and both were important to the survival of these small creatures. [9] As their eyesight became more acute, they were able to manipulate more precisely the objects they held, and this led to the evolution of separate fingers. [10] At the same time they were evolving larger parts of the brain to receive and interpret visual and tactile impressions. [11] Information that had previously been filtered through older parts of the brain was now beginning to be filtered through the new developing brain tissue. [12] These first primates displayed traits that have been developed and refined and are evident today in you and me.

> —From Mendoza and Napoli, *Systems of Society: An Introduction to Social Sciences.*

1. In sentence 1, *Homo sapiens* means
   a. nonhuman beings
   b. human beings
   c. tool-using animals
   d. non–tool-using animals

2. In sentence 5, *social scientists* are those who
   a. deal with human evolution
   b. deal with chemical formulas
   c. deal with social events
   d. deal with laboratory science

3. In sentence 7, *prosimians* are
   a. prosquirrels
   b. presquirrels
   c. premonkeys
   d. promonkeys

4. In sentence 8, *arboreal life* refers to
   a. creatures living in an arbor
   b. nighttime hunting animals
   c. imaginary (unreal) creatures
   d. tree-living creatures

5. In sentence 10, *tactile* refers to
   a. things you see
   b. things you touch
   c. things you hear
   d. things you taste

6. In sentence 12, *primates* refers to
   a. prosimians
   b. early man
   c. early animals in general
   d. early pairs of animals

[1] Have you ever examined your paper money closely? [2] See if you can locate a $5, $10, or $20 bill printed before 1964 and marked "Federal Reserve Note" over the portrait. [3] In the upper-left portion above the seal, a statement written in fine print says that the note is *legal tender* and that it "is redeemable in lawful money at the United States Treasury, or at any Federal Reserve Bank." [4] Does this mean that the bill is *not* lawful? [5] At the bottom center the same bill says, "Will pay to the bearer on demand X dollars." [6] Does this mean that your X-dollar bill is *not* X dollars?

[7] Much confusion exists about the real nature of money. [8] Many people believe that money has no value unless it is backed by gold or silver. [9] They think that the Federal Reserve note is only a symbol for money, and that real money is the precious metal backing the note. [10] Some people look on money as wealth and believe that it must have *intrinsic* value.

[11] If we were to study the history of money, we would find that in different places and at different times a variety of things have been used as money. [12] Cattle, shells, beads, tobacco leaves, and various metals—including iron, zinc, bronze, and copper—have all been used as a basis for exchange. [13] The precious metals, particularly silver and gold, have proved most satisfactory for this purpose and have been most commonly used in modern times.

[14] Until early 1968, the United States backed its Federal Reserve notes with 25 percent gold, but this did not mean that citizens could use gold as money or convert paper dollars to gold. [15] Clearly, *it is not what money is but what it does* that is important.

—From Gordon and Dawson, *Introductory Economics.*

7. In sentence 2, *Federal Reserve Note* means to the lay reader
   a. debt   b. precious metal
   c. wealth   d. money

8. In sentence 3, *legal tender* means to the lay reader
   a. lawful reading   b. not counterfeit
   c. soft and legal   d. usable as money

9. In sentence 10, *intrinsic* means
   a. extraordinary   b. inherent
   c. secret   d. limitless

[1] The magnetic properties of the mineral lodestone (magnetite, Fe_3O_4) were known to the Greeks as early as 600 B.C. [2] Thales of Miletus (640–546 B.C.), an early Greek mathematician and astronomer, was aware of the properties of attraction and repulsion of lodestone; he also knew of an electrostatic effect called the amber effect, that is, the attraction of bits of straw to an amber rod that had been rubbed with wool.

[3] The word "magnet" seems to have been derived from Magnesia, a province in Asia Minor, where the Greeks first discovered lodestone. [4] The Chinese were probably the first to use the lodestone as a compass, both on land and sea. [5] Early records indicate that ships sailing between Canton, China, and Sumatra as early as 1000 A.D. were navigated by the use of the magnetic compass.

[6] In the thirteenth century, a Frenchman, Petrus P. de Maricount, described the magnetic compass in some detail and applied the term "pole" to the regions on the compass where the fields of influence were the strongest. [7] The north-seeking pole he called N, and the south-seeking pole he called S. [8] The attraction of unlike poles, the repulsion of like poles, and the formation of new unlike poles when a magnet was broken into two pieces were also described by de Maricount.

[9] In 1600 Dr. William Gilbert (1540–1603), court physician to Queen Elizabeth, published his book on magnetism, *De Magnete*. [10] The book contained all information then known about electricity and magnetism, plus experiments carried out by Gilbert. [11] These experiments included information on the dip (the angle the Earth's magnetic field makes with the Earth's surface) and declination (the angle the compass needle deviates from the geographical north) of the compass, the loss of magnetism by a magnet when heated, and experiments with a sphere-shaped magnet, which led him to the conclusion that the Earth acts like a huge magnet.

[12] Gilbert was also aware of the amber effect. [13] We now know that this effect is due to repulsion and attraction of electric charges. [14] Gilbert carried out many experiments on the amber effect with an instrument he called a versorium (Latin, *verso*, to turn around). [15] The versorium was nothing more than a slender arrow-type nonconducting material balanced on a pivot point so as to give a high degree of sensitivity to the force of attraction when an amber rod or other substances were placed in its vicinity. [16] With his versorium he discovered that many substances possess the amber effect. [17] Gilbert is responsible for the word "electron," which is very familiar today. [18] He classified those substances possessing the amber effect as "electrics" (Greek, *electron*, amber).

—From Shipman et al., *An Introduction to Physical Science.*

10. In sentence 1, the word *lodestone* refers to

a. gravel   b. magnetite

c. sandstone   d. amber

11. In sentence 2, *electrostatic effect* refers to

a. attraction of amber to other amber   b. attraction of amber to wool

c. attraction of bits of amber to straw   d. attraction of straw to an amber rod

12. In sentence 3, *Magnesia* refers to
   a. a medicine
   b. a place in Asia Minor
   c. a type of automobile wheel
   d. a chemical that burns brightly

13. In sentence 8, the word *repulsion* refers to
   a. pulling close
   b. pushing away
   c. being offended
   d. feeling sick

14. In sentence 9, *De Magnete* refers to
   a. a magnet
   b. an early occult play
   c. a medical treatise
   d. a book on magnetism

15. In sentence 11, *dip* refers to the
   a. angle of the Earth's magnetic field
   b. movement of the Milky Way
   c. angle of compass deviation
   d. loss of magnetism when heated

16. In sentence 14, *versorium* refers to
   a. a small book of poetry
   b. a few lines in a song
   c. an instrument to measure the amber effect
   d. a place to grow exotic plants

[1] The next phase in the progression of the American Indian's forebears is the *Clovis Phase,* named for a type of weapon point first found near Clovis, New Mexico. [2] The ancient hunting culture associated with the Clovis point is sometimes called Llano. [3] Clovis points are carefully formed, lance-shaped projectiles, three to six inches long, made by pressure flaking; that is, pressing off stone flakes with a piece of pointed stone or bone. [4] Each Clovis point is distinctive because of its beauty, slenderness, length, and fluting —the channels cut on either side of the projectile face. [5] Clovis hunters also made stone scrapers, mauls, and knives as their methods became more refined. [6] Besides weapon making their crafts included fashioning clothing from skins and making sandals from shredded sagebrush.

   [7] Clovis hunters used the *atlatl,* the spear thrower, a short stick two feet long with a pair of animal hide loops at the end to grasp it and a hook and a weight for balance and whip action. [8] With the *atlatl,* the hunter could throw his spear with greater velocity and with more accuracy than with his arm only. [9] Archeologists have concluded that ancient hunters fastened the slender fluted points into long spear shafts with thongs of animal skin or plant-fiber twine. [10] A spear launched by an *atlatl* easily reached a target 300 feet away. [11] Probably Clovis hunters used the *atlatl* to launch spears at deer, elk, horses, camels, and other game from a distance, but used the spear alone to jab mammoths and mastodons when the huge creatures became mired in the mud of swamps and bogs.

   —From Gibson, *The American Indian.*

17. In sentence 4, *fluting* refers to
    a. sounds
    c. channels
    b. hunting
    d. archeologists

18. In sentence 7, *atlatl* refers to
    a. fashioning clothing
    c. a spear thrower
    b. making sandals
    d. knife making

19. In sentence 8, *velocity* refers to
    a. accuracy
    c. speed
    b. craftsmanship
    d. creativity

20. In sentence 1, *Clovis Phase* means
    a. a period of time
    c. a period of adolescent growth
    b. a lack of food
    d. a geographic area

EXERCISE 4

Use context clues to define *in your own terms* the underlined words in these sentences. Don't attempt to come up with formal definitions like those in the dictionary. Write working definitions demonstrating that you understand how the words are used in context.

Peter Corless, an art illustration major at Carnegie-Mellon University, picks up his artist's tools in the classroom and begins the assignment: draw a self-portrait.

He starts with his sloping nose, moves swiftly to the bushy eyebrows, then makes a sweeping semicircle for the facial outline. Slowly he fills in the features, using a brilliant color for each: green for the forehead, purple for hair, red for the mouth, gold for the face.

Finally he stares intently at the canvas—a computer screen. Satisfied, he jerks a <u>disk</u> out of the computer and lays down the <u>electromagnetic stylus</u> that is his paintbrush. Later he will insert the disk into another computer to show his professor his work.

Whether in the classroom or dormitory, the cafeteria or library, the computer has become very much a part of Mr. Corless's everyday life on campus. By plugging into special "accounts," he uses <u>computer terminals</u> to write papers for his creative writing class and turn them in, to send and receive <u>electronic mail</u>, and even to find out whether a certain soft drink machine is empty.

Mr. Corless generally accomplishes these miracles at the art building or the University Computation Center, but other terminal rooms and personal-computer clusters are scattered about the campus. Not counting individual students' own computers, more than 3,500 terminals are on campus now, compared with fewer than 50 two decades ago.

... Corless's daily life shows how a computer these days practically becomes an <u>appendage</u>. On Thursday mornings, for example, he goes to his art-and-the-computer class, where a software program enables him to choose from up to 16 million color mixtures to design pictures like his self-portrait. After class, he dashes to lunch, where a computerized cash register credits his hamburger, fries, and soft drink to his room-and-board bill. The only time he needs cash is when the computer tells him he has exceeded his meal limit for the week. If there is time before his illustration class in the afternoon, Mr. Corless seeks out a nearby terminal to check his electronic mail or catch up on classwork.

One recent night, Mr. Corless spent nearly 13 hours <u>pecking</u> away at a terminal keyboard, first creating two self-portraits, then struggling to convert Celsius temperatures to Fahrenheit for his introduction to programming course. By the time he forwarded the work directly into his professor's computer file, it was 7:30 A.M. He stayed awake to play computer games, tapping into <u>Rogue</u>, a computerized version of the popular Dungeons and Dragons game, until a 9 A.M. class.

On Thursday nights, Mr. Corless works at the library and shows other students how to use the computerized card catalog system, with its 550,000 book and 500 journal entries. This system is a good example of what computers can do.

—From The Wall Street Journal, © Dow Jones & Co., Inc., 1984. All Rights Reserved.

1. disk: ....

....

2. electromagnetic stylus: ....

....

3. computer terminals: ....

....

4. electronic mail: ....

....

5. appendage: ....

....

6. pecking: ....

....

7. Rogue: ....
....

EXERCISE 5

From this passage on Neptune, list the words that you are not familiar with in the spaces provided at the end. Reread the list and put a plus (+) next to the words for which you believe you could figure out the meaning from the context. Put a circle next to the words that are still a mystery to you and for which the context gives little help in determining the meaning

NEPTUNE

Neptune was discovered in 1846 by John G. Galle (1812–1910), a German astronomer at the Berlin Observatory. Partial credit is also shared by Englishman John Couch Adams and Frenchman U. J. J. Leverrier, two mathematicians. Using Newton's law of gravitation, Adams and Leverrier made calculations that produced information on where to look for a supposed planet that was disturbing the motion of the planet Uranus. The name Neptune was proposed by D. F. Arago, a French physicist who had suggested that Leverrier begin the critical investigation of the planet. He first suggested Leverrier as the name, but later withdrew this suggestion because it received little acceptance outside France.

The planet cannot be observed with the naked eye and appears to have a greenish hue when viewed through a telescope. The physical makeup of the planet is similar to that of Uranus. Methane and hydrogen have been detected spectrographically, so the planet probably has a gaseous atmosphere.

Neptune has two known satellites. Triton, which is larger than our moon, revolves retrograde once every six days. The revolving speed is decreasing and within a few million years Triton will be torn apart by Neptune's tidal forces, and the planet will develop a ring system similar to the other Jovian planets. A faint single ring fragment around Neptune was detected by a group of American and European astronomers during an occultation of the planet on July 22, 1984. The background star dimmed briefly as the faint ring passed between the star and the receiving telescope recording infrared wavelengths. The ring fragment is calculated to be 10 to 15 kilometers wide, about 100 kilometers long, and located some 70,000 to 80,000 kilometers from the planet.

Voyager 2 will encounter Neptune in August 1989 and more precise data will be obtained concerning Neptune, its faint ring and its satellites, assuming the spacecraft functions properly during the encounter.

Neptune's other satellite, Nereid, is very small. Its diameter is estimated to be less than 400 miles. Nereid has the most eccentric orbit (0.749) of any satellite in the solar system. The highly elliptical orbit takes the tiny moon from 870,000 miles to over six million miles from Neptune.

—From Shipman et al., *An Introduction to Physical Science.*

....

....

....

....

....

....

What kind of words have a circle next to them? technical? scientific? literary? short? long?

Does this list indicate anything about the new words you may be exposed to in your college reading?

Answers to Selected Exercises

EXERCISE 2

Answers may vary.

1. a writer who receives no credit or recognition for the writing
2. (The sentence itself is a definition of *incongruous*.)
3. someone who is unfamiliar with the sea
4. purple-red color
5. a delay of any action
6. to witness and authenticate a signature
7. an infantry formation with overlapping shields and spears
8. sorrowful
9. a small splash
10. native Americans who lived in the western United States

EXERCISE 3

1. b	2. a	3. c	4. d	5. b
6. a	7. d	8. d	9. b	10. b
11. d	12. b	13. b	14. d	15. a
16. c	17. c	18. c	19. c	20. a

EXERCISE 5

Words selected will vary.

Part Two

Critical Comprehension Skills

The literal comprehension skills you have studied in Chapters 2, 3, and 4 enable you to determine what it is that the author has said on the page. But *really* understanding written material takes more than just being able to identify ideas that have been stated; you need to evaluate them. Often you will want to be able to recognize the author's purpose, the overall organization in the writing, or relationships within and between sentences. Many times you will need to be able to detect bias in the writing, recognize the author's tone, and spot invalid arguments. Nearly every time you read you can expect to draw inferences and come to conclusions.

These are the critical skills in comprehension you are about to study in the next nine chapters. These skills will be invaluable in your college courses because they will help you accurately understand the ideas you read, and the patterns they establish in your thinking will help you think critically about everything you do. That's a valuable skill too!

Chapter 5

Recognizing the Author's Purpose

The better shall my purpose work on him.
—Othello

We always read for some purpose—unless
some sad, bad, mad schoolteacher has got
hold of us.

—I. A. Richards

This chapter will help you to:

1. understand why you need to recognize the author's purpose when you read.
2. understand how writing can manipulate the reader.
3. understand how the author's purpose is related to the main idea.
4. identify the many purposes a writer can have.
5. learn the seven clues to identifying the author's purpose.

G ood writing is organized writing. In good writing authors determine what they want to say (the main idea) and then organize it and write it in the most effective way so as to communicate exactly the message they intend to communicate.

Writing to Manipulate

Behind this planned and organized presentation lies the author's purpose. Most writers expect to modify our attitudes, actions (as we do in this book), thoughts, or knowledge in some way with their writing. In a very real sense most of the things we read are manipulative—everything from advertising to scholarly articles in research journals. The degree of manipulation employed is determined by the author's purpose. Whether or not you read something efficiently depends a lot on knowing the author's purpose for writing.

Often the purpose is simply to inform, but not always. Sometimes the author has another purpose and knowing that may affect your viewpoint or conclusions about the materials. The problem occurs when you believe the author has but one purpose—to inform. You assume objectivity, as if the author were simply presenting information; in reality the purpose may be something else—to persuade.

Our awareness of the author's purpose *before, while,* and *after* reading is a way of keeping ourselves from being fooled about the real message. Your objective of being an effective reader includes more than just comprehending the *ideas* that are written; it includes critically thinking about and analyzing the way in which they are written.

In any reading passage an author may or may not state outright his or her purpose for writing, but it should always be discernible.

What Are Your Thoughts?

1. How does subtle manipulation, or skill with words, hide the author's purpose? Are some works so "well written" that readers don't know they are being manipulated? When does this handling occur? Is it acceptable? Under what conditions?

   ....

   ....

   ....

2. Writers have many purposes, some of which seem to predominate in the materials you are expected to read in college. If you had to identify the three purposes that appear most often in your study reading, which would they be?

   ....

   ....

   ....

3. Where in your reading of something should you be able to make a judgment about the author's purpose? Must you wait until you have finished reading to make that determination? Why or why not?

....

....

....

4. Are you aware of being manipulated by the ideas you are reading *when you are reading them?* Always? Sometimes? What determines your awareness during reading, and what is your response?

....

....

....

Writing to Comprehend

1. Writing intended to manipulate the reader is common in everything we read. What examples of strong manipulative intent are you familiar with? How about advertising? Does advertising have degrees of manipulation? Explain your thinking.

....

....

....

....

....

2. How would you summarize the ideas that should be presented in this chapter? Pretend that you are explaining these ideas to a younger brother or sister. What would you say?

....

....

....

....

....

3. How important is it to be able to modify your reading strategies for

different purposes? When should you read for general impressions—
skim—and when should you read for specific details—*scan*.

....

....

....

....

....

4. Is all this information about skill in reading comprehension *really*
necessary to know if you are to succeed in college?

....

....

....

....

....

Purpose Is Related to Main Idea

This vital skill in critical comprehension, recognizing the author's purpose,
is commonly tested by college teachers when they question students about their
reading assignments. This skill is closely related to one that we discussed in
Chapter 2: recognizing the main idea. Usually it is helpful to determine the main
idea and how it is stated before you determine the author's purpose.

If the purpose is not stated, the main idea and how it is developed should provide clues to that purpose. On examinations, questions asking you to identify
the author's purpose are usually more difficult than those about the main idea
because you must select an answer usually not stated in the passage. Nevertheless, by grasping the author's main idea, you should at least be able to *reject*
answers pointing to purposes the author does *not* have.

Possible Purposes for Writing

Of the many purposes for writing, the most usual are listed here. Reminding
yourself about them from time to time will help you spot a purpose when it
appears.

to inform

to describe some idea or thing

to state a problem

to analyze something

to classify

to offer a solution

to suggest an alternative

to defend an idea or action

to entertain

to tell a story

to discuss some idea or thing

to define something

to compare

to convince, persuade

to evaluate

to present new information

to criticize

Clues to Identifying Purpose

Identifying the author's purpose is not really as difficult as it sounds because often clues are provided.

1. *Statement of purpose:* Occasionally an author will say something like "My purpose is ...." Your responsibility then is to make certain as you read that the stated purpose in fact *is* the purpose and not just a smokescreen. The more likely arrangement, however, is that the purpose will be implied, and you'll have to look for other clues.

2. *Word clues:* Words or phrases like *This discussion is focused on ..., My intention is ..., realize that ...* all point to the author's intent.

3. *Author's tone:* The tone, or mood, of the writing may also give you a clue to the author's purpose. If the tone is humorous and lighthearted, then the author's purpose is not likely to be a serious one. Watch for emotion-laden words; they are good clues.

4. *Titles, headings, boldface, and italics:* Titles, headings, and subheadings (which you can glance at when you do a quick preview of the reading) often give a clue to the author's purpose. An article entitled "Fire Dangers in Wok Cooking" will not simply explain the art of cooking with a wok, but instead probably will present wok cooking from a negative perspective. Boldface type and italics often signal and summarize key purpose words (words that signal mood, tone, feelings).

5. *Introductions, summaries, and conclusions:* Often the author's purpose is clearly seen in brief introductions, summaries, and conclusions. These are clearly a good investment for your previewing time before you start reading.

6. *Author's background:* Knowing the author's background can signal purpose very effectively. Observing that a writer is the state Grand Master of the Ku Klux Klan can help make you aware that the article he wrote entitled "The Role of Minorities in Building Our Nation" may not be as objective as the title suggests.

7. *Publication date:* Yes, the times do put different slants on things, and *when* something was written often is a clue to its purpose. An article on investing government funds in Japan written in the 1950s will certainly have a different purpose than one written today. The opinion prevailing at the time the article was written may have changed by the time you read the material.

What to Look Out for

A common error often occurs when students are asked questions testing their ability to identify the author's purpose.

Misstatement or misinterpretation. Not being clear about the author's purpose may fool students into believing that a misstatement or a misinterpretation correctly reflects the author's purpose. *To suggest an alternative* is not the same purpose as *to offer a solution.* If you are clear about what the author is saying, the correct answer should stand out.

Author's Purpose Margin Mark ✳

The margin mark for identifying the author's purpose is *. Put this mark in the margin *each* time you read something that is a clue to the writer's purpose, or opposite any statement specifically declaring that purpose.

Don't forget to preview your readings before you read. Use the suggestions and reading techniques you learned in Chapter 1.

Did you pace yourself as you read this section?

Words to Read by

Glance quickly over the reading selections (but not the questions) in the exercises for this chapter. From these passages select ten unfamiliar words that seem to stand out, circle them so that you will be able to find them again easily, and write them below. Put the number of the page where each word appears in the parentheses provided. Then define the words, using context clues. Even if you are not certain, guess at the meaning.

Next, look up each word in the dictionary and write the appropriate definition under your context definition. Notice that each word may have more than one definition. Select the definition that fits the word's context.

How close is your definition to the dictionary definition?

1. .... (...........)   Your definition: ....

....

Dictionary: ....

Is your definition close? not so close?

2. .... (...........) Your definition: ....

....

Dictionary: ....

Is your definition close? not so close?

3. .... (...........) Your definition: ....

....

Dictionary: ....

Is your definition close? not so close?

4. .... (...........) Your definition: ....

....

Dictionary: ....

Is your definition close? not so close?

5. .... (...........) Your definition: ....

....

Dictionary: ....

Is your definition close? not so close?

6. .... (...........) Your definition: ....

....

Dictionary: ....

Is your definition close? not so close?

7. .... (...........) Your definition: ....

....

Dictionary: ....

Is your definition close? not so close?

8. .... (...........) Your definition: ....

....

Dictionary: ....

Is your definition close? not so close?

9. .... (............) Your definition: ....

....

Dictionary: ....

Is your definition close? not so close?

10. .... (............) Your definition: ....

....

Dictionary: ....

Is your definition close? not so close?

Anticipate the Topics

As you have done in other chapters, write the first few words or phrases you think of on the line next to each word as you read it. Are you aware of satisfaction or disappointment when you read the exercise passages and find out that the things you associated with the topic were, or were not, written about in the passages? What do these questions have to do with your comprehension?

television ....

copperhead ....

drinking alcohol ....

nervousness ....

animal aggression ....

book and record burning ....

free-enterprise system ....

bombing ....

Ku Klux Klan ....

American revolution ....

drug dependence ....

common cold ....

throwaway children	....
sperm donors	....
writing	....
sexism	....
illicit birth	....
sneakers	....
offshore dumping	....
movie vacation	....
World War II	....
dust bowl	....
education	....
listening	....
cartoon noir	....
Great Depression	....

Practice Exercises

EXERCISE 1

For these passages select the purpose that *could not be* the primary intent for the selection. The first one is done for you.

1. The primary danger of the television screen lies not so much in the behavior it produces—although there is danger there—as in the behavior that it prevents: the talks, the games, the family festivities and arguments through which the child's learning takes place and through which his character is formed. Turning on the television set can turn off the process that transforms children into people.

    —From Bailey and Kennedy, *The American Pageant.*

    ...*a*... a. to entertain   b. to analyze something

2. What is the relationship between risk and free enterprise?

    —From Megginson et al., *Business.*

    .... a. to compare   b. to offer a solution

137

3. A better mousetrap would be hard to find. Indeed, once a copperhead snake senses prey, it moves so swiftly that a victim like this white-footed mouse has little chance of escape.

Throughout its eastern U.S. range, the reptile often hides in woodland debris beside what herpetologists call a "mouse run"—a trail the snake locates by "smelling" the ground with its highly sensitive tongue. There, the copperhead lies in wait until something crosses its path. Then, homing in with heat-sensing organs located in depressions below each of its eyes, the snake springs to life and, in an instant, pumps venom through its fangs into the prey. In minutes, the mouse is dead.

Instinctively, the reptile then locates the rodent's head—the most stream-lined point from which to begin swallowing its meal. Slowly, the snake plies its jaws up the mouse's body, until only two white feet and a tail remain visible.

Finally, replete with a meal requiring a week to digest, the copperhead retires to a quiet den. A month or more may pass before the snake will again conceal itself beside a woodland trail, waiting for another victim to beat a path to its jaws.

> —From *National Wildlife,* October/November, 1988, page 23. Copyright ©
> 1988 by the National Wildlife Federation.

.... a. to classify   b. to describe something

4. We can easily argue that drinking alcohol is an American institution. When the Puritans set sail for America, their cargo included fourteen tons of water. It also included forty-two tons of beer and ten thousand gallons of wine. Today, alcohol consumption supports a multibillion dollar business in the United States alone.

> —From Ingersoll, *Adolescents.*

.... a. to present new information   b. to offer a solution

5. When I was in the fifth grade, I was chosen to recite a poem in an auditorium filled with recess-minded 11-year-olds. Waiting nervously in the wings for my turn, I smoothed and resmoothed my skirt, tucked in and retucked the edges of my blouse. I yanked at my knee socks and pulled up on my half-slip.

When I finished all that smoothing and pulling, I walked out onto the stage to a burst of applause—with my skirt tucked into my underpants.

> —From Newman, *Communicating in Business Today.*

.... a. to tell a story   b. to evaluate

6. Animals feel secure when at home and afraid when in unfamiliar environ-ments, and this feeling influences their communication and their willingness and ability to fight. What results is a *balance between aggression and fear.* Animals frequently fight, but rarely do they fight to the death.

> —From Lowry and Rankin, *Sociology: Social Science and Social Concern.*

.... a. to inform   b. to entertain

7.   Blue Springs, Neb.—Books and records have been burned by members of an independent church.

They said they were destroying the work of witches, demons, and druids. The burning was organized by teenagers.

"In rock and roll, the drumbeat hypnotizes the listener, and the words are a coded spell," said Dave Kruse, one of the teenagers.

"The record production companies have witches write songs, and the companies have old druid manuscripts containing melodies and drumbeats. They hire top musicians ...."

About 30 members of the Gospel Fellowship Church gathered Saturday in the back yard of Doc Barton, the church leader, to burn several dozen albums and single records and about a dozen books.

Among the records destroyed were ones by Johnny Horton, the Kingston Trio and the rock group, Pipeline.

Included was a book authored by John Hershey.

—From Allgeier and Allgeier, *Sexual Interactions*.

.... a. to convince or persuade   b. to describe something

8.   In a free enterprise system, businesses are organized, owned, operated, and controlled by private individuals who have the right to a profit (or must suffer the loss) from operations. The system results from the free association of people in a free society. Under this system, you can organize any business the law allows, produce whatever you wish, charge whatever you want, or even sell your interest in the firm. In reality, however, a business can succeed only if it produces a product or service that the public wants, sells it at a price people are willing to pay, does the job somehow better than the competition, and makes a profit for its efforts. In addition, government regulations and the legal system set limits on certain types of products, businesses, and pricing.

—From Megginson et al., *Business*.

.... a. to analyze something   b. to suggest an alternative

9.   In Bootle, England, a city of 55,000, people were bombed nightly for a week during World War II with only 10 percent of the houses escaping serious damage. Yet one fourth of the population remained asleep in their homes during the raids. Only 37 percent of the London mothers and children who were eligible for evacuation left the city during the war crisis. Furthermore, even during periods of heavy bombing in London, evacuees drifted back nearly as rapidly as they were being evacuated. Similar findings are on record for Germany and Japan during World War II. This should not be surprising. Human beings have a very strong tendency to continue with their established behavior patterns rather than initiating new courses of behavior.

—From Lowry and Rankin, *Sociology: Social Science and Social Concern.*

.... a. to criticize   b. to convince, persuade

10.   Antisocial secret societies, like the Ku Klux Klan, utilize both the appeal of former roles and values and the appeal of special uniforms and ritual which symbolize new roles and values. The recruit is taught that the Klan stands for white Christianity (the cross) and 100-percent Americanism (the flag). At the same time, hoods and robes, a burning cross, and special uniforms for leaders distinguish the group as separate and different from larger society. Klan members, therefore, are willing to use violence and other disapproved methods to achieve racial purity in the name of God and country.

—From Lowry and Rankin, *Sociology: Social Science and Social Concern.*

.... a. to classify   b. to analyze something

EXERCISE 2

Occasionally a writer's purpose may not be clear, or the author may have more than one purpose. For each of these passages, three purposes are suggested; two of them are possible. Select the one that is *least* likely to represent the writer's purpose in the passage. The first one is done for you.

1.   Could entrepreneurship have a part in a pure communist system? Why or why not?

...**C**.... a. to compare
        b. to evaluate
        c. to offer a solution

2.   The American Revolution was not a revolution in the sense of a radical or total change. It did not suddenly and violently overturn the entire political and social framework, as later occurred in the French and Russian revolutions. What happened was accelerated evolution rather than outright revolution. During the conflict itself people went on working and praying, marrying and playing. Most of them were not seriously disturbed by the actual fighting, and many of the more isolated communities scarcely knew that a war was on.

—From Bailey and Kennedy, *The American Pageant.*

.... a. to offer a solution
        b. to analyze something
        c. to present new information

3. Psychological dependence occurs when an individual has a preoccupation with the altered states of consciousness brought on by drugs or feels unable to cope with stress in the absence of drugs. Not all drugs lead to physical dependence, but all drugs may lead to psychological dependence. Not all drug abusers are drug dependent.

   —From Ingersoll, *Adolescents.*

   .... a. to defend an idea
   b. to inform
   c. to present new information

4. No wonder Richard Nixon sweated so in front of the cameras. No wonder his beard grew visibly and sinisterly before its unblinking eye. No wonder Jimmy Carter couldn't begin a speech at all without giving that small pursed-lip, goody-goody smile that the world found so infuriating. These people were *nervous*; they were experiencing stage fright.

   —From Newman, *Communicating in Business Today.*

   .... a. to describe something
   b. to criticize
   c. to analyze something

5. *New Attack on Common Cold.* The common-cold virus is fighting back in the war against the sniffles. A Purdue University team researching the structure of one cold virus—rhinovirus 14—has found that the virus changes its structure in order to prevent antiviral drugs from interacting with it. The antiviral agents work to prevent the virus from reproducing, but the virus adapts, blocking the ability of drugs to bind. "It's as if the cold virus sticks out its arm—like a running back fending off a tackler," says one researcher. The team hopes that further research into the atomic structure of viruses can bring modern medicine closer to curing the common cold.

   —From *The Futurist,* September/October 1988, page 6. Reprinted with permission from *The Futurist,* published by the World Future Society, 4916 St. Elmo Avenue, Bethesda, Maryland 20814.

   .... a. to present new information
   b. to state a problem
   c. to offer a solution

6. Leslie Ann and her stepfather did not get along, and her mother sided with her new husband. Feeling betrayed, Leslie Ann rebelled by staying out late, smoking marijuana and flouting family rules. Finally, after she spent a night away from home without permission, her mother called the police. Leslie Ann was placed in a group foster home.

   The girl still loves her mother and misses her. Each Sunday, visiting day, she and the other girls dress up and look forward to seeing their families.

> The visitors arrive. As her friends laugh and talk with their mothers, fathers, brothers and sisters, Leslie Ann sits alone by the window, watching.
>
> Each Sunday it's the same. She sits waiting for the mother who never comes, wondering why she isn't wanted, why she has been thrown away.
>
> —From Ingersoll, *Adolescents.*

.... a. to entertain
b. to describe something
c. to state a problem

7. One of the easiest ways to deal with male infertility is to inseminate the wife with sperm collected from an anonymous donor. At times, the husband's sperm is mixed with the donor sperm so that there is always the possibility that the child is fathered by the husband. The parents are advised to keep the procedure a secret, even from their own gynecologist, so that, in time, they come to believe that the father as well as the mother are biologically related to the baby.

> —From Zigler and Finn-Stevenson, *Children: Development and Social Issues.*

.... a. to criticize
b. to inform
c. to offer a solution

8. Experienced writers routinely wait for the heat of creativity to cool and then reread their work with a critical eye. Knowing that almost any first draft will contain deadwood, they look for the stylistic weaknesses that breed verbosity, and they eliminate them.

> —From Newman, *Communicating in Business Today.*

.... a. to suggest an alternative
b. to describe something
c. to define something

9. *Sexism* is another term that will be relevant to some of the discussions in this book. Sexism can be defined as discrimination or bias against people based on their gender. Some people use the term "reverse sexism" for discrimination against males, although it would seem preferable to use the term "sexism" for discrimination against either females or males on the basis of their gender.

> —From Hyde, *Half the Human Experience: The Psychology of Women.*

.... a. to define something
b. to analyze something
c. to defend an idea or action

10. From 1938 to 1958 in the United States, the estimated annual number of illicit births increased 42 percent (to over 200,000); the proportion of illicit births to all births increased 8 percent; and the proportion of illicit births for unmarried females in the childbearing ages increased 33 percent. By 1973, annual illegitimate births totalled about 407,300 (Bureau of Census, 1975). Thus, by any measure, illegitimacy is becoming a problem of concern to many.

—From Lowry and Rankin, *Sociology: Social Science and Social Concern.*

.... a. to classify
          b. to present new information
          c. to state a problem

EXERCISE 3

In Exercise 2 you selected the answer least likely to represent the author's purpose. Now, look back over those passages and select from the two remaining answers the *most* likely purpose for each passage. For some, you may have a fairly difficult time deciding on the *best* choice because the purposes are similar, or both could be correct. But choose one anyway and be prepared to discuss the reasons for your choice.

1.   *a*   2.   ....

3.   ....   4.   ....

5.   ....   6.   ....

7.   ....   8.   ....

9.   ....   10.   ....

EXERCISE 4

In these sentences indicate the author's purpose. Next to the sentence write the letter of the appropriate purpose from the list below. It will be apparent that more than one purpose may fit each selection and that some purposes are quite similar; therefore be ready to explain your reasons for selecting your choice of purpose for each passage. The first one is done for you.

a. to inform	b. to entertain
c. to describe a thing or an idea	d. to state a problem
e. to analyze something	f. to classify
g. to offer a solution	h. to suggest an alternative
i. to defend an idea or action	j. to tell a story
k. to define something	l. to compare
m. to convince, persuade	n. to evaluate
o. to present new information	p. to criticize

1. *Sneaker Power.* The latest advance in shoe engineering is "energy return" —that is, the ability of an athletic shoe to return the wearer's expended energy. Energy return is measured by how much pressure a material pushes back, rather than absorbing, when it is pressed. For instance, Converse, Inc., claims its new "Energy Wave" shoe returns 50% of an athlete's expended energy. Such "spring" in the step could mean a 3- to 5-minute reduction in a marathon runner's time or a 1-inch increase in a basketball player's vertical leap. Athletes may also experience fewer injuries and less fatigue, allowing them to work out longer and more safely.

   —From *The Futurist,* September/October 1988, page 6. Reprinted with permission from *The Futurist,* published by the World Future Society, 4916 St. Elmo Avenue, Bethesda, Maryland 20814.

2. *Navy Pledges to Stop Dumping Plastic Wastes.* In a major effort to reduce the ocean dumping of plastics which kill and maim millions of marine mammals, sea turtles, fish and seabirds each year, the U.S. Navy is implementing plans to halt its dumping of plastic waste by the end of 1992. Among its major initiatives: stopping the purchase of foods packaged in plastic; storage of plastic waste for onshore disposal or recycling; and installation of specially designed trash compactors. Presently, Navy ships hold all trash on board within 25 miles of shore; beyond this limit, all trash is dumped overboard. The Navy has already cancelled a contract for millions of plastic shopping bags and plans to eliminate six-pack rings and plastic overwrap for soft drink containers.

   —From *National Wildlife,* October/November, 1988, page 29. Copyright © 1988 by the National Wildlife Federation.

3. A man was going from Jerusalem to Jericho, and he fell among robbers, who stripped him and beat him, and departed, leaving him half dead. Now by chance a priest was going down that road; and when he saw him he passed by on the other side. So likewise a Levite, when he came to the place and saw him, passed by on the other side. But a Samaritan, as he journeyed, came to where he was; and when he saw him, he had compassion, and went to him and bound up his wounds, pouring on oil and wine; then he set him on his own beast and brought him to an inn, and took care of him. And the next day he took out two denarii and gave them to the innkeeper, saying, "Take care of him; and whatever you spend, I will repay you when I come back."

   —Luke 10: 29–37.

4. *Dream Vacations for Movie Buffs.* Movie fans now have a new treat for their vacations. Instead of just touring studios, they can now act in a movie simulation and take home videotapes of their performance. Universal Studios has introduced "The Star Trek Adventure," in which Trekkies can dress as their favorite *Enterprise* crewmember and perform in a seven-minute scene from a *Star Trek* script. With special effects, the fan appears to work alongside actors William Shatner and Leonard Nimoy as Kirk and Spock. A similar

tour of the Disney-MGM Studios at Walt Disney World will allow vacationers to "experience" such movie special effects as earthquakes, explosions, collapsing bridges, and floods.

.... —From *The Futurist,* September/October 1988, page 6. Reprinted with
permission from *The Futurist,* published by the World Future Society,
4916 St. Elmo Avenue, Bethesda, Maryland 20814.

5. What I want to recommend is that it makes sense to understand the world in a way and do life in a manner that puts the particular "fantasy" of science fiction in the limited box where it belongs.

.... —From Scherman, *A Preface to Politics.*

6. To seek freedom through drugs is, at once, to misunderstand freedom and to give in to the very dynamic that is causing many of the problems.

.... —From Scherman, *A Preface to Politics.*

7. *Student Alcoholic Recounts "Hitting Bottom," Recovery.* I discovered I was an alcoholic when I was 18 years old. I had been drinking for four and a half years.

I remember vividly my first experiment with alcohol. I went to a friend's house on a weekend night. I was looking forward to socializing with new friends. I didn't plan to drink. I didn't even know drinks would be available.

People were already there when I arrived. Almost immediately I saw the booze and someone told me to make a drink. Without even thinking, I grabbed a large glass and added what seemed to be the right proportion of alcohol and juice.

There were about six ounces of hard liquor in the drink. I had to choke down the first few swallows, but afterward I felt warm and comfortable.

From then on, I lived for the weekends. One gulp of alcohol would start me yearning for more of the warm feeling.

During one indiscreet weekend, I went to three parties, got drunk three times, and necked with three different guys. After that, I was labeled "loose." I kept thinking, "They're not talking about me." If I had been sober, I would never have necked with three guys in one weekend.

.... —Lisa Gorski, *The Minnesota Daily,* University of Minnesota, Twin Cities.

8. World War II proved to be terribly costly. American forces suffered some 1 million casualties, about one-third of which were deaths. Compared with other wars, the proportion killed by wounds and disease was sharply reduced, owing in part to the use of blood plasma and miracle drugs, notably penicillin. Yet heavy though American losses were, the Russian allies suffered casualties many times greater—perhaps 20 million persons killed.

.... —From Bailey and Kennedy, *The American Pageant.*

9. *Computer virus:* A program that resides, unknown to the computer user, on his or her hard or floppy disks, either damaging or destroying programs, files and data. Damaging and destroying may entail regenerating mistakes, altering other programs or erasing memory banks. Viruses do not discriminate; they affect personal computers as well as computer systems/networks.

.... —Source unknown.

10. Drug dependence may take two forms—*physical dependence* and *psychological dependence.*

.... —From Ingersoll, *Adolescents.*

11. Runaways usually suffer a poor self-image and lack interpersonal skills. Typically, they see themselves in conflict with others and are plagued by feelings of self-doubt and anxiety. Although they see themselves as living lives filled with problems, they feel they are victims of fate and are resigned to the idea that their problems will never be solved.

.... —From Ingersoll, *Adolescents.*

12. *Drought and Erosion Create Mini Dust Bowl in Great Plains.* Parched by severe drought, much of the Midwest's prime topsoil is gone with the wind. By late spring, nearly 12 million acres in ten states were badly damaged by wind erosion, and another 19 million acres were judged ready to blow away if dry, windy conditions persisted, according to the U.S. Soil Conservation Service. This year's damage was the fourth worst since the government started measuring wind erosion in the Great Plains in 1935. Hardest hit has been North Dakota, where "black blizzards" have ravaged 3.5 million acres of farmland, leaving ditches and fencerows under deep drifts of dust. When erosion occurs, fine, nutrient-rich particles blow away first, leaving behind soil that is less fertile and less able to hold water. Damage would have been even worse if many farmers had not left crop residue on the land to protect fragile topsoil, say soil experts.

.... —From *National Wildlife,* October/November, 1988, page 19. Copyright © 1988 by the National Wildlife Federation.

13. Why are you in school? Just what are your motives? In an amazingly optimistic way, let's start our list with something nice. It is possible that people go to college to gain wisdom. Or (less grand and noble) we fear ignorance; or (more accurate probably) we don't want to appear stupid. That, of course, is the top of our list—the most impressive of our motives.

Why the hell are you in school? For future money? Maybe. For a wife or a husband with a college degree? Maybe. 'Cause your friends or parents silently (or not so silently) demanded it? Could be. Just a terrific set of reasons.

.... —From *National Wildlife,* October/November, 1988, page 23. Copyright © 1988 by the National Wildlife Federation.

14. *Party Time! It's the Best of "Louie, Louie."* It is one of the most enduring, unintelligible, and most covered songs of all time. "Louie, Louie" has since become a staple at fraternity parties, happy hours and beach barbeques. The *Los Angeles Daily News* calls "Louie, Louie" the "song that wouldn't die." And Rhino Records has now come out with *The Best of Louie, Louie,* which includes the original track by Richard Berry, the Kingsmen's famous version, the Sand Pipers and even punk rockers Black Flag.

.... —Bruce Beckwith, *The Technique,* Georgia Institute of Technology.

15. In another study, Vener and Stewart (1974) reported that many preadolescents answered that they had engaged in sexual intercourse. When interviewers questioned further, they discovered that the youngsters thought that sexual intercourse was talking to someone of the opposite sex.

.... —From Ingersoll, *Adolescents.*

16. When your words are well chosen and you have used them effectively, your writing style will exhibit *clarity, conciseness,* and *vigor.* These three characteristics represent the broad objectives you should set for your business writing style. *Clarity* implies that, with no more than the expected effort, a reader can grasp your meaning. *Conciseness* means that you have no wasted words in your sentences. And *vigor* is the quality in your writing that keeps the reader awake, even when the content of the piece is routine or highly technical.

.... —From Newman, *Communicating in Business Today.*

17. Whether participating in a telephone conference or giving a presentation, you will find that it is important to use your voice effectively. Listening skills are also critical to interacting well with others, especially if you are called on to supervise other employees.

.... —From Newman, *Communicating in Business Today.*

18. As guerrillas normally cannot match regular soldiers in discipline or firepower, they rely chiefly upon isolation and surprise. They avoid open or prolonged combat, preferring sudden assaults, sabotage, and terrorism. Knowing the landscape and its people intimately, they use both to conceal their activities and to achieve surprise.

.... —From Risjord, *Representative Americans: The Revolutionary Generation.*

19. It just might be that *Who Framed Roger Rabbit* will create a new film genre: Cartoon Noir—films in which both real and cartoon characters seek meaning for their existence in realistic and animated universes with one world only slightly less wacky than the other. But however film historians attempt to classify the film's incredible and ingenious use of live action combined with animation, they will note that it's one of the most amazing and hilarious movies of all time.

.... —Source unknown.

20.   What caused the Great Depression? One basic explanation was overproduction by both farm and factory. Ironically, the depression of the 1930s was one of abundance, not want. It was the "great glut" or the "plague of plenty."

The nation's ability to produce goods had clearly outrun its capacity to consume or pay for them. Too much money was going into the hands of a few wealthy people, who in turn invested it in factories and other agencies of production. Not enough was going into salaries and wages, where revitalizing purchasing power could be more quickly felt.

....   —From Gordon and Dawson, *Introductory Economics.*

EXERCISE 5

Write a one-paragraph summary of this reading selection. After you have written your summary, identify the purpose in the reading selection and then identify the purpose of your summary paragraph. Are they the same? Is more than one purpose possible here? Is it easier to identify the purpose in a reading selection or a summary? Why?

THE ELUSIVE OCTOPUS

The cephalopod, *Octopus vulgaris,* occurs offshore. It inhabits crevices, large shells, or empty cans and is nocturnal in its habits. *Octopus* has a larger brain than any other invertebrate and can learn to discriminate among objects of different sizes and shapes for a reward and can retain the memory for at least three weeks. Along the underside of its eight legs, *Octopus* has two rows of suckers which can grasp objects securely. Its mouth lies in the center of the web of tentacles. The eyes are well developed and image-forming. When orienting to its prey the octopus only uses one eye. In estimating the distance of the object it raises and lowers its body. An octopus stalks its prey by gliding over the bottom and stopping within 15 or 20 centimeters of it. It then gathers itself together and leaps on the prey, trapping it beneath the web of tentacles.

Octopus exhibits a variety of colors and can change the surface texture of its skin. It responds to the color of its environment and exhibits the same color changes even when blinded. This behavior is protective; when the octopus is moving and changing colors at the same time, it confuses potential predators. During mating the male octopus deposits a spermatophore in the female's mantle cavity. This capsule breaks open, releasing the spermatozoa, which enter the oviduct and fertilize the eggs. The eggs are attached in strings to the roof of the octopus' burrow. As many as 150,000 eggs may be produced over a week's time. The female cares for them, cleaning and aerating them with spurts of water from her siphon. The young hatch in approximately 6 weeks, when they are nearly 1 millimeter long. The diminutive octopuses then spend weeks or months in the realm of the plankton and settle to the bottom when they have grown to a length of 5 millimeters or more.

—From Fotheringham, *The Beachcomber's Guide to Gulf Coast Marine Life.*

YOUR SUMMARY

....

....

....

....

....

....

Answers to Selected Exercises

EXERCISE 1

1. a	2. b	3. a	4. b	5. b
6. b	7. a	8. b	9. a	10. a

EXERCISE 3

1. a	2. b	3. a	4. b	5. c
6. a	7. a	8. c	9. c	10. a

Chapter 6

Identifying the Author's Overall Pattern of Organization

I always have two things in my head—I always have a theme and the form. The form looks for the theme, theme looks for the form, and when they come together you're able to write.

—W. H. Auden

This chapter will help you to:

1. become familiar with the ten common overall patterns of organization.
2. become familiar with the clue words that signal the presence of a specific pattern.
3. recognize when a writer mixes the overall patterns.

We have all begun to read something and then, because we couldn't tell how the author was developing the idea or couldn't identify the overall pattern of organization, we would lose the train of thought, get frustrated, and start over again. Sometimes we just quit reading.

The author's way of arranging the material to best accomplish his or her purpose and to express the ideas clearly is called the pattern of organization. You need to be aware of this organization because if you recognize the method of development the author employs, you can think along with the author and you are less likely to lose the main point, get frustrated, waste time, or quit reading.

Common Overall Patterns of Organization and Their Clue Words

Even though most reading materials a college student is required to read are *expository prose*—that is, written to inform or to explain something—within that *exposition* different patterns of organization are applied. The pattern a writer chooses can vary greatly, but in well-written material it is recognizable. The pattern in most textbooks is likely to be either cause and effect (showing how something occurs because of other factors); comparison and contrast (pointing out likenesses and differences among ideas and events); time order (putting facts and events into a sequence); statement and classification (statement of a fact or problem followed by discussion or solution intended to make things clear); or simple listing (enumeration, in order, of facts, events, and ideas). Other patterns too are used. To increase your comprehension of the works you read, become aware of the ten commonly used organizational patterns; see the table on page 153. Also, notice the clue words that help you determine which pattern is employed.

Mixed Patterns

Although authors generally follow *one* overall organization when they write, they often mix their patterns to more easily or more efficiently accomplish their objectives. Finding both *comparison* and *contrast* mingled is very common, as is mixing *definition* and *classification*. Don't be alarmed if when reading a piece of writing you see an author moving from one pattern to a different one, or combining two patterns. That you are able to spot this combination indicates *you are successful* in this important technique in reading comprehension. It doesn't matter which pattern an author uses as long as *you* recognize it.

What to Look Out for

Be aware of two things.

1. Often students confuse the clue words and attribute them to the wrong pattern of organization. Be clear about the patterns and which clue words go with each.
2. The *summary* pattern is especially confusing because often authors *employ* summary in their organization, but that does not necessarily mean the *pattern* is summary. The author's overall pattern may be, for example, definition.

Patterns of Organization and Their Clue Words

Pattern of Organization	Clue Words
1. *Time order:* Events or ideas are discussed in relation to passing time.	after, afterward, at last, at that time, before, during, immediately, now, presently, shortly, since, thereupon, until, while
2. *Simple listing:* Emphasis on the order in which something occurs.	next, then, first, second, third, last
3. *Definition:* Emphasis on meaning of a word, phrase, idea.	means, can be defined as, the same as, like, is
4. *Statement and clarification:* Statement of fact with discussion intended to make that statement clear.	clearly, evidently, in fact, in other words, obviously, of course, too
5. *Classification:* Analysis of where events, ideas, or facts fit in with other events, ideas, and facts.	category, field, rank, group, various elements, characteristics, some feature, types, parts
6. *Summary:* Condensed statement of the principal points in a larger statement or idea.	in brief, in conclusion, in short, on the whole, to sum up, to summarize
7. *Comparison:* Discussion of similarities in two or more ideas, events, or things.	also, likewise, in like manner, similarly, similar to, compared with
8. *Contrast:* Discussion of the differences in two or more ideas, events, or things.	although, however, but, conversely, nevertheless, yet, on the contrary, on one hand ... on the other hand, at the same time
9. *Generalization and example:* Statement with examples designed to illustrate or clarify the statement.	for example, e.g., for instance, that is, thus, to illustrate, as demonstrated
10. *Cause and effect:* A reason or condition and the subsequent effect or conclusion.	accordingly, affect, as a result, because, consequently, hence, in short, may be due to, reasons, results, then, therefore, thus

Organizational-Pattern Margin Mark ℘

As soon as you see indications (clue words) of an author's organization, jot a P in the margin opposite the indicating word or words.

Writing to Comprehend

1. Try writing a brief statement (three or four paragraphs) on your feelings about illegal drug use, but write it according to a preselected organization. Be ready to discuss the ease or difficulty in doing this exercise. Use one or more sheets of paper, as necessary.

2. Explain as clearly as you can why knowing the overall organization in a passage you are reading—while you are reading it—is good for your comprehension.

   ....

   ....

   ....

   ....

3. What is the overall pattern of organization in this chapter? in this book? Give reasons for your conclusions.

   ....

   ....

   ....

   ....

4. Why is it important to be able to answer these three questions as you are reading?
   a. Do I understand this material?
   b. Could I repeat this writing?
   c. Where does all this writing lead?

   ....

   ....

....

....

....

Words to Read by

For each of these words we list four possible choices for a definition. Only one of the four, however, is a definition of the word as it is used in the reading selection in this chapter. You will need to refer to the passage (page number in parentheses) to establish the context for each word. If you do not know the meaning of a word, including answer choices, look it up in the dictionary. Circle the correct definition.

1. *economics* (158)
   a physical science
   a social science
   a natural science
   a mathematical science

2. *cartilage* (159)
   material on a motorcycle
   a kind of doctor
   connective tissue
   means of transportation

3. *chronic* (160)
   angry
   continuing
   ticklish
   medical

4. *fantasy* (162)
   trashy reading
   product of the imagination
   gimmick writing
   a delusion

5. *lobotomies* (165)
   health food
   television programs
   illegal marriages
   surgical operations

6. *altruistic* (166)
   actively ill-willed
   hating women
   believing in God
   unselfish

7. *migration* (168)
   movement from region to region
   having one color
   having similar parts
   multiple births

8. *nurturant* (169)
   a star-shaped symbol
   hostile activities
   ancient traditions
   something that nourishes

9. *erosion* (169)
   medical science
   expansion
   wearing away
   calculations

10. *modem* (169)
    way of life
    computer equipment
    platform
    real estate directory

What Are Your Thoughts?

1. Some things we read don't seem to have an overall organization. Is that possible? Under what circumstances might something we are reading not have such a pattern?

   ....

   ....

   ....

2. Are some organizations easier to identify than others? Which ones, and why?

   ....

   ....

   ....

3. Discuss the difference between the *statement and clarification* and the *generalization and example* patterns.

   ....

   ....

   ....

4. Are the *time order* and *simple listing* patterns close in structure and easily confused? How do you remember which is which?

   ....

   ....

   ....

5. Where in your reading are you usually first aware of what the structure may be? What do you think about when that pattern becomes evident?

   ....

   ....

   ....

Anticipate the Topics

These words suggest the topics in the reading passages in the exercises in this chapter. On the line next to each topic, write a brief sentence indicating the idea you guess is the main one in that passage. The first one is done for you.

economics *Economics is one of the hardest courses in college.*

military ....

snoring ....

depression ....

drug use ....

college ....

science fiction ....

minimum wage ....

aspirin ....

attorneys ....

Carter and Nixon ....

taxes ....

Kennedys ....

profit ....

Lassie ....

lunar effects ....

population growth ....

madman ....

insect and animal cooperation ....

languages ....

real estate ....

work ....

Practice Exercises

EXERCISE 1

On the line following each of the patterns of organization, jot down at least two clue words that signal each pattern. After you have finished (and not before), turn back to page 153 and check to see if your clue words are among those listed for the patterns. The first one is done for you.

1. time order .... *after, since, shortly* ....

2. simple listing ....

3. definition ....

4. statement and clarification ....

5. classification ....

6. summary ....

7. comparison ....

8. contrast ....

9. generalization and example ....

10. cause and effect ....

EXERCISE 2

Read these passages and decide which overall pattern of organization each follows. Indicate your choice by circling the letter of the correct technique among those listed with the paragraphs. Then, on the lines following, give reasons for your choice. The first one is done for you.

1. Economics is classified as a social science. Like political science, sociology, and geography, it concerns people's attempts to organize the environment to satisfy their needs. Economics concentrates on satisfying material needs such as the need for food and shelter. Specifically, it concerns *production, distribution, and consumption of goods and services.*

    —From Gordon and Dawson, *Introductory Economics.*

    a. time order
    b. simple listing
    c. definition

    The subject, economics, is explained.
    The clue word: is.

2. The military must teach the recruit new roles (professional killer) and values (destroying an enemy is good) that are opposed to civilian roles and values. In order to do this, a period of desocialization (basic training) deliberately separates the recruit from former socialization experiences (no leave to visit family, new dress and short haircuts, specified hours to go to bed and to eat, and so on). In this context, the recruit becomes totally dependent upon the drill instructor for a new sense of self and identity. During bayonet practice, D.I.s frequently yell "Kill, kill, kill!"

> —From Lowry and Rankin, *Sociology: Social Science and Social Concern.*

a. cause and effect

b. generalization and example

c. classification

....

....

3. *Help for Snorers.* Snoring, which can get as loud as a motorcycle, threatens marriages and can be a health hazard. But help is on the way. Werner Mang, a West German physician, reports successfully treating snorers with an injection of cattle cartilage to stiffen the palate. In the United States, doctors are experimenting with a nighttime dental mouthpiece that opens the airways in the back of the snorer's throat.

> —From *The Futurist,* September/October 1988, page 5. Reprinted with permission from *The Futurist,* published by the World Future Society, 4916 St. Elmo Avenue, Bethesda, Maryland 20814.

a. contrast

b. summary

c. statement and clarification

....

....

4. In general, disaster victims work out their own private withdrawal arrangements. For example, when a tornado hit Worcester, approximately 10,000 persons were made homeless. However, only about 50 individuals were housed by the public authorities. Displaced persons instead moved in with other family members, intimates, neighbors, and generally ignored the formal agencies.

> —From Lowry and Rankin, *Sociology: Social Science and Social Concern.*

a. generalization and example

b. comparison

c. cause and effect

....

....

5. Three characteristics of this book—its readability, comprehensiveness, and scholarship—were well received in previous editions, and I have worked to retain and improve these qualities.

     —From Hyde, *Half the Human Experience: The Psychology of Women.*

  a. definition
  b. summary
  c. classification

....

....

6. Treatments for depression vary. The first step is to have a medical checkup. Therapy may be appropriate if you are grieving an important loss, such as a long-term relationship or job, when symptoms have become chronic or if you are acting destructive or are inclined to do so.

     —Source unknown.

  a. simple listing
  b. contrast
  c. cause and effect

....

....

7. It makes sense to go about knowing in several ways.

     —From Scherman, *A Preface to Politics.*

  a. generalization and example
  b. time order
  c. classification

....

....

8. The question of when we can call drug *use* drug *abuse* is not an easy one to answer. In the strictest sense, any use of an illegal drug can be called abuse because the user has broken the law. Such a definition is thus not very useful. Experimental use of drugs, although it might reasonably be discouraged, often goes no further than experimentation, and no long-term or short-term, negative impact occurs. Although we cannot consider all drug use to be drug abuse, clearly certain kinds of use create problems for the individual and society. I will define *abuse* for purposes of this chapter as any drug use that interferes with an individual's performance at school, home, or work, or in society.

—From Ingersoll, *Adolescents.*

a. cause and effect
b. definition
c. comparison

....

....

9. What started out as leisurely activity among friends, then became a new way of playing fetch with the dog, has now reached its newest and most exciting stage. The Ultimate stage.

    Ultimate combines the elements of other sports, mostly soccer and football, using a Frisbee.

    The seven players on each team can only advance the disc by tossing it to a teammate. Each player has 10 seconds to release the disc, and the goal is to advance to the opponent's end zone.

    The sport requires a great deal of stamina, as players may play up to three or four games each day of a tournament while running, catching, throwing and diving for the disc.

    "Ultimate is a sport which is built on good spirit and attitude," said Ed Lane, a second-year Ultimate player. "There is a great comradery among both teammates and the opposition. We all feel very good about the sport and the spirit behind it."

    This may explain why there are no referees. Lane said the game is quite unique because it is governed solely by the players.

    —Source unknown.

a. statement and clarification
b. contrast
c. classification

....

....

10. For example, most of us either do not know why we are in college or are here just because it seemed the thing to do. Either our parents wanted us to go or all our friends were doing it. More self-consciously, we are here to find a wife or a husband, or so that we can get a good job when we graduate.

    —Source unknown.

a. generalization and example
b. summary
c. simple listing

....

....

EXERCISE 3

Read these passages and decide which overall pattern of organization is used.
Indicate your choice by circling the letter of the correct technique among those
listed with the paragraphs. Then, on the lines following, give reasons for your
choice. The first one is done for you.

1.   Science fiction and similar kinds of fantasy can be interesting and instructive
     and even good escape. There are lessons to be learned from "Star Trek," *Star
     Wars,* and *Dune,* and what passes for the future on TV and in the movies.
     But an amazing amount of "science" "fiction" is pretty lightweight stuff. Fun
     for sure, and certainly a way to play, but it is generally just a logical exten-
     sion of what we have and know.
         —Source unknown.

   a. definition
   b. time order
   c. contrast

   *Notice the clue word, But. A contrast is
   suggested between "instructive" and "lightweight" science fiction.*

2.   Nearly 5,000 years ago, in Sumer (present-day Iraq), the government en-
     forced minimum wages and controlled employee working conditions. Nearly
     4,000 years ago, the Code of Hammurabi (king of Babylon) contained several
     laws relating to business, especially liability and minimum wages for
     workers.
         —From Megginson et al., *Business.*

   a. classification
   b. generalization and example
   c. time order

   ....

   ....

3.   Let us review what the Federalists, as exemplified by Madison, believed:

1. People could not be trusted to rule themselves. Indeed, the only thing worse than a few people trying to rule themselves was many people trying to rule themselves.
2. The morality of the system was in almost no sense public. Morality was a private thing, a commodity of the individual based on self-interest.
3. Citizenship was based upon an individual's remaining private. The system depended upon materialism, self-seekingness, and self-interestedness, and the citizen became trapped in this self-view.
4. The system was created by people of the Enlightenment who believed that if only the right (read *rational*) set of institutions were discovered, then the system could run indefinitely, in spite of people.

   —From Scherman, *A Preface to Politics.*

a. summary
b. cause and effect
c. classification

....

....

4. *What a Headache.* Over-the-counter drug abuse has some university health officials worried. "Students overuse and abuse over-the-counter drugs without knowing the physical consequences that are caused by them," said David F. Duncan, professor of health education at Southern Illinois U., Carbondale. In a campus study of drugs most commonly used by students, Duncan found the statistics on aspirin use frightening. The study, taken from a random sample of about 223 students enrolled in undergraduate and graduate classes, revealed that about 12 percent of those surveyed took aspirin with other drugs, 6 percent used aspirin daily, 3 percent reported taking at least 12 aspirin a day and the same percent said they experienced abdominal pain, rectal bleeding or frequent vomiting. "Far more people die from aspirin abuse than heroin or cocaine," Duncan said.

   —Source unknown.

a. generalization and example
b. summary
c. comparison

....

....

5. A second way to get a view of the law (get a view of ourselves) is to look at how lawyers structure and do their work.

   —From Scherman, *A Preface to Politics.*

a. time order
b. simple listing
c. contrast

....

....

6. The attorneys believe the problems of the Indians they represent can, in a rough way, be understood as: (1) the poverty of the individuals, (2) the lack of power—both personally and tribally, and (3) the lack of education and skills of the people. These are all problems we can relate to; after all, we sort out much of the world with those very categories.

    —From Scherman, *A Preface to Politics*.

a. statement and clarification
b. cause and effect
c. classification

....

....

7. While it is always helpful to have Nixon as a bad example, it is important to remember that he was not the first—nor will he be the last—to show us rotten things.

    The next elected president after Nixon was the self-proclaimed Religious Carter. Self-righteous, morally upstanding, and as interested in being reelected as Nixon was. In his effort to be renominated, Carter used federal money in the "right" places to ensure votes; he refused to open his decisions to public debate; he was ever ready to use the Iranian crisis to his political advantage.

    It is certainly fair to call that politics as usual. To contend that it is not unusual would be correct. It would be truthful to say that others have done the same thing.

    All this is so, but to say that Carter's actions are normal is not to say that they are either good or right or, in the long run, helpful to anyone but the president.

    For years and years Richard Nixon had a terrible reputation. He was seen as ruthlessly ambitious and not altogether moral. Jimmy Carter was different: We did not know he was equally ruthlessly ambitious and not altogether moral until he became president.

    —From Scherman, *A Preface to Politics*.

a. mixed comparison and contrast
b. cause and effect
c. summary

....

8. Income tax regulations frequently incorporate special provisions for groups that feel they are not being sufficiently rewarded for their work. For example, salesmen and college professors can deduct travel expenses for business purposes. Problems with this method include the following: tax deductions can be misused (vacation travel becomes business travel by merely attending a meeting for a few hours); tax loopholes frequently favor those who are already privileged (oil depletion allowances).

   —From Lowry and Rankin, *Sociology: Social Science and Social Concern.*

   a. generalization and example
   b. time order
   c. contrast

9. The Kennedys satisfy another part of ourselves. In fact, they are so popular because they help us with two things. First, of course, we get a kind of long running soap-opera about life in the fast lane. At that level, we have gotten three generations of fast lane: from the patriarch's affairs to the grandchildren's drugs.

   In all of that, there have been huge successes (there is certain status in having a president in the family) which are nothing if not fast lane. We Americans like to look, and to dream.

   Second, and not fun at all, the Kennedys have fast-lane troubles. Automobile accidents, drug deaths, frontal lobotomies, divorces, being soft on fascism, and so on. We are able, at some level, to see that they are human. In fact, we can even judge that some of them (even with all that money and all those connections) aren't even as good as we are.

   —From Scherman, *A Preface to Politics.*

   a. classification
   b. simple listing
   c. comparison

10. The most common motive for entering business is the *profit motive*, the desire to make a profit as a reward for taking the risks of running a business. *Profit* is a term we've been using freely so far, in the same breath with *business*. It is income received, minus the costs of operating the business. Profit serves both as a reward for undertaking the risks of business and as a yardstick of one's success at it. Simple as it is, though, a profit isn't always made. Sometimes there are losses.

    —From Megginson et al., *Business.*

    a. definition

    b. statement and clarification

    c. contrast

....

....

EXERCISE 4

Do the same thing in this exercise that you have been doing in exercises 2 and 3, but add an element. This time, margin-mark the passages as you are reading them, using the P to indicate clue words or other indicators of the writer's purpose. The first one has been done for you.

1. Exposure to models again proves to have a significant influence on the child's P response. In one experiment a television film was used as the modeling stimulus. First graders watched either a "Lassie" episode in which a boy risks his life to rescue the dog or a "Lassie" episode without a response-to-stress theme. Subsequently, each child was placed in a conflict situation in which he or she could come to the assistance of some distressed puppies, but at the cost of giving up a game involving a valuable prize. The children who viewed the altruistic "Lassie" episode gave more help to the puppies.

    —From Feshbach and Weiner, *Personality.*

    a. time order

    (b.) generalization and example

    c. simple listing

A statement is made about "exposure to models" and examples are given to illustrate it.

2. You're on the couch again. You've been there a lot lately.

    While you watch soapy reruns on the tube, you remind yourself of the half-dozen other things you should do—finish homework, write overdue letters, face the corroded lasagna pan in the sink—but you know won't get done.

    Life is a drag and you're not sure why. Friends call, but you let the answering machine take your place. The pajamas you've been living in for days are grimy, you're choking up at commercials and purposeful work seems like a fantasy.

    —Source unknown.

    a. time order

    b. summary

    c. classification

....

3. It has often been suggested that the moon directly influences human behavior. The moon has been thought to increase sexual powers, affect births and deaths, cause the onset of epilepsy, promote mental disturbances and, of course, be responsible for werewolves. These effects have been written about throughout history and in fictional literature. Inasmuch as the moon provides light at night and exerts a powerful gravitational force that influences the tides and weather, these effects could be thought of as having physical mediators.

To examine possible lunar effects on mental disturbances, Campbell and Beets (1978) reviewed the psychological literature related to psychiatric hospital admissions, suicides, and homicides. They noted no correlation between a full moon and any of these indicators of psychological disturbance. Perhaps the widespread use of electric lights masks the influence of the presence or absence of a full moon. But for whatever reason, it seems that a full moon has no significant consequences for mental stability. On the other hand, there are data suggesting a relation between the absence of sunlight and depression, and one experimental approach to the alleviation of depression merely bathes the patient in light!

—From Feshbach and Weiner, *Personality*.

a. statement and clarification

b. classification

c. cause and effect

4. *Three U.S. States Will Show Biggest Growth.* Half of the total population growth in the United States through the end of this century will occur in just three states: California, Texas, and Florida. California will remain by far the most-populous state at the turn of the century; by 1995, Texas will have moved past New York into the second spot, and Florida will remain fourth, according to the U.S. Bureau of the Census. Wyoming will continue as the least-populous state.

—From *The Futurist*, September/October 1988, page 5. Reprinted with permission from *The Futurist*, published by the World Future Society, 4916 St. Elmo Avenue, Bethesda, Maryland 20814.

a. classification

b. statement and clarification

c. cause and effect

5. The madman's repeated clashes with authority fit a maddeningly familiar pattern: since arriving in the U.S. from Cuba as part of the Mariel boatlift in 1980, Jorge Delgado had been arrested at least eleven times for petty crimes and hospitalized as a mental patient seven times. Once he had smashed a chalice during a service at St. Patrick's Cathedral. Twice in the past six months, city psychiatrists had examined him and failed to discover any reason not to return him to the streets.

They obviously overlooked something. Outside St. Patrick's last Wednesday night, the 6-ft. 5-in. Delgado stripped off his clothes, entered the soaring Manhattan landmark and began to strike worshippers. Police officer James McMann, 50, radioed for help before Delgado knocked him out with a wrought-iron prayer stand and then struck and killed usher John Winters, 77. Lunging at one of three newly arrived policemen, he was shot dead.

—From *Time*, October 3, 1988. Copyright © 1988 by Time, Inc. Reprinted by permission.

a. statement and clarification
b. contrast
c. time order

....

....

6. Each tribe was a group of bands, a practical association for hunting and subsisting according to the pattern of bison migrations. Most of the year these animals grazed over the Plains in small groups but during the late summer rutting (mating) season "they came together in huge herds that blackened the Plains." The Indians responded with a parallel social cycle, uniting for the summer encampment and for the conduct of tribal business and ceremony.

—From Gibson, *The American Indian.*

a. comparison
b. contrast
c. summary

....

....

7. The complex cooperative societies of social insects like the ant and the bee have been described in countless popular articles, and the interaction of genetic programming with environmental influences in these insects has been extensively studied. But cooperation and sharing are by no means restricted to social insects. Chimpanzees, for example, display unusual cooperation and coordination when in pursuit of prey. Also, when the food supply is limited, chimpanzees will beg from one another and share food.

Positive social behaviors are common even among African elephants. "Young calves of both sexes are treated equally and each is permitted to suckle from any nursing mother in the group. Adolescent cows serve as 'aunts,' restraining the calves from running about and nudging others awake from their naps." When a young bull elephant was felled with an anesthetic dart, "the adult cows rushed to his aid and tried to raise him to his feet." The African wild dog provides a striking contrast between savage behavior displayed when attacking prey and gentle, nurturant behavior extended to others in its pack. When the pack have eaten their prey, they return to the den and regurgitate, making it possible for the young and other adults who remained behind to share in the bounty. The sick and the crippled, unable to participate in the hunt, are thus maintained by the pack.

—From Feshbach and Weiner, *Personality.*

   a. generalization and example
   b. cause and effect
   c. simple listing

....

....

8.   *Glottochronology* is the technique used to determine the age of a particular culture from characteristics of its language. Linguists have found that languages go through predictable changes—they tend to lose words in what is called language erosion. The rate of change, about 19 percent of the original words lost each thousand years, has been calculated and is predictable. Glottochronological analysis of American Indian languages indicates that the many tongues spoken in 1500 required at least 15,000 to 20,000 years to evolve.

—From Gibson, *The American Indian.*

   a. contrast
   b. definition
   c. classification

....

....

9.   Breaking into the tightly knit world of Manhattan real estate brokerage isn't easy, but Clark Halstead has technology on his side. The managing partner in the Halstead Property Management Co. opened for business this fall with an IBM System 36 minicomputer and 14 terminals in his townhouse office. But his real edge may be parked out front. The cab is not only a rolling billboard—it is a way of shuttling clients around with the office computer virtually in tow. The cab is outfitted with an IBM Portable Computer, cellular telephone and 2400-baud modem.

From the backseat a broker can type in the apartment hunter's requirements. Calls are transmitted from a small antenna above the rear window. If an apartment description appeals to the client's fancy, the show, as they say, is already on the road.

To keep the backseat more spacious, the computer and modem are kept on foam padding in the trunk. Both are plugged into a 120-volt generator, which feeds off the car's electrical system. Only the keyboard, phone and monitor are inside with the passengers....

—From Slotnick et al., *Computers and Applications.*

a. simple listing
b. time order
c. generalization and example

....

....

10. The common meaning of the word *work* refers to the accomplishment of some task or job. When work is done, energy has been expended. Hence, work and energy are related.

A student performs a certain amount of work during the day and becomes tired. He or she must obtain rest and food in order to continue the work. We know that rest alone is not sufficient to keep the student going; thus, the food must serve as fuel to supply the necessary energy.

The technical meaning of the word *work* is quite different from the common meaning. A student standing at rest and holding several books is doing no work, although he or she will feel tired after a time. Technically speaking, work is accomplished only when a force acts through a distance.

—From Shipman et al., *An Introduction to Physical Science.*

a. definition
b. summary
c. cause and effect

....

....

EXERCISE 5

This excerpt is the conclusion to Stephen Crane's short story, "The Bride Comes to Yellow Sky." Read the passage and then, as if you were the instructor in the class, prepare a brief five-question multiple-choice test similar to the questions you have been answering in the exercises in this and preceding chapters.

Using this story portion and what you have learned so far, prepare one multiple-choice question—and the answer choices—to measure each of these reading-comprehension skills.

1. recognizing the main idea
2. identifying supporting details
3. determining meaning of words from context
4. recognizing the author's purpose
5. identifying the author's overall pattern of organization

Make these questions as fair as you can, being careful, though, to create questions that are clear. After you write your questions, be ready to answer in class the analysis questions that follow.

THE BRIDE COMES TO YELLOW SKY

Potter and his bride walked sheepishly and with speed. Sometimes they laughed together shamefacedly and low.

"Next corner, dear," he said finally.

They put forth the efforts of a pair walking bowed against a strong wind. Potter was about to raise a finger to point the first appearance of the new home when, as they circled the corner, they came face to face with a man in a maroon-coloured shirt, who was feverishly pushing cartridges into a large revolver. Upon the instant the man dropped his revolver to the ground and, like lightning, whipped another from its holster. The second weapon was aimed at the bridegroom's chest.

There was a silence. Potter's mouth seemed to be merely a grave for his tongue. He exhibited an instinct to at once loosen his arm from the woman's grip, and he dropped the bag to the sand. As for the bride, her face had gone as yellow as old cloth. She was a slave to hideous rites, gazing at the apparitional snake.

The two men faced each other at a distance of three paces. He of the revolver smiled with a new and quiet ferocity.

"Tried to sneak up on me," he said. "Tried to sneak up on me!" His eyes grew more baleful. As Potter made a slight movement, the man thrust his revolver venomously forward. "No; don't you do it, Jack Potter. Don't you move a finger toward a gun just yet. Don't you move an eyelash. The time has come for me to settle with you, and I'm goin' to do it my own way, and loaf along with no interferin'. So if you don't want a gun bent on you, just mind what I tell you."

Potter looked at his enemy. "I ain't got a gun on me Scratchy," he said. "Honest, I ain't." He was stiffening and steadying, but yet somewhere at the back of his mind a vision of the Pullman floated: the sea-green figured velvet, the shining brass, silver, and glass, the wood that gleamed as darkly brilliant as the surface of a pool of oil—all the glory of the marriage, the environment of the new estate. "You know I fight when it comes to fighting, Scratchy Wilson; but I ain't got a gun on me. You'll have to do all the shootin' yourself."

His enemy's face went livid. He stepped forward, and lashed his weapon to and fro before Potter's chest. "Don't you tell me you ain't got no gun on you, you whelp. Don't tell me no lie like that. There ain't a man in Texas ever seen you without no gun. Don't take me for no kid." His eyes blazed with light, and his throat worked like a pump.

"I ain't takin' you for no kid," answered Potter. His heels had not moved an inch backward. "I'm takin' you for a damn fool. I tell you I ain't got a gun, and I ain't. If you're goin' to shoot me up, you better begin now; you'll never get a chance like this again."

So much enforced reasoning had told on Wilson's rage; he was calmer. "If you ain't got a gun, why ain't you got a gun?" he sneered. "Been to Sunday-school?"

"I ain't got a gun because I've just come from San Anton' with my wife. I'm married," said Potter. "And if I'd thought there was going to be any galoots like you prowling around when I brought my wife home, I'd had a gun, and don't you forget it."

"Married!" said Scratchy, not at all comprehending.

"Yes, married. I'm married," said Potter, distinctly.

"Married?" said Scratchy. Seemingly for the first time, he saw the drooping, drowning woman at the other man's side. "No!" he said. He was like a creature allowed a glimpse of another world. He moved a pace backward, and his arm, with the revolver, dropped to his side. "Is this the lady?" he asked

"Yes; this is the lady," answered Potter.

There was another period of silence.

"Well," said Wilson at last, slowly, "I s'pose it's all off now."

"It's all off if you say so, Scratchy. You know I didn't make the trouble." Potter lifted his valise.

"Well, I 'low it's off, Jack," said Wilson. He was looking at the ground. "Married!" He was not a student of chivalry; it was merely that in the presence of this foreign condition he was a simple child of the earlier plains. He picked up his starboard revolver, and, placing both weapons in their holsters, he went away. His feet made funnel-shaped tracks in the heavy sand.

—From "The Bride Comes to Yellow Sky" by Stephen Crane (1897).

YOUR QUESTIONS

1. ....

   a. ....   b. ....

   c. ....   d. ....

2. ....

    a. ....   b. ....

    c. ....   d. ....

3. ....

    a. ....   b. ....

    c. ....   d. ....

4. ....

    a. ....   b. ....

    c. ....   d. ....

5. ....

    a. ....   b. ....

    c. ....   d. ....

ANALYSIS

What was difficult about creating these questions?

Which was the most difficult question to create? Why was it so difficult?

What did this exercise teach you about these five specific reading-comprehension skills? Are you now better able to read with increased awareness of how to answer these kinds of questions yourself, because you worked hard to create fair, clear questions?

Does creating questions give you an idea about how teachers create the questions *you* have to answer?

In your own words, what's the value of learning to write specific types of questions on skills in reading comprehension?

Answers to Selected Exercises

WORDS TO READ BY

1. a social science
2. connective tissue
3. continuing
4. a product of the imagination
5. surgical operations
6. unselfish
7. movement from region to region
8. something that nourishes
9. wearing away
10. computer equipment

EXERCISE 2

1c. The subject, economics, is explained. The clue word: *is.*

2b. General statements are made and then examples are given.

3c. Help for snorers is on the way, is the statement, which is then clarified on what form the help will take.

4a. The first sentence is the generalization. The second sentence begins with the clue words *for example.*

5b. This is a condensed statement of the characteristics: readability, comprehensiveness, scholarship.

6a. Notice the phrase "the first step." If this passage were longer, we would anticipate reading clue words like *then* and *next.*

7c. Knowing will be analyzed according to different standards, types, or classifications.

8b. The words *definition* and *define* are actually used in this extended definition.

9a. A statement is made in the first sentence, followed by a discussion intended to make that statement clear.

10a. Notice the clue words *for example.* We can infer that a general statement (about going to college) has already been made.

EXERCISE 4

1b. A statement is made with examples designed to illustrate it.

2a. Events are discussed in order of their occurring. Time is passing. Notice the clue word *while.*

3c. This is a discussion of a potential cause and its effects, even though the conclusion is that there is no relation.

4b. This is a statement of fact followed by a discussion intended to make that statement clear.

5c. The events are discussed in relation to the passing time: 1980, the past six months, last Wednesday.

6a. The comparison is made between the pattern of bison migration and the *parallel* (clue word) Indian social cycle.

7a. This generalization about cooperation and sharing is supported by numerous examples.

8b. A clear definition of glottochronology.

9c. Several examples are given of how the general statement "but Clark Halstead has technology on his side" applies.

10a. This is an extended definition of the word *work.* Clue words like *is* and *refers to* are strong indicators of organization.

Mid-Course Review and Diagnostic Test

Read carefully but quickly the passages and the questions that follow each passage. Circle the letter of the correct answer for each question.

PASSAGE 1

1 Sue Benson gathered some notes into her briefcase and told
2 her secretary she'd be having lunch with a potential client at
3 The Cordon Bleu.
4   After her pleasant telephone conversation with business-
5 man John Kingsley, Sue was looking forward to explaining
6 how her agency could promote his new enterprise. Listening
7 to Kingsley's dynamic, resonant voice, Sue had conjured up
8 mental images of a young, attractive, athletic entrepreneur.
9 Thus, on entering the restaurant, she paused only briefly
10 before heading toward a tall blond wearing a sporty cashmere
11 sweater, tweed jacket and beige corduroy slacks.
12   When a short, stout redhead in a well-tailored navy suit
13 stepped into her path and introduced himself as John Kings-
14 ley, Sue concealed her surprise with professional composure.
15   Inwardly, however, she resolved never to make assump-
16 tions about appearances based on telephone conversations.
17   Even though the voice is an "influential factor" in nonver-

175

18 bal communication, Sue was correct in recognizing the rela-
19 tive inaccuracy of predicting physical appearances based on
20 "blind" nonverbal cues.
21   But if telephone contact does not reveal whether you're
22 talking to a stunning Venus or a stocky brunette, studies
23 show that most people can accurately gauge several charac-
24 teristics based solely on this nonverbal information, including
25 a person's general age, level of education or sophistication,
26 regional or ethnic background, and mood.
27   One trait commonly detectable on vocal cues is the speak-
28 er's gender. As with all nonverbal cues, however, the obvious
29 is not always as it seems.
30   One experienced telephone interviewer recalls, "I had
31 conducted an entire interview believing my deep-voiced re-
32 spondent was a man until I asked 'his' wife's occupation.
33   "'That's me, baby,' was the gruff reply."
34   Limitations of judgment based solely on telephone conver-
35 sations should not obscure the importance of Alexander Bell's
36 invention as a tool for projecting positive images.
37   John Kingsley, the young entrepreneur who was success-
38 ful despite a less-than-Olympic physical appearance, obvious-
39 ly knew how to use the telephone to his advantage, projecting
40 attractiveness, energy and enthusiasm. And his success on
41 the telephone was based less on what he said than on how he
42 said it.

—From Newman, *Communicating in Business Today*.

1.   The details in the first three paragraphs do which of these?
     a. Expand the passage.
     b. Give an example of the main idea.
     c. Illustrate the difficulties in meeting people in a restaurant.
     d. Show a person's inability to detect any characteristics over the phone accu-
        rately.

2.   The sentence beginning in line 40 of this passage is a statement of
     a. fact   b. opinion

3.   In this passage the author shows bias against
     a. short, stout redheads in well-tailored suits
     b. deep-voiced women who sound like men when speaking on the telephone
     c. assumptions about appearances based on telephone conversations
     d. stocky brunettes and stunning Venuses

4. The word or phrase that identifies the relationship within the sentence beginning in line 15 ("Inwardly, however ...") is

a. time order   b. generalization and example

c. classification   d. contrast

PASSAGE 2

1 Once inside the retail location, the shopper receives contin-
2 uous messages at three levels. *Store atmosphere* is the overall
3 setting of the store, its design, lighting, fixtures, color, and
4 sound. These are developed to convey a mood or feeling that
5 separates the store from others that sell similar merchandise.
6 The more similar the product offerings of competitors, the
7 more important it is to create a unique environment.
8   By going into any large shopping mall and walking from
9 one clothing store to another, a shopper can easily experience
10 atmosphere differences. One store will be brightly lit with
11 neatly lined-up pastel plastic racks and pastel walls. Another
12 will be in seeming disarray, with loud rock music and strobe
13 lights. A third will have a wood decor, soft lights, and soft
14 music. Each type of atmosphere is aimed at a particular
15 target market, and each serves as a screen to tell shoppers
16 whether or not they will feel comfortable in the store and
17 what type of merchandise they might expect.
18   "Establishing a mood of shopping ambiance has never
19 been more important than it is now," says Lois Patrich, vice
20 president of sales promotion and advertising with Carson
21 Pirie Scott & Co., a Chicago-based retailer. "Department
22 stores have always had a preponderance of merchandise that
23 you can get at any store. How then does a retailer get a
24 customer to buy at his store? By creating a shopping atmo-
25 sphere that will motivate him to buy and one that he wants
26 to come back to."
27   *Store layout* is the arrangement of merchandise to facili-
28 tate shopping. The layout tells consumers how to proceed
29 through the store and what pace is expected. An open layout
30 invites shoppers to browse. A cluttered layout sends a signal
31 of busyness and rushing.
32   An effective layout maximizes customer exposure to mer-
33 chandise and keeps the customer in the store longer. Studies
34 show that the longer the customer is in the store, the more
35 money is spent. The layout also should have the high-margin

36 merchandise in the high-traffic areas and the most desired
37 merchandise in the back so that consumers must walk past
38 many other goods. In a supermarket, for example, the meats,
39 dairy products, and produce have the greatest constant
40 demand and are placed at the perimeters so shoppers will
41 need to pass other products to get to them.
42   *Merchandise display* refers to the organization of goods at
43 a specific place in the store's layout. Displays communicate at
44 still another level to attract attention to the product, enhance
45 product appeal, and increase the shopper's propensity to pur-
46 chase. While these tasks might lead the display design in one
47 direction, the display also needs to be consistent with the
48 store's atmosphere.

—From Rothschild, *Advertising.*

5.   The subject in this passage is
      a. store atmosphere   b. store layout
      c. merchandise display   d. ways in which stores
                                  communicate

6.   All these are factors the writer says help create communication between shoppers and individual stores *except*
      a. merchandise display   b. advertising
      c. store layout   d. store atmosphere

7.   In line 18, the word *ambiance* means
      a. appearance   b. smell
      c. sound   d. atmosphere

8.   The first sentence in this passage ("Once inside the …") indicates that the author's purpose is
      a. to discuss three things   b. to suggest an alternative
      c. to offer a solution   d. to define something

9.   In developing this passage, the organization the author uses can be described as
      a. summary   b. definition
      c. contrast   d. cause and effect

10.   From this passage you could infer that
      a. store layout is more important than quality of merchandise.
      b. store atmosphere matters more than quality of merchandise.
      c. getting customers to purchase depends mostly on location of product.
      d. successful department stores motivate buyers to purchase.

PASSAGE 3

1 American public and private agencies spend millions of
2 dollars annually attempting to persuade citizens to drink
3 alcohol only in "moderate" amounts or not at all, particularly
4 when operating a motor vehicle. Studies indicate that this
5 propaganda and advertising approach is almost totally inef-
6 fective. Alcohol consumption continues to rise nationally, and
7 alcohol-related traffic deaths, especially for teenage drivers,
8 have increased. In contrast to the American approach, Nor-
9 way has severe, but meaningful, penalties for driving while
10 drunk. These include periods of compulsory public work
11 (picking up trash along highways), mandatory jail sentences
12 that do not interfere with one's work (a person goes to jail for
13 the night and is released during the day to go to work), and
14 application of the law without exception (a member of the
15 Norwegian royal family will be equally punished if guilty). As
16 a result, many Norwegians use taxis, or the driver for the
17 evening does not drink when spending a night on the town.

—From Lowry and Rankin, *Sociology: Social Science and Social Concern.*

11. In this passage the author shows bias in favor of
   a. American treatment of drunk driving
   b. Norwegian treatment of drunk driving
   c. anti–drunk-driving propaganda
   d. rise in alcohol consumption

12. The author of this passage has created a tone that could be described as
   a. frustrated   b. impassioned
   c. evasive   d. serious

13. The word or phrase indicating the relationship within the sentence that begins in line 15 ("as a result ...") is
   a. comparison   b. cause and effect
   c. time order   d. definition

14. What does the sentence beginning in line 10 ("These include periods ...") do in relation to the sentence beginning in line 8 ("In contrast to ...")?
   a. It gives specific examples of ideas stated in the sentence beginning in line 8.
   b. It summarizes what was said in the sentence beginning in line 8.
   c. It indicates an idea to be added to what is stated in the sentence beginning in line 8.
   d. It indicates the order of something discussed in the sentence beginning in line 8.

15. In this passage, you could infer all these *except*
   a. Alcohol-related traffic fatalities are not decreasing.
   b. Meaningful penalties for driving while drunk could be effective in America.
   c. More money should be spent on anti-alcohol advertising.
   d. Severe penalties do not have to be improper penalties.

PASSAGE 4

1 Gibbons's categories are the following:

2   1. The *predatory gang delinquent* is the type of youth that
3 fits the stereotyped image of the gang delinquent. He makes
4 his primary association with the gang and is regularly in-
5 volved in violent delinquent behavior that will show him to
6 be "cool" or "tough." This individual is antisocial and hostile
7 toward society.

8   2. The *conflict gang delinquent* identifies with a gang and
9 may join in street fights, "rumbles," or "bopping." Typically,
10 however, his association is less well defined. He is cynical
11 about society rather than hostile, and his commitment to the
12 gang varies.

13   3. The *casual gang delinquent* is less committed to the
14 gang. His association with the gang is loose, and although he
15 joins in gang activities, his participation is primarily for
16 "kicks." Mostly, this youth sees himself as a nondelinquent
17 and has aspirations of getting an education or at least a well-
18 paying job. His parents are typically blue-collar workers who
19 are themselves law abiding and interested in his welfare.
20 Further, his gang "membership" may not be totally of his own
21 choosing.

22   4. The *casual delinquent, non-gang member* is what has
23 been termed the "hidden delinquent." His delinquent behav-
24 ior is intermittent, but he is seldom in trouble with the
25 police. Neither he nor adults think of him as delinquent. He
26 is generally committed, in the long run, to the goals of society
27 and describes his delinquent behavior as "having fun."

28   5. The *auto-theft joyrider* steals cars for joyriding and not
29 for profit. This adolescent typically engages in delinquent
30 behavior in a casual, nonplanned fashion. Like the *casual*
31 *delinquent,* he usually comes from a middle-class family who
32 gives him close supervision and discipline. He does not see
33 himself as delinquent; however, he likes to think of himself
34 as tough.

35 6. The *heroin user* thinks of himself more as a drug user
36 than a delinquent. His motives for delinquent behavior are to
37 support his habit. He feels harassed by society and typically
38 rejects it.
39 7. The *overly aggressive delinquent* is not a member of a
40 gang. He is a loner who engages in seemingly irrational
41 senseless assaults on others. His behavior is sometimes
42 described as sociopathic.

—From Ingersoll, *Adolescents.*

16. The main idea in this passage is
a. Delinquents choose to associate with gangs for security.
b. Some delinquents are not really "bad" kids.
c. There are several categories of delinquents.
d. Commitment to a gang is always a sign of a delinquent.

17. The different delinquents identified in each paragraph
a. provide concrete illustrations of the main idea.
b. point the finger at different delinquents who need help.
c. warn readers of youths who may live nearby.
d. contrast the not-so-bad delinquents with the dangerous.

18. In line 17, the word *aspirations* means
a. fears   b. promises
c. hopes   d. fantasies

19. The pattern of organization the author used in developing this passage can
be described as
a. statement and clarification   b. comparison
c. generalization and example   d. classification

20. The assertion in lines 28–34, that the "auto-theft joyrider ... comes from a
middle-class family who gives him close supervision and does not see himself
as delinquent; however, he likes to think of himself as tough" is
a. valid   b. invalid

PASSAGE 5

1 The manner in which the family was formed and the direc-
2 tion it took varied among the tribes. The formulas for a
3 couple joining in matrimony ranged from parental
4 commitment of male and female infants to future marriage to
5 bride capture by men in wars with neighboring tribes.

6 Several tribes followed a system of purchase called "bride
7 price" and "bride service" or "suitor service" where male or
8 female youth lived with and worked for future parents-in-law
9 for a year to prove one's worth as a homemaker or as a pro-
10 vider. Most tribes practiced exogamic marriage, that is the
11 bride and groom were required to be from different clans.
12   Among the Southeastern tribes where courtship in the
13 modern sense was permitted, a suitor might declare his
14 matrimonial intentions by sending the hoped-for bride a
15 small present, perhaps a trinket or a fine deerskin garment.
16 Her acceptance meant that the couple was engaged. At the
17 simple public marriage ceremony, the groom divided a choice
18 ear of corn into two parts before witnesses, handing the bride
19 one half and keeping the other half as a sign of his
20 willingness to share, or giving her a deer's foot "as an emblem
21 of the readiness with which she ought to serve him; in return,
22 she presents him with some cakes of bread, thereby declaring
23 her domestic care and gratitude.... When this short ceremony
24 is ended they may go to bed like an honest couple."
25   Native Americans practiced both monogamy and polyg-
26 amy. Of the forms of plural marriage—polygyny, marriage of
27 a male to more than one female, and polyandry, marriage of a
28 female to more than one male—the latter was rare. Where it
29 existed, it was a response to harsh economic conditions as
30 found in the Great Basin or Arctic where supporting a wife
31 and children might be too much of a burden for one man. In
32 many polygynous marriages a man had chosen a woman with
33 several sisters, and he wed them all.

—From Gibson, *The American Indian.*

21. The first sentence in this passage ("The manner in ...") indicates that the author's purpose is
   a. to classify things   b. to tell a story
   c. to define something   d. to describe something

22. The statement beginning in line 25 of this passage ("Native Americans practiced ...") is a statement of
   a. fact   b. opinion

23. If the author were delivering this passage orally, his or her tone of voice would probably be
   a. amused   b. serious
   c. outspoken   d. satiric

24. What does the sentence beginning in line 16 ("Her acceptance meant ...") do in relation to the sentence beginning in line 12 ("Among the Southeastern ...")?

    a. It contradicts something stated in the sentence beginning in line 12.

    b. It amplifies and adds to something stated in the sentence beginning in line 12.

    c. It indicates a subsequent effect of something stated in the sentence beginning in line 12.

    d. It discusses the similarities between something and something else discussed beginning in line 12.

25. The assertion in lines 26–28 that among Southeastern tribes "polyandry, marriage of a female to more than one male ... was rare" is

    a. valid   b. invalid

Chapter 7

Distinguishing Between Statements of Fact and Statements of Opinion

Opinion is that exercise of the human will which helps us to make a decision without information.

—John Erskine

Next t' a fourteen-year-ole boy ther hain't nothin as worthless as th' average opinion.

—Frank McKinney Hubbard

This chapter will help you to:

1. distinguish between fact and opinion when you read.
2. understand the place of opinion in your reading.
3. recognize when a fact is a fact.
4. learn seven ways of differentiating between fact and opinion.

Continued development of your critical reading skills is necessary if you are to be as successful in college (and after college) as you can be. These skills will enable you to determine the value of works that you read and whether you should accept or reject the ideas, or seek additional information. High-comprehension reading requires that you *question, compare,* and *evaluate* as you read.

What Are Your Thoughts?

1. Just what is it that separates fact from opinion?

....

....

....

2. Are opinions ever valuable, or are facts the only things worth reading and remembering?

....

....

....

3. Do opinions ever become facts? If so, under what circumstances?

....

....

....

4. How can you turn statements of fact into statements of opinion? How can you (if it's possible) turn statements of opinion into statements of fact?

....

....

....

5. What did you read in this book so far that you think you should remember for a test? What did you learn that is so important you want to remember it always? Which of these questions identifies information that you think the teacher wants you to know? What does the other question identify?

....

....

....

"Fact" May Be Opinion

Often students assume that because it is written in a textbook or journal article, a statement is automatically a fact. That connection just does not follow. To be a successful and efficient reader, you will need to know if you are being presented an opinion, a fact, or fact and opinion combined. Much writing that you read in college is the writer's opinion, or in different degrees combines statements of opinion with statements of fact; you will need to develop your ability to distinguish between those statements.

The Difference Between Fact and Opinion

Why is it vital to distinguish fact from opinion?

1. A fact is anything that can be *validated or proved.* If a statement can be proved right *or* wrong by verifiable measurement or testing, it is a fact.
2. An opinion *cannot be validated.* If no validation can be arrived at, if no right or wrong can be established, the statement is an opinion.

Statements of Opinion

Keep in mind that an opinion is not necessarily *incorrect,* but it hasn't been proved. An opinion may seem true, but if it *hasn't yet been proved,* it is an opinion.

Statements of opinion express an author's *impressions, beliefs,* and *judgments* about something. Those opinions cannot be judged true or false, right or wrong because they are that author's individual impressions about something. This truth gives rise to the familiar statement, "You have the right to your own opinion."

These are statements of opinion. Do you understand why?

1. President Kennedy's death significantly affected elementary-school pupils.
2. The Big Mac is the best hamburger around for the money.
3. Cats are more loving than dogs.
4. Toronto is the best city to visit in North America.
5. Fishing relaxes you better than sleeping.
6. It is better when eaten hot.

These sentences present statements of opinion about real things, but they are still *unverifiable* opinions.

Statements of Fact

Statements of fact present information without interpreting it. They imply neither judgment nor evaluation. Unlike statements of opinion, statements of fact can be verified in records, tests, or historical or scientific documents.

These are statements of fact. Do you understand why?

1. British Columbia receives 47 inches of rain yearly.
2. The temperature in the oven is 35°.
3. My friend Jim Patterson is a resident of Port Huron, Michigan.
4. He died in 1520.
5. *E.T.* has grossed more money than any other film in history.
6. It is sunny outside.

For each of these statements, you can *verify* the accuracy by going to source books, measurements, or even personal experience. Thus, these are statements of fact.

Remember These Guidelines

1. Statements dealing with persons, places, objects, occurrences, or processes which exist or did exist, and which can have their truth or falsity *proved,* are facts.

   In last night's class, Dr. Joan Kaywell spoke on methods of teaching English.

2. Statements whose truth or falsity can be proved or disproved are statements of fact even when they could be in error and proved false. A fact, then, is not always accurate or correct.

   Three-hundred twenty-seven teachers from forty-nine schools attended the school-board meeting.

   It is sunny outside.

   These are statements of fact, even if a mistake was made in counting people and schools, or even if it is not sunny outside but cloudy. If truth *or falsity* can be proved, it is a statement of fact.

3. Statements that deal with evaluations, attitudes, or probabilities are statements of opinion because they cannot be proved true or false.

   Not enough people care about the political situation to ensure any change.

   The remark may be true, but it is *opinion* because it cannot be proved by objective means. Statements of opinion are often presented in an authoritative voice

—don't be confused. If it cannot be proved, it is still opinion no matter how definite it sounds.

4. Statements about future events are opinion even when those events seem very probable.

> Eventually, consumption of water will be strictly regulated by the federal government.

Perhaps one day this will come to pass, but perhaps it won't. Either way, this statement is still an opinion.

5. Statements of fact often use more *concrete words* referring to things, events, or measurable characteristics. Words such as *blue, rock, bottle, ten years, 130 pounds, sycamore tree* are all concrete words.

6. Statements of opinion may rely on *abstract* words. Abstract words refer to things that can't be touched or measured, such as faith, love, hope, courage, patriotism, health. Because these words cannot be *specifically* defined and limited, people use them to mean different *degrees* of the same things, or often to mean something completely different. As we all know, the word *love* may mean one thing to one person but not necessarily the same thing to another.

7. Watch for clue words and phrases in statements of opinion. Frequently you can spot *value-judgment* words such as *good, bad, unattractive, necessary, quality;* or *opinion phrases* such as *I believe, it appears, we suggest* in your reading. These words and phrases should tip you off to the strong probability that *opinion,* not fact, is present.

Writing to Comprehend

1. What does it suggest to you when you read statements of opinion that are presented as if they were statements of fact? Clearly identify what you are thinking by giving examples where possible.

....

....

....

....

....

2. In a brief essay, explain how it is possible for a statement with facts in it that are wrong to still be called a statement of fact. Give examples.

> ....
>
> ....
>
> ....
>
> ....
>
> ....
>
> ....
>
> ....
>
> **3.** What is the funniest, saddest, most frustrating example of your believing a statement which you thought was fact but which turned out to be opinion?
>
> ....
>
> ....
>
> ....
>
> ....
>
> **4.** What do you do when you read? Discuss what you think occurs that gets the meaning of the words on a page turned into meaning in your mind. Is it the same meaning? How and why does that meaning stay in your memory?
>
> ....
>
> ....
>
> ....
>
> ....
>
> ....

Fact-or-Opinion Margin Mark

The margin-mark symbol indicating where you have identified an example of the writer's opinion being expressed is an O (for *opinion*).

Remember, you're not marking facts when you read them, just *opinions*.

Words to Read by

Locate the words listed here in the reading passages in this chapter on the pages indicated. On the lines that follow, suggest a definition for each word as it was used in the passage. If you cannot come up with a definition based on the context and use of a word, look it up in the dictionary and write it down here. Be ready to discuss how you arrived at your definition for each word. Remember, don't read now the questions that go with each passage.

nuclear (192) ....

absolute (193) ....

diabetes (195) ....

lavish (196) ....

electromagnetic (196) ....

blight (196) ....

pseudonym (196) ....

apathy (197) ....

recession (191) ....

spree (199) ....

sporadic (200) ....

sleuths (200) ....

immigrants (201) ....

affects (202) ....

characterized (202) ....

Practice Exercises

EXERCISE 1

These statements are all opinions. Underline the part of the sentence that helps you know it is an opinion. Also, on the lines following each statement briefly explain why it is an opinion. The first one is done for you.

1. Restaurant employees are <u>always overworked and underpaid</u>.

   Not all restaurant workers are overworked and underpaid; some are overpaid and underworked. A survey would show this balance.

2. She is the most beautiful woman in the office.

   ....

   ....

3. The television soap operas are getting better scripts.

   ....

   ....

4. Installing a new hot-water heater is an easy job.

   ....

   ....

5. Students in public schools should be required to say the Pledge of Allegiance every day.

   ....

   ....

6. Jimmy Carter was the worst president in the twentieth century.

   ....

   ....

7. *Playboy* and *Penthouse* magazines should not be sold in drugstores and supermarkets.

   ....

   ....

8. The nuclear-arms ban was the best treaty ever signed by two countries.

   ....

   ....

9. Playing in a band can only result in a life of poverty.

   ....

   ....

10. All the athletes should be required to take drug tests before they play each game.

....

....

11. This has been the nicest day all month.

....

....

12. Everybody agrees: she is an absolute doll!

....

....

13. He has an outstanding record in the Senate.

....

....

14. The Grand Canyon is easily the most spectacular sight in the world.

....

....

15. Working hard is the most important element in becoming wealthy.

....

....

16. The paintings of Renoir are better than those of any painter living today.

....

....

17. There is nothing more annoying than being caught in freeway traffic at rush hour.

....

....

18. It is clear that dentists are the least popular of professionals and least likely to be invited to parties.

....

....

19. A 1965 Mustang is the best car for a sixteen-year-old.

....

....

20. If more people would complain about spending excesses by congressmen, their spending would decrease.

....

....

EXERCISE 2

Read these passages. These are "possible facts." After each passage, place a check mark beside the question you would want to answer before accepting the statement as fact. Avoid the tendency to check more than one question even though that may seem a good idea. Focus on the *one* question that is most likely to validate or invalidate the statement as a fact. If none of the questions is appropriate, write your own question on the lines provided.

1. Construction workers are better protected from injury than children at playgrounds. (reported in *USA Today*)

.... Can you find another reliable source to consult?

.... Is the writer a known authority on this subject?

.... Does the newspaper, magazine, or book have a good reputation for truth and accuracy?

.... Does the writer have a reason for not being objective?

....

....

2. It's not who blinks first, but who blinks most that shows stress. (reported in *Newsweek*)

.... Can you find another reliable source to consult?

.... Is the writer a known authority on this subject?

.... Does the newspaper, magazine, or book have a good reputation for truth and accuracy?

.... Does the writer have a reason for not being objective?

....

....

3. Mary Tyler Moore was secretly hospitalized with a flare-up of her diabetes, reveal insiders—who say her medical problems resulted from the star's desperate efforts to make her new TV show a success. (reported in *The National Enquirer*)

.... Can you find another reliable source to consult?

.... Is the writer a known authority on this subject?

.... Does the newspaper, magazine, or book have a good reputation for truth and accuracy?

.... Does the writer have a reason for not being objective?

....

....

4. Sunlight beats the daylights out of the skin, but Retin-A appears to reverse some of the damage. (reported in *The Bradenton Herald*)

.... Can you find another reliable source to consult?

.... Is the writer a known authority on this subject?

.... Does the newspaper, magazine, or book have a good reputation for truth and accuracy?

.... Does the writer have a reason for not being objective?

....

....

5. Shocking new evidence discloses that heartless space aliens have been snatching terrified tots from their beds for monstrous medical experiments, warns a top UFO investigator. (reported in *Weekly World News*)

.... Can you find another reliable source to consult?

.... Is the writer a known authority on this subject?

.... Does the newspaper, magazine, or book have a good reputation for truth and accuracy?

.... Does the writer have a reason for not being objective?

....

....

6.   Nancy Reagan's fondness for designer couture that she once contended was beyond her ability to buy has not abated. Mrs. Reagan has been borrowing costly dresses, matched outfits and jewelry from leading fashion houses on both coasts on a lavish scale. (reported in *Time*)

.... Can you find another reliable source to consult?

.... Is the writer a known authority on this subject?

.... Does the newspaper, magazine, or book have a good reputation for truth and accuracy?

.... Does the writer have a reason for not being objective?

....

....

7.   The production of electromagnetic waves with frequencies greater than radio waves is accomplished by molecular excitation. (reported in a physical-science textbook)

.... Can you find another reliable source to consult?

.... Is the writer a known authority on this subject?

.... Does the newspaper, magazine, or book have a good reputation for truth and accuracy?

.... Does the writer have a reason for not being objective?

....

....

8.   In an effort to escape the blight of fame, Elvis has taken the pseudonym John Burrows and moved to Kalamazoo, Michigan. (reported in *US* magazine)

.... Can you find another reliable source to consult?

.... Is the writer a known authority on this subject?

.... Does the newspaper, magazine, or book have a good reputation for truth and accuracy?

.... Does the writer have a reason for not being objective?

....

....

9.   The first settlers came to New England to establish a Godly community with a

true church. They soon found that righteousness was a never-ending struggle against apathy and evil. (reported in a history textbook)

.... Can you find another reliable source to consult?

.... Is the writer a known authority on this subject?

.... Does the newspaper, magazine, or book have a good reputation for truth and accuracy?

.... Does the writer have a reason for not being objective?

....

....

10. A one-foot fall headfirst onto concrete or a four-foot fall headfirst onto packed earth can be fatal. (reported in *USA Today*)

.... Can you find another reliable source to consult?

.... Is the writer a known authority on this subject?

.... Does the newspaper, magazine, or book have a good reputation for truth and accuracy?

.... Does the writer have a reason for not being objective?

....

....

EXERCISE 3

In this exercise, do the same thing you did in Exercise 2.

a. Check the best question to ask to help you determine if the statement is a fact.
b. Write your own question to ask if you can think of a better one.

In addition, make a preliminary decision on whether each statement is likely to be fact or opinion. Put a check mark next to your choice. The first one is done for you.

1. He was 3,000 miles away as his $1.25-million home burned to the ground, but Merv Griffin, 63, is determined to rebuild his jewel of the desert and rekindle his hopes of retiring there with longtime love Eva Gabor. (reported in *Star*)

.... Can you find another reliable source to consult?

.... Is the writer a known authority on this subject?

....✓.... Does the newspaper, magazine, or book have a good reputation for truth and accuracy?

.... Does the writer have a reason for not being objective?

....

....

.... Fact   ....✓.... Opinion

2.   On any given night, an estimated 735,000 people in the U.S. are homeless. As many as 2 million may be without shelter for one night or more during the year. (reported in *Time*)

.... Can you find another reliable source to consult?

.... Is the writer a known authority on this subject?

.... Does the newspaper, magazine, or book have a good reputation for truth and accuracy?

.... Does the writer have a reason for not being objective?

....

....

.... Fact   .... Opinion

3.   Foreign, older and wealthy-looking travelers are at high risk of becoming victims of airport crime. (reported in *USA Today*)

.... Can you find another reliable source to consult?

.... Is the writer a known authority on this subject?

.... Does the newspaper, magazine, or book have a good reputation for truth and accuracy?

.... Does the writer have a reason for not being objective?

....

....

.... Fact   .... Opinion

4.   Within the power of the Japanese government and its financial institutions is

the total collapse of the U.S. currency. The Japanese hold so many dollars that the island nation could float away on them. Dumping them on financial markets could cause a world recession, if not a depression. (reported in *The Bradenton Herald*)

.... Can you find another reliable source to consult?

.... Is the writer a known authority on this subject?

.... Does the newspaper, magazine, or book have a good reputation for truth and accuracy?

.... Does the writer have a reason for not being objective?

....

....

.... Fact .... Opinion

5. Sharon Head's one-woman crime spree averaged 11 burglaries a week, and police said she stole $1,836,062 worth of property, including 291 Ferraris, Porsches, Jaguars, and other luxury autos. (reported in *The National Examiner*)

.... Can you find another reliable source to consult?

.... Is the writer a known authority on this subject?

.... Does the newspaper, magazine, or book have a good reputation for truth and accuracy?

.... Does the writer have a reason for not being objective?

....

....

.... Fact .... Opinion

6. Republicans over the last 20 years have made themselves far more adept than Democrats in using the marketing tools of Madison Avenue and the power of television to sell their candidates. (reported in *Newsweek*)

.... Can you find another reliable source to consult?

.... Is the writer a known authority on this subject?

.... Does the newspaper, magazine, or book have a good reputation for truth and accuracy?

.... Does the writer have a reason for not being objective?

....

....

.... Fact   .... Opinion

7.   By and large, drug use among teens is concentrated within a few types of drugs. Use of other drugs may occur in sporadic fashion, but it does not usually last long. What is curious is that the most widely used drug, alcohol, is often viewed with the least alarm by adults. (reported in a psychology textbook)

.... Can you find another reliable source to consult?

.... Is the writer a known authority on this subject?

.... Does the newspaper, magazine, or book have a good reputation for truth and accuracy?

.... Does the writer have a reason for not being objective?

....

....

.... Fact   .... Opinion

8.   America's so-called crackdown on crime isn't getting results—in fact, murderers, drug dealers, and thugs are spending less time in prison than they were 10 years ago, Justice Department figures show. (reported in *The National Enquirer*)

.... Can you find another reliable source to consult?

.... Is the writer a known authority on this subject?

.... Does the newspaper, magazine, or book have a good reputation for truth and accuracy?

.... Does the writer have a reason for not being objective?

....

....

.... Fact   .... Opinion

9.   The identity of Jack the Ripper has fascinated sleuths for a century. The gruesome murders of five women by the mystery madman in 1888 kept London gripped by fear, until the killings suddenly stopped. (reported in *Star*)

.... Can you find another reliable source to consult?

.... Is the writer a known authority on this subject?

.... Does the newspaper, magazine, or book have a good reputation for truth and accuracy?

.... Does the writer have a reason for not being objective?

....

....

.... Fact .... Opinion

10.　A man who lost his $3,800 wristwatch got it back a month later—when a vet retrieved it from his Doberman Pinscher puppy's stomach!

Veterinarian Jim Grantham of Spartanburg, S.C., said the Rolex was still ticking after it was surgically removed from the five-month-old pup. (reported in *Weekly World News*)

.... Can you find another reliable source to consult?

.... Is the writer a known authority on this subject?

.... Does the newspaper, magazine, or book have a good reputation for truth and accuracy?

.... Does the writer have a reason for not being objective?

....

....

.... Fact .... Opinion

EXERCISE 4

Some of the sentences below state facts, some express opinions, and some may include both facts and opinions. Use an *F* to identify statements of fact, an *O* to identify statements of opinion, and an *FO* to identify statements with both fact and opinion. The first one is done for you.

F
....　**1.** The drinking age in Florida is twenty-one.

....　**2.** I think the drinking age in California is twenty-one.

....　**3.** The only good reason for going to college is to learn.

....　**4.** Forty-eight percent of immigrants changed their names when they came to this country.

.... **5.** The Jaguar XJS has a twelve-cylinder engine and is the most beautiful car made.

.... **6.** Bill Cosby is a positive role model for television watchers.

.... **7.** Many universities provide condoms for sale in machines on campus, but they are morally wrong to do so.

.... **8.** Florida gets considerably hotter in July than California does, and that's why people move from Florida to California.

.... **9.** My daughter once secretly kept a kitten hidden in her bedroom for nearly three weeks.

.... **10.** Hitchhiking is a frequent method of traveling for college students.

.... **11.** The best way to eat cold chicken is to dip it in mayonnaise.

.... **12.** An expensive suit, pair of shoes, shirt, and tie are not always appropriate for work.

.... **13.** Pollution of various sorts affects everyone in some way.

.... **14.** Marigolds are usually gold-orange and are enjoyed by everyone.

.... **15.** I watched television last night until 4:00 am.

.... **16.** She is having a fiftieth birthday January 31 and will be emotionally upset.

.... **17.** Columbus discovered America in 1491, not 1492.

.... **18.** Time spent in the sun, tanning, causes cancer but not in everyone.

.... **19.** Christmas is characterized as a time when people feel better, but for many it is the reverse.

.... **20.** A tune-up will cost you $26.95 at the corner station and will make your car run better.

Answers to Selected Exercises

WORDS TO READ BY

You will find variation in definition.

nuclear: using atomic energy
absolute: complete, perfect
diabetes: a metabolic disorder
lavish: extravagant, profuse
electromagnetic: containing or exhibiting electromagnetism

blight: ruin
pseudonym: a fictitious name
apathy: uncaring
recession: decline in economic activity
spree: overindulgence in an activity
sporadic: occasional
sleuths: detectives
immigrant: a person who settles permanently in another country
affects: influences
characterized: was a quality of

EXERCISE 3

Student-suggested questions may be offered for each passage.
1. Does the newspaper ...? Opinion
2. Can you find another ...? Opinion
3. Does the newspaper ...? Fact
4. Is the writer ...? Opinion
5. Does the newspaper ...? Fact
6. Does the writer have a reason ...? Opinion
7. Does the newspaper ...? Fact
8. Can you find another ...? Opinion
9. Does the writer have a reason ...? Fact
10. Can you find another ...? Fact

EXERCISE 4

1. F	2. O	3. O	4. F	5. FO
6. O	7. FO	8. FO	9. F	10. F
11. O	12. O	13. O	14. FO	15. F
16. FO	17. F	18. F	19. O	20. FO

Chapter 8

Detecting Bias

Bias and prejudice are attitudes to be kept in hand, not attitudes to be avoided.
—Charles Curtis

I can promise to be frank. I cannot promise to be impartial.
—Johann Wolfgang von Goethe

This chapter will help you to:

1. understand what bias is.
2. understand why you need to detect bias.
3. recognize the five common signs that bias is present.
4. avoid the confusion that you often find in tests in which you are expected to detect bias.

You've heard it said that "It's *how* you say it that counts, not *what* you say." Propagandists know the saying is accurate and have been highly successful in molding public opinion on both political and social issues. By the time we get to college we are generally aware that public media are "loaded" with bias (a predisposition, prejudice, or prejudgment), especially in such things as commercials, political speeches, and even pep talks by religious and social-work fund raisers. This "loading" with words and phrases that play upon our emotions is meant to move our thinking—and thus our actions—in a chosen direction. In fact, we are so aware of this phenomenon that we usually don't even think about it unless our emotions are strongly touched in some way, and then we *may* question the cause.

Bias in Textbooks

Seldom, however, do we question statements that we read in college assignments or wonder if the author is being unbiased in presenting facts—and we must be sensitive to that possibility because bias in a textbook or article may negate its value.

We need to pay close attention not only to the *ideas* the author states, but to the *words* the author uses to express them. Being sensitive to the language in the argument or presentation matters just as much as being sensitive to the facts presented and the logic behind them. Often an author's words reveal a bias suggesting an attempt to influence the reader to like or dislike, agree or disagree with, support or refute a subject. In much reading matter, such as newspapers and magazines, writers attempt to influence your thinking and behavior in overt ways. Nothing is wrong with this intent unless you allow yourself to be *unknowingly* influenced. Being unable to tell that bias lurks in your reading is a severe handicap. Accepting every bit of information and interpretation you read without question would result in chaos.

Writing to Comprehend

1. Explain as carefully and clearly as you can in a few paragraphs, as if to a younger brother or sister, just what bias is. Use a separate sheet of paper. Give examples.

2. Are we ever biased in our thinking about our friends? Is that good? Always? What could being biased about our friends (or enemies) do to our objectivity about them and all they do and say?

   ....

   ....

   ....

   ....

   ....

3. What should you do when you realize that you do not understand a passage you are reading?

   ....

   ....

```
..............................................................................
..............................................................................
..............................................................................
```

The Need to Detect Bias

As skillful and efficient readers we need to learn how to detect bias expressed by authors and then allow for that slant when we evaluate the writing. Being alert to separate biased, emotional words from fact when you read is a very desirable comprehension skill and will make acquiring a high-quality education much easier.

How to Recognize Bias

Bias is often present when a writer's choice of words arouses the reader's emotions, but is *always* there when the material being read includes one or more of these elements.

1. *Name-calling*

    The presidential candidate was not able to continue speaking because of irresponsible interruptions by several ill-mannered, unkempt weirdos.

2. *Contradictions*

    Our religious organization is in no trouble at all. The recent scandal will blow over, people will resume their giving, and we will save the ministry.

3. *Highly emotional, even inflammatory statements*

    We all feel the same way: let them go back where they came from and stop causing trouble in our community. They don't belong here with normal people.

4. *False assumptions, based on weak or inaccurate information*

    Asian refugees have a hard time adjusting to Western society because they are used to being told when to do everything, and in this country everyone is his own boss and does what he wants to do.

207

5. *Stereotyping, often with overgeneralizations full of inaccuracies*

Everyone knows that men make much better airline pilots than women do.

Keep in mind that biased writing may be very interesting to read because of the slanted, colorful language designed to sway you. That doesn't mean you should be suspicious of all interesting writing, but you should heighten your sensitivity to bias.

What Are Your Thoughts?

1. Is it possible to be completely unbiased in anything we say or write? Why or why not?

....

....

....

2. Why is being able to recognize bias when it is present such a vital skill?

....

....

....

3. As you are reading, how and when do you become aware that bias is present? Does that awareness of bias come gradually? suddenly? both ways?

....

....

....

4. Just to remind yourself, pick up a copy (or two) of the tabloids that are usually sold near supermarket checkout counters and circle examples of bias reflecting such things as name-calling, contradictions, highly emotional statements, false assumptions, and stereotyping. Read them to the class and identify the ways in which the bias is reflected.

> ....
>
> ....
>
> ....

What to Look Out for

When you are given examination questions that test your ability to spot bias in your reading, there are a few things to keep in mind. In multiple-choice tests (the most frequent kind for determining your ability to spot bias) the answer choices can be confusing because the following may be present.

1. A statement with bias that wasn't biased in the reading. *Bias was added when it became an answer choice.* Now it looks familiar; though it has bias it must be the correct response. Wrong.
2. A statement which reveals bias but which was not expressed in the reading selection.
3. A quoted or paraphrased statement that reveals a fair, *unbiased* attitude. Because it looks familiar, it may be quickly (too quickly) pointed at as the wrong answer.

Bias Margin Mark   *B*

A B in the margin will indicate bias or slanted materials. Many B's in the margin should alert you to strong bias. You should then ask yourself, "What does the presence of this bias do to the truth or falsity, the accuracy of statements made by the writer?"

Anticipate the Topics

What do you think these reading passages are about? Jot down a few words describing ideas you think will be covered in the passages.

show-off ....

prison crime ....

schools ....

presidential campaign ....

cinema ....

voter registration ....

watch ....

Israel ....

George Bush ....

Shah of Iran ....

Words to Read by

The words in the left column are used in reading exercises in this chapter. Match as many as you can with the definitions in the right column by putting the letter of the appropriate definition on the line next to the word. When you finish, turn to the passage in which the word is used and check to see that your match is correct. Be ready to discuss the reasons for your selections. What were your clues to meanings?

.... abominable (211)   a. encouraged

.... feisty (211)   b. small bomb

.... grisly (213)   c. unreliable

.... sextuplet (214)   d. detestable

.... fanatic (214)   e. struck repeatedly

.... irresponsible (215)   f. one possessed by excessive zeal

.... lofty (216)   g. outside the city

.... grenade (216)   h. horrifying

.... parody (217)   i. imitation

.... abetted (217)   j. spirited

.... suburban (217)   k. noble

.... pummeled (218)   l. six offspring

Check your accuracy with the answers at the end of the chapter.

Practice Exercises

EXERCISE 1

In these sentences two words or phrases are given in parentheses, one neutral and one biased. Choose the word or phrase that if used would *add* bias to the sentence, and write it on the line indicated. Then briefly describe the bias. The first one is done for you.

1. We've long been aware that people are being used for these (abominable, medical) tests.

   Biased word: *abominable* .... Bias: *Abominable means horrible and makes the tests sound like something out of a horror movie.*

2. In one (bizarre, unusual) incident, a child reported a space creature hiding in the closet.

   Biased word: .... Bias: ....

   ....

   ....

3. When the doctor examined the injury, he found (extensive, disfiguring) damage.

   Biased word: .... Bias: ....

   ....

   ....

4. (Feisty, Active) grandmothers over sixty-five are now being recruited as bouncers for New York punk nightclubs.

   Biased word: .... Bias: ....

   ....

   ....

5. My brother (listens to, grooves on) country and western music.

   Biased word: .... Bias: ....

   ....

6. A local correctional facility has (racked up, experienced) fifty-one escapes in the past year.

Biased word: .... Bias: ....

....

....

7. The procedure will (cost, drain) the parents to the tune of about $30,000.

Biased word: .... Bias: ....

....

....

8. Her courage is an (inspiration, example) to everyone.

Biased word: .... Bias: ....

....

....

9. Being rejected by the fraternity was a (crushing, further) blow to the young man.

Biased word: .... Bias: ....

....

....

10. That's the (recent, astonishing) claim made by East German researchers.

Biased word: .... Bias: ....

....

....

EXERCISE 2

In this exercise, *three* words or phrases are given in parentheses, one neutral and two biased. Determine the *neutral* word or phrase and write it in the space indicated. Then select the *most biased* word in your opinion and write it down along with a brief explanation of why it's the most biased. The first one is done for you.

1. Mrs. Lopez says she knows of no way to (patch up, save, repair) her failed marriage.

    Neutral word: ..*save*........ Most biased word: "*Patch up*"...............
    trivializes the problems in the marriage. You "patch up" an old pair of jeans......................

2. People who frequent singles bars are (lonely, alone, needy).

    Neutral word: .... Most biased word: ....

    ....

    ....

3. A teenage girl who gets pregnant may simply refuse at first to believe that she is (pregnant, knocked up, ruined).

    Neutral word: .... Most biased word: ....

    ....

    ....

4. The Roman Catholic Church has (survived, triumphed, existed) for nearly 2,000 years.

    Neutral word: .... Most biased word: ....

    ....

    ....

5. The (challenge, task, obstacle) before us now is to figure out exactly how to use it efficiently.

    Neutral word: .... Most biased word: ....

    ....

    ....

6. The (inescapable, logical, thrilling) conclusion is that we have now confirmed the existence of the soul.

    Neutral word: .... Most biased word: ....

    ....

    ....

7. Climbers made a (recent, grisly, frightening) discovery in a glacier while scaling a mountain—the frozen bodies of two men.

   Neutral word: .... Most biased word: ....

   ....

   ....

8. A religious (believer, nut, fanatic) who believed Christ was about to return to earth gave away all his worldly goods one afternoon.

   Neutral word: .... Most biased word: ....

   ....

   ....

9. Backaches seem to be replacing headaches as the (excuse, reason, justification) people most often use to avoid sex.

   Neutral word: .... Most biased word: ....

   ....

   ....

10. He spent more than two hours (thinking about, pondering, stewing over) the letter she had sent him.

    Neutral word: .... Most biased word: ....

    ....

    ....

EXERCISE 3

In these passages a portion is unbiased and a portion is biased. Underline the biased portion of the passage. The first one is done for you.

1. The sextuplet daughters born to Mr. and Mrs. Ronald Johnson July 28 are the <u>most beautiful babies in the hospital.</u>

2. A tragic drama unfolded recently when my neighbor's canary drowned in a glass of wine.

3. Hapless Andy Taylor recently was stung eight times by wasps.

4. Wild rumors are terrifying people in six states as reports of killer bees arriving appear on television.

5. Most people consider him a buffoon because he regularly plays practical jokes on his friends.

6. Princess Caroline of Monaco regularly hangs out with the super-rich jet set.

7. My wife and I went to Mexico on a vacation and lived it up.

8. Poor, filthy rich, super-famous Madonna was in town for the opening of her new movie.

9. The average supermarket has nine incidents of shoplifting a day, proving that moral integrity is sadly lacking today.

10. Dying people who have important social events to go to can actually put off death because the will to live is stronger than the need to die.

EXERCISE 4

For each sentence indicate the letter for the type of bias being illustrated. The first one is done for you.

a... 1. People who do not keep their yards looking nice are irresponsible and inconsiderate.
    a. name-calling   b. contradictions
    c. emotional, inflammatory statements
    d. false assumptions   e. stereotyping

.... 2. We all know that there is no such thing as a gentle pit bull.
    a. name-calling   b. contradictions
    c. emotional, inflammatory statements
    d. false assumptions   e. stereotyping

.... 3. Women make much better child-care workers because they instinctively know how to respond.
    a. name-calling   b. contradictions
    c. emotional, inflammatory statements
    d. false assumptions   e. stereotyping

.... 4. If the cops would stop acting like tyrants and spend their time catching criminals, we would all be better off.
    a. name-calling   b. contradictions
    c. emotional, inflammatory statements
    d. false assumptions   e. stereotyping

.... 5. Certainly there is life on Mars because roadways are visible through powerful telescopes, and roads mean life.

     a. name-calling   b. contradictions
     c. emotional, inflammatory statements
     d. false assumptions   e. stereotyping

.... **6.** All presidents have represented the will of the people and continue to do so, but this president is representing his own best interests and needs to stop.
     a. name-calling   b. contradictions
     c. emotional, inflammatory statements
     d. false assumptions   e. stereotyping

.... **7.** If you want to win any political election you must be tall, slim, light complected, and an attorney.
     a. name-calling   b. contradictions
     c. emotional, inflammatory statements
     d. false assumptions   e. stereotyping

.... **8.** Pam has the combined qualities of a vampire and a werewolf: she will drain a man of everything without hesitation.
     a. name-calling   b. contradictions
     c. emotional, inflammatory statements
     d. false assumptions   e. stereotyping

.... **9.** Most delinquent girls who run away from the Midwest and become prostitutes in New York originally intended to become actresses or dancers and to succeed on Broadway.
     a. name-calling   b. contradictions
     c. emotional, inflammatory statements
     d. false assumptions   e. stereotyping

.... **10.** Many schoolteachers forget the lofty goals and good intentions that caused them to pick teaching as a career and quickly "burn out."
     a. name-calling   b. contradictions
     c. emotional, inflammatory statements
     d. false assumptions   e. stereotyping

EXERCISE 5

These passages include examples of biased language. On the line to the left of the passage, write the letter for the group of words that suggest the writer's bias. The first one is done for you.

1. Smart-aleck soldier Miguel Martinez whipped out a hand grenade trying to impress his girlfriend—and it was the last thing he ever did.

The stupid show-off was blown to bits, along with his sweetie, Marta Vargas, and 10 innocent bystanders. Twenty others were wounded in the blast.

"Apparently the pin had slipped out of the grenade when he grabbed it from his belt and he didn't know it," said Police Sgt. Jose Pinto of Playitas, El Salvador.

"He didn't have long to regret it," said Sgt. Pinto. "I'd say about three to seven seconds."

—From *Weekly World News,* November 1, 1988. Copyright © 1988 by *Weekly World News.*

......*c*..... a. police, Sgt. Pinto, grenade
   b. impress, girlfriend, twenty others
   c. smart-aleck, stupid show-off

2. After more than a year and a half of investigative work, the Philadelphia police and district attorney's office began moving last spring to break up a vast network of corrupt activity in the prison system. The web of graft they have uncovered is staggering in size and complexity. Within the city's jails, right and wrong were turned upside down in a bizarre parody of law and order. Inmates locked up to prevent further wrongdoing continued to commit exactly the same crimes they had committed on the outside. And correctional personnel sworn to guard the prisoners instead abetted their criminal acts.

—From *Newsweek,* October 24, 1988. Copyright © 1988 by Newsweek, Inc. All rights reserved. Reprinted by permission.

.... a. corrupt, staggering, bizarre parody
   b. prisoners, inmates, crimes
   c. network, law and order, investigative

3. *Hard line.* In Chicago, some black, inner-city parents save enough money to rent an apartment in a suburban district for one month—just long enough to establish residency. Then they move back to the city hoping that their children will continue in their new schools. Suburban officials are taking a hard line against such ploys; one district sends truant officers to monitor suburban-bound commuter trains, trying to catch kids sneaking into the district.

—From *Newsweek,* October 24, 1988. Copyright © 1988 by Newsweek, Inc. All rights reserved. Reprinted by permission.

.... a. suburban, residency
   b. ploys, sneaking
   c. apartment, schools

4. It was called the Star-Spangled Caravan, but the two busloads of Hollywood celebs that rolled into Stockton, Calif., to promote voter registration seemed more like a lost civics class on a misguided field trip. The klieg lights' harsh

217

glare, cameras flashing in air, gave proof through the day that the media were there, but would-be voters were a little harder to find.

—From *People,* October 24, 1988. Reprinted with permission of *People.*

.... a. voter registration, cameras flashing
    b. lost civics class, misguided field trip
    c. would-be voters, klieg lights' harsh glare

5. It was, in a way, the unkindest cut of all. For two months George Bush had tortured Michael Dukakis, strangling him with the flag, force-feeding him his own ACLU card, dunking him in the gunk of Boston Harbor, handcuffing him to furloughed homicidal rapists. Then in the Los Angeles debate Bush did a really dirty trick. He pummeled Dukakis with politeness. Will he stop at nothing?

—From *Newsweek,* October 24, 1988. Copyright © 1988 by Newsweek, Inc. All rights reserved. Reprinted by permission.

.... a. Bush, Dukakis, Boston Harbor
    b. strangling, dunking, gunk
    c. Los Angeles debate, politeness, two months

Answers to Selected Exercises

WORDS TO READ BY

d. abominable	j. feisty	h. grisly	l. six offspring
f. fanatic	c. irresponsible	k. lofty	b. grenade
i. parody	a. abetted	g. suburban	e. pummeled

EXERCISE 2

1. save. "Patch up" trivializes the problems in the marriage. You "patch up" an old pair of jeans.

2. alone	3. pregnant	4. existed
5. task	6. logical	7. recent
8. believer	9. reason	10. thinking about

EXERCISE 4

1. a	2. e	3. e	4. c	5. d
6. b	7. e	8. a	9. d	10. c

Chapter 9

Recognizing the Author's Tone

Take the tone of the company that you are in.
—Philip Dormer Stanhope

This chapter will help you to:

1. understand what tone is.
2. understand why tone is important.
3. recognize that tone is a clue to purpose.
4. learn common tone words.

Another critical comprehension skill that is not difficult to master is ability to recognize the author's tone. Often your professors will ask you questions about assigned readings such as, "What is the tone (or mood, or feeling) the author of this passage creates about the statements he or she makes?" or simply, "What is the tone in this work?" Your professor expects you to be able to recognize the *attitude* the author takes toward the material he or she discusses. That attitude can be anything: lighthearted or malicious, ironic or gentle, or any number of others.

Writing to Comprehend

1. If you were asked to explain as clearly as possible just what tone is, what would you say?

....

....

....

....

....

2. How does understanding and identifying the tone of something you are reading help you establish the author's purpose?

....

....

....

....

....

3. In just three sentences, identify the three most important pieces of information this chapter should include on the reading-comprehension skill of identifying an author's tone. Limit yourself to one sentence for each piece of information.

....

....

....

....

....

Why Is Tone Important?

Identifying authors' attitudes in their writing can tell you a great deal about their *purpose*. An author's feelings and attitudes toward the ideas being written *greatly* influence word choice and emphasis. In selecting words or phrases, authors are influenced by their feelings toward the subject. You, as reader, should also be aware of how the author feels so that you can read critically and objectively, putting the ideas expressed in perspective. If the tone in a work is ridicule and irony, the author may be trying to lead you to a position of not taking seriously some person, event, or idea that is being presented. If the tone is earnest or serious, formal or sympathetic, then perhaps the author intends to encourage your support or belief in some cause or idea.

Tone Is a Clue to Purpose

These paragraphs illustrate different tones and show how tone is a clue to an author's purpose.

> The federal government's policy on economic growth proved to be as liberal and unthinking as it had ever been when it gave away choice land to corporations and industrialists rather than to prospective farmers and hardworking ranchers.

> The federal government had an established policy to encourage economic growth that enabled it to give away large sections of valuable land to manufacturing and industrial corporations, land that otherwise would merely have been used for farming or ranching.

In the first paragraph, the author uses a condemning tone in discussing the government's policy, and the words *liberal, unthinking, choice* are meant to create an unfavorable effect on the reader thinking about the government's policy.

In the second paragraph, the same information is presented but the author's words such as *established, encourage, enabled, merely* create a positive and accepting tone, clearly designed to encourage the reader to *approve* of the ideas written.

Don't Let Tone Confuse You

Tone often confuses students because they may think it hard to define. If you think of tone merely as the impression you have after reading the author's *attitude* toward the ideas being presented, then it is easier to identify.

In thinking of a word or phrase with which to identify the tone in a reading passage, think of the passage as being read aloud or even set to music. The same words you use to describe a speaker's tone of voice or the mood created by a piece of music (joyous, intimate, hard, uneasy) are those used to describe the tone in a reading passage.

221

Learn Common Tone Words

You face no real difficulties in learning to identify correctly tone in a reading. The most difficult task is coming up with a word or phrase that *fits* the tone as you recognize it. One good way (and about the only way) to become more proficient at recognizing the author's tone is to become familiar with a lot of "tone words."

In the table below, place a check mark next to any word whose meaning is not familiar to you, or whose meaning you are not sure of, and look up those words in the dictionary. Doing so will increase your vocabulary of tone words and will help you more accurately appraise the tone in a passage.

Recognizing-Author's-Tone Margin Mark T

Whenever in your reading the author's tone becomes obvious, mark T in the margin. If that tone changes later on, make a double T (TT) in the margin where you recognize that change. For each tone change that you spot, just add another T (or a number: T3, T4, and so on).

Tone Words

compassionate	disapproving	frustrated	awestruck	distressed
earnest	cruel	melancholy	wondering	sensational
comic	serious	formal	ridiculous	ironic
bitter	vindictive	playful	intimate	gentle
absurd	amused	intense	hard	detached
tragic	malicious	reverent	impassioned	irreverent
abstruse	farcical	sympathetic	mocking	reticent
depressed	prayerful	righteous	pathetic	cynical
pessimistic	loving	solemn	outspoken	ambivalent
complex	optimistic	condescending	arrogant	indignant
ghoulish	evasive	objective	obsequious	critical
caustic	angry	apathetic	satiric	cheerful
excited	joyous	nostalgic	outraged	straightforward
condemning	celebratory	incredulous	uneasy	grim

What Are Your Thoughts?

1. Can you think of tone words that are not listed in the table? If so, what are they, and what do they express? Could some current slang words or contemporary expressions which may not yet even be in the dictionary but which are widely used be tone words? How about *nerdy*? Think of others. What words did they replace, if any?

    ....

    ....

    ....

2. Think about your college reading materials. Are the tones in materials you are required to read diverse, or all about the same? Do you find exceptions in which tone seems to change periodically, or maybe drastically, within the material?

    ....

    ....

    ....

3. What is the tone in this chapter? this book?

    ....

    ....

    ....

Words to Read by

Answer these questions by looking up the key word from each sentence in your dictionary. The page numbers in parentheses indicate the passages that include each key word. You may wish to read that key word in its context. Write the answer on the lines provided. How do you determine which words to look up?

1. In the context of this passage, what is a *gumshoe*? (226)

    ....

2. What is a *bumbling burglar*? (226)

....

3. What are *ligaments* composed of? (228)

....

4. Does *classic* mean *classy, with class*? (230)

....

5. Does *finesse* mean *subtlety and tact,* or *completeness*? (230)

....

6. Is there such a thing as *inhuman bias*? (231)

....

7. When something is *hideous,* it is extremely unpleasant, especially to which sense: vision, hearing, smell, or taste? (232)

....

8. How many pronunciations for *nausea* does your dictionary give? (233)

....

9. Is a person smiling *genially* about to be sick? (233)

....

10. In this passage, *impotent* doesn't mean sexually inadequate. What does it mean? (234)

....

11. What did the word *catapulting* originally mean? (235)

....

12. Can you vaporize *vapor*? (236)

....

13. If a person is *alienated,* is that person still a citizen? (237)

....

14. What is another expression for *pseudoscientific*? (237)

....

Compare your answers with those at the end of this chapter.

Anticipate the Topics

Jot down the first couple of thoughts that enter your mind as you read each of these words or phrases. Also put a check mark next to each topic when you read the passage and you have guessed correctly the subject that may be covered.

Dr. Benjamin Spock ....

disaster victims ....

MasterCard ....

flight-panic ....

discrimination ....

Samuel Adams ....

chimpanzees ....

backaches ....

hogs ....

evil statue ....

women as property ....

boy ....

high wire ....

behavior ....

interaction ....

poverty ....

Connie Chung ....

buffalo ....

Alaska ....

Love Boat ....

template ....

phrenology ....

skin bleaching ....

Practice Exercises

EXERCISE 1

Each of these six passages illustrates one of the six tone words listed. In the space provided next to each passage, put the letter for the tone word that applies to each passage. It may seem that a tone word will fit more than one passage; be ready to discuss with class members the clues you saw in the passages that helped you choose the tone word you did for each passage. Do not use a tone word more than once. If you are unfamiliar with any word on this list, look it up before you begin. The first one is done for you.

a.	amused	b.	intense	c.	detached
d.	objective	e.	playful	f.	mocking

1.　Gumshoe Mike Hammer wouldn't like the idea, but 40 percent of all private eyes are women.

e
　　　　　—From *Weekly World News,* November 1, 1988. Copyright © 1988 by *Weekly World News.*

2.　Private ownership isn't the only form of ownership in our business system. *Public ownership,* in which some level of government owns and operates a company for the public's benefit, has grown rapidly in recent decades. The government in one form or another now buys more goods and services than any other institution in the world. And the federal government owns about a third of the land, and hires nearly one out of five employees, in the United States.

　　　　　—From Megginson et al., *Business.*

3.　When oddball Emperor Menelik of Ethiopia had the aches, he munched on pages from the bible the way some folks munch on aspirin.

　　　　Then one day in 1913, miserable Menelik felt so lousy he gobbled both books of Kings—and keeled over dead.

　　　　　—From *Weekly World News,* November 1, 1988. Copyright © 1988 by *Weekly World News.*

4.　A terrified family of nine was trapped for hours behind closed doors when a huge swarm of 20,000 angry wasps invaded their home in Bristol, England. Horror-stricken Terry Hoskins, his wife, Kay, and their seven children escaped when alert neighbors called pest control experts.

　　　　　—From *Weekly World News,* November 1, 1988. Copyright © 1988 by *Weekly World News.*

5.　Bumbling burglar Barrington Turner was in such a hurry to get away from police that he jumped into the icy waters of Canada's Humber River—then remembered that he couldn't swim!

　　　　　—From *Weekly World News,* November 1, 1988. Copyright © 1988 by *Weekly World News.*

6.   *The Morning After.* An accidental pregnancy is not something many students want to deal with. The answer for some California State U., Chico, students is found in the form of a "morning-after pill." The pill is a form of post-coital contraception available at the Student Health Center. The most common use for the morning-after pill is for intercourse occurring without any contraception, according to a 1986 Health Center brochure, and treatment must begin within 72 hours after unprotected intercourse. The morning-after pill contains a higher-than-usual estrogen and progesterone dose, found in the birth control pill Ovral 28.

....   —Source unknown.

EXERCISE 2

In this exercise select *two* tone words from the list, both of which seem to fit the passage. Again, as in Exercise 1, be ready to discuss your choices with the class. Look up in the dictionary any words you do not know. Do not use any words more than once. The first one is done for you.

a. straightforward	b. ironic	c. serious
d. absurd	e. objective	f. playful
g. grim	h. disapproving	i. wonderstruck
j. amused	k. cynical	l. incredulous

1.   If you had been a German gentleman in the 1300s, you would have been a real Tinkerbelle—because the fashion then was to trim your clothing with hundreds of tiny bells.

f, j   —From *Weekly World News,* November 1, 1988. Copyright © 1988 by *Weekly World News.*

2.   Child-rearing expert Dr. Benjamin Spock says kids with regular chores are more likely to grow up to be well-adjusted adults.

       The reason, says Dr. Spock, is that routine household chores give children a healthy sense of self-esteem and the belief that they are contributing to the family.

....   —From *Weekly World News,* November 1, 1988. Copyright © 1988 by *Weekly World News.*

3.   Victims of disaster tend to act independently of official command and control. While this may prove awkward and disruptive at times, it can also function to relieve public agencies of an impossible burden and to engage formal social groups (family and friends) in crisis recovery.

....   —From Lowry and Rankin, *Sociology: Social Science and Social Concern.*

4.   More than a million people are expected to apply for the new Elvis Presley MasterCard in the next couple of months alone!

The jet black card is being issued by Leader Federal Savings & Loan of Memphis, Tenn., and features a color portrait of The King.

Brochures say cardholders can "become part of the (Presley) legend."

....
—From *Weekly World News*, November 1, 1988. Copyright © 1988 by *Weekly World News*.

5. Know why your muscles ache when you have the flu? Neither do doctors.

....
—From *Weekly World News*, November 1, 1988. Copyright © 1988 by *Weekly World News*.

EXERCISE 3

For each passage, select the word from the six choices following each that best describes the tone the writer has created. Write the letter of the tone word you chose on the line provided. The first one is done for you.

1. Scientists Thursday said they have successfully tested a proposed nuclear warhead that could smash through the Earth to destroy underground Soviet command centers. Physicist Harry Vantine at the Lawrence Livermore National Laboratory, a government research lab in California, called the test a "major milestone" in developing the controversial Earth-penetrating bomb.

—From *USA Today*, October 21, 1988, page 4A. Copyright © 1988 by *USA Today*. Excerpted with permission.

c
....
a. distressed   b. gentle   c. straightforward

d. sensationalist   e. ironic   f. irreverent

2. *Customs Surprise.* U.S. Customs Service inspectors in Buffalo seized a shipment they said was illegally coming in from Canada since it didn't bear identification of the country of origin. Inside: 5,000 patches ordered by Customs chief William van Raab for agents to wear on their uniforms marking the service's 200th anniversary.

—From *USA Today*, October 21, 1988, page 4A. Copyright © 1988 by *USA Today*. Excerpted with permission.

....
a. ironic   b. grim   c. awestruck

d. uneasy   e. detached   f. reticent

3. Don't bother trying to build up the muscles in your fingers. Our fingers don't have muscles—only ligaments.

—From *Weekly World News*, November 1, 1988. Copyright © 1988 by *Weekly World News*.

....
a. cynical   b. ambivalent   c. indignant

d. playful   e. critical   f. cheerful

4. Data from American scenes of disaster substantiate this finding. For example, in Port Jervis, New York, during a flood crisis in the 1950s, there was rumor of a broken dam and newspapers reported that most of the 9000 inhabitants had fled. Actually only an estimated one fourth fled. Analysis of those who did flee Port Jervis points up another misconception: It is often assumed that when people flee they do so in "flight-panic." Panic is flight where the individual ceases to play any social role whatsoever and merely flees. Withdrawal of this type is extremely rare. Most withdrawal behavior involves definite role playing, especially within primary group relationships. Thus in the so-called panic flight from Port Jervis, there was no solitary flight, and 23 percent of those escaping even made attempts to assist community members outside of their original fleeing group.

—From Lowry and Rankin, *Sociology: Social Science and Social Concern.*

....   a. outraged   b. satiric   c. obsequious
         d. arrogant   e. outspoken   f. serious

5.   *Speaking of Pap Smears.* While a pap smear is not something that comes up in everyday conversation, Northern Arizona U.'s Fronske Health Center officials said they believe it should be a topic of concern to all women who are sexually active. A number of abnormal pap smears have been caused by the Human Papilloma or HPZ virus, which leads to genital warts, said Dr. Donald Allred, physician at the health center. If left untreated, the virus may develop into cancer of the cervix. High risk behavior encompasses those who are sexually active before the age of 18, those who engage in sexual intercourse with three or more partners, or those who are sexually involved with one partner who has had previous involvement with three or more partners. Through pap smear testing, the virus can usually be found in its earliest stage and treated quickly and easily.

—Carrie O'Connor, *The Lumberjack*, Northern Arizona U.

....   a. earnest   b. pathetic   c. mocking
         d. impassioned   e. hard   f. intimate

6.   I knew I was a dead man.

The monstrous wave seemed to come from nowhere, suddenly looming over my frail boat like a row of three-story houses. It was moving like an express train as it smashed into the boat with unbelievable power and knocked me into the ice-cold water.

I struggled with all my strength and finally surfaced—only to see my boat floating upside down!

—From *The National Enquirer*, October 25, 1988.

....   a. awestruck   b. sensationalist   c. wonder
         d. ridicule   e. intimate   f. hard

7.   Here's a shocker for America: The U.S. Congress—which has passed laws

229

forbidding discrimination on the basis of race, religion, sex and age—has exempted itself from those very same laws!

What's more, our Capitol Hill hypocrites also don't have to obey the laws that they have passed regulating working conditions, occupational health and safety, and wages.

It's a disgusting, classic case of "Don't do as I do—do as I say."

—From *The National Enquirer*, October 25, 1988.

.... a. outspoken   b. compassionate   c. tragic
         d. abstruse   e. depressed   f. pessimistic

8. The First Continental Congress was a triumph for Samuel Adams, who managed it with the finesse learned from years in the Boston Caucus. It approved all his suggestions; it endorsed his view of imperial power. The outbreak of war, and after that true independence, was only a matter of time. The revolution, for which he had worked so long, had dawned.

—From Risjord, *Representative Americans: The Revolutionary Generation.*

.... a. bitter   b. absurd   c. vindictive
         d. overused   e. optimistic   f. prayerful

9. Chimpanzees are more like humans than any other creatures on earth, says world-famous chimp expert Dr. Jane Goodall.

The animals clearly demonstrate amazingly humanlike emotions and thought patterns, said the animal researcher, who has spent 28 years studying chimps in the wilds of Africa.

"Some chimps who have been taught sign language and raised as humans don't even know they are chimpanzees. They actually think they are humans."

—From *The National Enquirer*, October 25, 1988.

.... a. disapproving   b. cruel   c. serious
         d. malicious   e. farcical   f. angry

10. Backaches, which lame an estimated 5.4 million Americans each year, have resisted all medical miracles. A leading treatment for recurring low back pain is still the sofa, upon which a patient is supposed to recline, usually for at least a week and often much longer, until the pain goes away. Lingering backaches keep more workers off the job than any other ailment, costing the nation $16 billion in medical bills and lost wages annually. But it now appears that you shouldn't take a bad back lying down. Medical researchers in Sweden have shown that the best remedy for the most common type of backache is exercise—and that the afflicted should be active even if it hurts.

—From *Newsweek*, October 24, 1988. Copyright © 1988 by Newsweek, Inc.
All rights reserved. Reprinted by permission.

.... a. reverent   b. condemning   c. straightforward
          d. celebratory   e. playful   f. incredulous

EXERCISE 4

In this exercise, write the letter for the word that best completes the statement following each passage. The first one is done for you.

1.   *Happy Hogs Make Better Bacon.* Pig farmers can really bring home the bacon if they reduce the stress in their swine's lives.

        That's because happy hogs produce pork that's tastier, more tender, and sells for more at the market. That's why Canadian food scientist Andre Fortin is developing a list of stress factors that pig farmers should consider.

        First, to give your porkers peace of mind, don't force them to co-mingle with strange pigs in marketing yards. That's a disturbing ordeal. Likewise, rides to the slaughterhouse should be as long as possible because short rides are stressful.

        And don't make your pigs wait around to be killed. Waiting for the butcher to slit a throat is unsettling for hogs.

                 —From *The National Examiner*, October 25, 1988. Reprinted by permission
                   of *The National Examiner*.

...*b*... The author of this passage has created a tone that can be described as
     a. evasive   b. farcical   c. joyous   d. frustrated

2.   All science is subject to human bias. This is especially true for social scientists. Since human behavior is their area of study, they are actually part of the subject matter. Furthermore, human behavior patterns vary from one place to another and from one group to another. This is in contrast to the subject matter of the natural sciences. When a chemist studies hydrogen, he can assume that one hydrogen atom is very much like another, wherever it is found, and that the conditions surrounding it can be quite accurately controlled. The same is true when a physicist measures a metal bar; he can be quite sure that it will not stretch or shrink in length as long as natural conditions are the same. This is why Earl Babbie quotes economist Daniel Suits, who calls the natural sciences the "easy sciences" because of the predictable nature of their subject matter.

             —From Megginson et al., *Business*.

.... If the author were delivering this passage orally, his or her tone of voice would probably be
     a. loving   b. ghoulish   c. excited   d. objective

3.   An occult expert warned a couple to destroy a valuable Egyptian statue and purge its evil forces.

"It's evil," Paul and Karen Graham were told after they fished the foot-high statue from a river. "Build a bonfire and hurl the cursed thing into the flames!"

The Grahams received the warning from medium Michael Biswell, who thinks the statue was used in occult worship. Biswell threw the figure into the river in an attempt to exorcise its evil influence.

—From *The National Examiner*, October 25, 1988. Reprinted by permission of *The National Examiner*.

.... The author of this passage has created a tone (mood, feeling) that can be described as

a. ironic   b. hard   c. outraged   d. straightforward

4. A loving mother has promised to buy a new face for her hideously deformed daughter born with no nose and two tiny slits for eyes.

—From *The National Examiner*, October 25, 1988. Reprinted by permission of *The National Examiner*.

.... The author of this passage has created a tone that can be described as

a. intimate   b. sensationalist   c. outspoken   d. obsequious

5. The notion of women as property is also reflected in some Old Testament views regarding prostitution and rape. Because each woman belonged to a man, rape was essentially theft. A man who raped the daughter of another man had to either pay the father or marry the daughter in order to be absolved. It was not considered a crime for a father to sell sexual access to his daughter to other men. A daughter who was "legitimately" prostituted in this way could marry another Jew; later some religious leaders even maintained that she could marry a priest. But if a daughter gave herself sexually to a man of her choosing, depriving her father of a fee, she committed a capital crime.

—From Allgeier and Allgeier, *Sexual Interactions*.

.... If the author were delivering this passage orally, his or her tone of voice would probably be

a. solemn   b. excited   c. pathetic   d. nostalgic

6. According to the principle of insurable interest, no one can be insured unless he or she stands to suffer financially or emotionally when a loss occurs. The main reason for this requirement is to permit measurement of the extent of the loss. For example, ownership conveys an insurable interest in property, since its loss by fire, theft, or disaster would mean a loss of assets.

—From Megginson et al., *Business*.

.... The author of this passage has created a tone (mood, feeling) that can be described as

a. awestruck   b. intimate   c. formal   d. pathetic

7. In the United States a *real* boy climbs trees, disdains girls, dirties his knees, plays with soldiers, and takes blue for his favorite color .... In college the boys smoke pipes, drink beer, and major in engineering or physics .... The real boy matures into a "man's man" who plays poker, goes hunting, drinks brandy, and dies in the war.

—From Hyde, *Half the Human Experience: The Psychology of Women.*

.... The author of this passage has created a tone that can be described as

    a. ridiculing   b. cynical   c. distressed   d. evasive

8. Helen Wallenda began urging Karl, her husband, to retire from the high wire in 1970 when he was sixty-five years old. He'd reply: "Look, honey, let me do it as long as the good Lord lets me. He's up there with me." She'd respond: "How will you know when He tells you to stop?" "When He leaves me, I'll know," Karl said. Before stepping out on the wire, the greatest high-wire performer in circus history always put a piece of hard candy into his mouth to prevent nausea and said silently, "God, please ...."

—From Megginson et al., *Business.*

.... If the author were delivering this passage orally, his or her tone of voice would probably be

    a. reverent   b. grim   c. nostalgic   d. evasive

9. They want me to make a few remarks at the start of tonight's meeting? No problem, I say.

I bring along an index card scribbled over with key phrases, and, when the moment arrives, I mount the stage.

The hall is packed. I sit among the other speakers, hands folded, smiling genially and remembering not to sprawl in my chair.

But as the meeting is being called to order, strange things start happening to my body.

My legs go rubbery, for one thing. Unaccountably, my knees begin knocking like castanets. I grasp the lectern firmly with both hands to prevent fainting, and resist the temptation to drape myself over it like one of those melting watches in a painting by Dali. I'm sure it wouldn't do to speak from a sitting position on the floor *behind* the thing, but still—it's an appealing notion.

—From Newman, *Communicating in Business Today.*

.... The author of this passage has created a tone (mood, feeling) that can be described as

    a. cruel   b. serious   c. sympathetic   d. playful

10. Stop wishing and dreaming. A beautiful bosom—one that you've always wanted can be yours in the privacy of your own home. Why be unhappy, settle for less or consider costly or painful alternatives? If you are not completely satisfied with your bust, we have good news for you.

We are proud to introduce FORM U, the breast creme formulation that takes over and gives you a beautiful bust. FORM U breast creme is completely safe to use, manufactured with the purest and finest ingredients. Thousands of women have used FORM U creme with great success.

> —From *The National Examiner,* October 25, 1988. Reprinted by permission of *The National Examiner.*

.... The author of this passage has created a tone that can be described as

    a. optimistic   b. prayerful   c. critical   d. uneasy

EXERCISE 5

For each of these passages, write a tone word of your choice (or pick one from the list of tone words on page 222) that best completes this statement: "If the author were delivering this passage orally, his or her tone of voice would probably be ...." Be ready to discuss your choice of tone word. The first one is done for you.

1. Even in an age when the computer is king, 95 percent of all information is still stored on good old-fashioned paper.

light

> —From *Weekly World News,* November 1, 1988. Copyright © 1988 by *Weekly World News.*

2. Such behavior also suggests that the belief that kinship and primary ties have been greatly weakened in modern mass societies and that the protective functions of the family have been transferred entirely to large-scale organizations is an exaggeration of fact. Other evidence is similarly convincing and leads to the conclusion that most people in crisis do not become "completely irresponsible and totally impotent." In fact, most do not even turn to public agencies for help.

> —From Lowry and Rankin, *Sociology: Social Science and Social Concern.*

3. Socrates loved to jog but he finally gave it up—because he kept tripping over his toga.

> —From *Weekly World News,* November 1, 1988. Copyright © 1988 by *Weekly World News.*

4. There are thinkers who believe that knowledge is the result of more than objective reality, more than those things we can touch. They argue that knowledge is the result of the interaction between the object and the individual; a kind of mingling of the "what is" with the "what might be"; the personal and the impersonal; and I and the thou. Let us begin with two individuals who meet and talk. They are strangers who view each other with what we know as typical insecurity and fear—two Madisonian people in our modern world. Each views himself or herself as "I" and the other person as an "it." There is no real exchange of anything between them. Each has his or her own little social act, own game to put on the other. Both become dehumanized, both objects.

.... —Source unknown.

5. The smiling citizens of Seattle, Wash., buy more toothbrushes than do folks in any other U.S. city.

.... —From *Weekly World News,* November 1, 1988. Copyright © 1988 by *Weekly World News.*

6. There were times—weak moments—when he longed for people to blind themselves to him. He was a scarecrow catapulting himself along the streets with a light step and a professional habit of cheerfulness, but in broken boots, a tall hat so limp he wore it back to front to avoid doubling the brim when raising it, cuffs whose margins had been refined with his mother's scissors, trousers whose holes were hidden by a tailed coat fading from black to green. He was an example of poverty.

.... —From *Newsweek,* October 24, 1988. Copyright © 1988 by Newsweek, Inc. All rights reserved. Reprinted by permission.

7. The world in which we live is changing continually, and people are continually seeking to discover and understand these changes. Work in this area is resulting in advances in technology related to all aspects of our daily life, making it most important that each individual knows and understands the physical concepts behind this advancing technology. It is only through an understanding of the basic physical concepts that the individual today can hope to remain abreast of this technology concerning the natural environment.

.... —From Shipman et al., *An Introduction to Physical Science.*

8. *Eyeliner Notes.* NBC News's Connie Chung says that without her eye makeup, her good looks would be an optical delusion. "I know what I look like without eye makeup," says Connie. "We're talking refugee. You know that scene in *Twilight Zone: The Movie* where the guy turns to the other guy in the car and says, 'Do you want to see something really scary?' Well, every night I take off my makeup and open the bedroom door and say to my husband, Maury [Povich, host of Fox TV's *A Current Affair*], 'Do you want to see something *really* scary?'"

.... —From *People,* October 24, 1988. Reprinted with permission of *People.*

9. A terrified bison, or buffalo, can hightail it at speeds up to 40 miles an hour—about the speed of a thoroughbred racehorse.

.... —From *Weekly World News,* November 1, 1988. Copyright © 1988 by *Weekly World News.*

10. To a then young lad like myself, it sounded like a cumbersome, slow-moving, and slightly terrifying beast. It was, of course, creeping socialism. My impulse was always to look around to see if it was near, to prepare to stomp that dreaded creep right into the ground.

As it turns out, neither socialism nor capitalism was much to get excited about, but that's not the point.

.... —From Scherman, *A Preface to Politics.*

11. We did, however, see a great deal of nature. Alaska is almost completely covered with nature, including several million spectacular snow-capped mountains, any one of which is so awesome that if you were to relocate it to an average semiflat state such as Indiana, the residents would all quit their jobs and form cults and worship it. But Alaska has so many amazing mountains that after a while you hardly notice them, which is a good thing because it frees you to watch out for the moose poop, which is all over the place in the form of egg-shaped units known as "moose nuggets," which local people use—this is also the truth—to make earrings and other souvenir items to sell to tourists who have no taste. We bought some.

.... —From *The Bradenton Herald,* Bradenton, Florida, July 3, 1988.
Copyright © Dave Barry. Reprinted from *The Miami Herald.*

12. Behind the idyllic, Love Boat scenes, though, the cruise ship industry harbors a dirty little secret that would make many of its passengers sick if they knew the truth. That is, that the industry has treated the very oceans that provide its livelihood as a garbage dump. Living up to an ancient mariner's tradition, each day most of the cruise ships that ply the oceans dump over the side all of their garbage—and not merely the uneaten food from overindulged passengers. This is the same mixture of plastic, paper, glass and metal waste with which your family fills several garbage cans a week. Imagine every home in your neighborhood dumping all of its bags of garbage into the Manatee River this week, and you get some idea of the effect one cruise ship has on the Gulf of Mexico.

.... —From *The Bradenton Herald,* Bradenton, Florida, July 31, 1988.
Copyright © Dave Barry. Reprinted from *The Miami Herald.*

13. The big difference between Premier and a standard cigarette is that it doesn't burn tobacco. There's nothing unusual about its shape, size or color, but the inside looks a little like a four-stage rocket. At one end is a piece of charcoal that, when lit, vaporizes the nicotine and other volatile substances housed in an adjacent aluminum "flavor capsule." Puffing on the mouthpiece draws the flavored aerosol through two filters and out the end. But since the charcoal heating element is the only thing that burns, the stick doesn't shrink as it's smoked. It just runs out of fuel.

.... —From *Newsweek,* October 24, 1988. Copyright © 1988 by Newsweek, Inc.
All rights reserved. Reprinted by permission.

14.   Before we started mucking around and moving and murdering the Indians, they seemed to live as they wished. Their tribes were strong communities; their relationship to the environment was one not of control but of respect; they were, mostly, peaceful people. To fast-paced, alienated, bureaucratized, controlling, standard Americans, the Indian—both in fact and myth—seemed to be more whole and together than we are.

....   —From Scherman, *A Preface to Politics.*

15.   Tender young things are sampling sex before its season—before they are out of dental braces—and then feeling the anguish of remorse. Many are less sexually liberated than they would like to think.

....   —From Ingersoll, *Adolescents.*

16.   Word recognizers on the market today rely mainly on a pattern-recognition technique called template matching. A microphone translates sound waves of a spoken word into an electrical signal from which the recognizer derives a pattern, or template, similar to the voice spectrograms used by researchers to study pronunciation. Like the fairy tale prince with the glass slipper, the recognizer then tries to match the pattern against templates stored in its memory.

....   —From Slotnick et al., *Computers and Applications.*

17.   There are several episodes in the history of psychology that exemplify the fallibility of measurements obtained without controlling for observer bias and other sources of error. None is more telling than the pseudoscientific movement of *phrenology* that achieved wide acceptance during the first half of the nineteenth century. Even Edgar Allan Poe attempted to "explain" some of the behavior of his book characters by including a description of their head shapes.

....   —From Feshbach and Weiner, *Personality.*

18.   A staggering $500,000,000—that's half a billion bucks—is spent each year treating victims of shootings in the United States.

....   —From *Weekly World News,* November 1, 1988. Copyright © 1988 by *Weekly World News.*

19.   A growing number of young, black African women—and, increasingly, men —are bleaching their skin in an effort to be more attractive to the opposite sex, reports *World Development Forum.* The practice, which involves overuse of lightening creams, oils, lotions, and powders, could do irreparable damage to the skin. Already, health officials in Ghana, Nigeria, Kenya, and Tanzania, where skin bleaching is most common, are reporting a high incidence of skin cancers and lesions—once very rare among blacks. The bleaches also produce "brittle" skin that does not allow rashes and cuts to heal.

....   —From *The Futurist,* September/October 1988, page 7. Reprinted with permission from *The Futurist,* published by the World Future Society, 4916 St. Elmo Avenue, Bethesda, Maryland 20814.

20. Law changes you. It does a head job.

You don't have a chance. Not only is it silly to assume *you,* as a lawyer, are going to change the system: it is especially wrongheaded to believe you will escape being changed. They'll get you. Count on it.

.... —From Scherman, *A Preface to Politics.*

EXERCISE 6

Read this selection on nuclear materials and identify tone. Next, *change* the tone and purpose significantly by writing a sentence or two of your own and inserting them at appropriate spots in the passage.

Nuclear reactors use uranium enriched to 3% ^{235}U while nuclear weapons use uranium enriched to 30–95% ^{235}U. Thus, it is not possible to use reactor fuel for nuclear weapons. The plutonium produced in reactors, if separated from the ^{238}U, and so on, could be used in weapons. For this reason, international control of uranium and plutonium is utilized to prevent the spread of nuclear weapons material.

As technology in small nations improves, more and more countries will have the ability to produce weapons-grade nuclear material. We can only hope that no country will ever use these awesome forces.

Radioactive substances from the fission process are dangerous and must be handled with extreme caution. Radioactive nuclei with short half-lives are not too troublesome, because they decay away rather quickly. However, nuclei such as ^{14}C and ^{90}Sr, with half-lives of 5730 and 28 years, respectively, are quite hazardous and must be stored or disposed of with the utmost care.

The isotope ^{90}Sr is particularly harmful because its chemical properties are similar to calcium. Thus, it combines chemically in the bones and, through subsequent radioactivity, greatly increases the likelihood of bone cancer.

In the 1950s a number of nuclear tests were carried out in the atmosphere by the United States and Russia. This led to alarming increases in radioactivity in such things as milk. For this reason, an atmospheric nuclear test ban treaty between the United States and Russia was signed in the early 1960s. Since that time, all weapons testing of nuclear materials by these two countries has been carried out below the ground. However, other countries that did not sign the treaty, most notably France, China, and India, have exploded nuclear devices in the atmosphere.

The radioactive material that falls to the ground after a nuclear explosion is called fallout. This fallout is hazardous primarily because it consists of small dustlike particles that can be breathed into the lungs, where they can cause lung cancer. Once the fallout has fallen to the ground, it is not nearly so dangerous. During the days following a nuclear explosion, it is best to be inside with the doors and windows closed, so that the radioactive dust from the fallout is not inhaled.

If many nuclear explosions were to be detonated, there is a high probability that a lot of smoke would be created from fires raging out of control. Studies have shown that the smoke and dust created would circulate in the atmosphere and significantly decrease the amount of sunlight striking the Earth. This would result in a lowering of the temperature in the Northern Hemisphere by 5°C to 15°C. The resulting nuclear winter would be very difficult for the entire Northern Hemisphere. Certainly, it would drastically alter civilization as we know it.

—From Shipman et al., *An Introduction to Physical Science.*

The present tone is: ....

Write sentences that change the tone of the passage to:

1. highly emotional and inflammatory ....

....

....

Insert where? ....

2 pessimistic and distressed ....

....

....

Insert where? ....

3. cheerful and excited ....

....

....

Insert where? ....

4. mocking and cynical ....

....

....

Insert where? ....

5. comical and amused ....

....

....

Insert where? ....

Answers to Selected Exercises

WORDS TO READ BY

1. detective
2. a burglar who behaves clumsily
3. tough, fibrous tissue
4. No. In this passage *classic* means being in accordance with established methods.
5. subtlety and tact
6. No.
7. vision
8. Answer may vary; probably 4.
9. Probably not.
10. being powerless, ineffective
11. ancient machines that hurled large objects
12. No. Vapor is already vaporized.
13. Yes, but perhaps unfriendly or set apart.
14. false, fake, deceptively scientific

EXERCISE 2

1. f, j	2. a, e	3. b, c	4. d, l	5. b, i

EXERCISE 4

1. b	2. d	3. d	4. b	5. a
6. c	7. b	8. a	9. d	10. a

Chapter 10

Recognizing Relations Within Sentences

With sixty staring me in the face, I have developed inflammation of the sentence structure....

—James Thurber

This chapter will help you to:

1. see the similarity between this skill and identifying the author's *overall* pattern of organization.
2. understand how relationships are mixed in reading material and how that happens.
3. gain experience in identifying the relation within sentences from two perspectives.

Another reading competency which you will be expected to use in college (and afterward) and which you must demonstrate often on exams is ability to recognize the organizational relationship *between the parts of a sentence.* This relationship may be explicit (stated) or implicit (unstated). You will need this skill in comprehension because it enables you to perceptively think along with the author, *sentence by sentence,* as the author develops the presentation or argument. Being able to recognize the relationship between the parts of a sentence will make you less likely to lose the thought or to let your mind wander while reading.

A Similar Skill

This skill should be fairly easy for you to develop because it is so similar to one you have already covered: identifying the author's *overall* patterns of organization. In Chapter 5 you studied the ways of determining an author's organization, the ten common patterns, and the clue words that indicate each pattern. If you studied those patterns and clue words carefully, you will have an easy time with this skill because the names describing the patterns *within* sentences are the same as those used to describe the *overall* patterns in writing. You see, recognizing relations within sentences is the same as recognizing overall patterns of organization.

Thus, if you learn the ten overall patterns of organization discussed on page 153 and the words that go with each pattern, you will easily recognize those similar relations *within* sentences.

Mixing Relations

Relations *within* a sentence, though, will not form the same pattern as the *overall* organization in the reading material. That organization may be statement and clarification, but the author may employ one or more organizational relations within sentences, such as time order or simple listing, to strengthen and accomplish the overall pattern.

Two Perspectives

The exercises in this chapter are designed to give you experience in identifying the relation within sentences from two perspectives.

1. In some of the exercises you are asked to read a sentence carefully and then choose the word or phrase (definition, contrast, and so on) that identifies the relation between parts of the sentence. You will need to get a good grasp on the content of the sentence, but it is just as important to keep your eyes open for relationship words (after, next, like, also, nevertheless, and so on). These "clue words" (listed on page 153) will help you quickly identify internal relations in the sentences.

2. In other exercises you will find a passage with one or more relationship words deleted; you are asked to choose the word from several listed that best completes the passage. Just read the sentence with the missing word and insert each of the answer choices in the space. One of the words will be an appropriate fit. Watch that in answering a question you don't come to a conclusion too quickly. Try *all* the choices in the blank before deciding. All may fit *gram-*

matically, but only one fits in a way that makes the *most* sense. That word can then be matched to one of the organizational pattern words or phrases (cause and effect, classification, and so on).

Important Note

A good investment of your time will be to learn the ten organizational patterns and their clue words (Chapter 6, page 153) because by knowing them you can successfully improve your reading comprehension in *three* ways. The same patterns and clue words are used for these three competencies: identifying the author's overall pattern of organization (Chapter 6), recognizing relations within sentences (Chapter 10), and coming up, recognizing relations *between* sentences (Chapter 11). Therefore, go back and review thoroughly the ten patterns and their clue words in Chapter 6.

Recognizing-Relations-Within-Sentences Margin Mark ( )

To indicate clue words signaling relations within sentences, use *parentheses* as your mark in the margin. Margin marks (and you've learned nine so far) can be very helpful in studying, reviewing, and taking tests.

Writing to Comprehend

1. How does recognizing relationships within a sentence differ from recognizing the author's overall pattern of organization?

....

....

....

....

....

2. Of the comprehension skills discussed so far in Chapters 2–10, which three do you believe will be most useful while you are in college and after you graduate? Why did you select these three?

....

....

....

....

....

3. If in a short story or novel you suddenly realize that descriptions of the characters don't match their behavior, what does the discrepancy mean?

....

....

....

....

....

....

Words to Read by

Glance quickly over the reading selections (but not the questions) in the exercises for this chapter. From these passages select ten unfamiliar words that seem to stand out, circle them so that you will be able to find them again easily, and write them below. Put the number of the page where each word appears in the parentheses provided. Then define the words, using context clues. Even if you are not certain, guess at the meaning.

Next, look up each word in the dictionary and write the appropriate definition under your context definition. Notice that each word may have more than one definition. Select the definition that fits the word's context.

How close is your definition to the dictionary definition?

1. .... (............) Your definition: ....

....

Dictionary: ....

Is your definition close? not so close?

2. .... (...........) Your definition: ....

....

Dictionary: ....

Is your definition close? not so close?

3. .... (...........) Your definition: ....

....

Dictionary: ....

Is your definition close? not so close?

4. .... (...........) Your definition: ....

....

Dictionary: ....

Is your definition close? not so close?

5. .... (...........) Your definition: ....

....

Dictionary: ....

Is your definition close? not so close?

6. .... (...........) Your definition: ....

....

Dictionary: ....

Is your definition close? not so close?

7. .... (...........) Your definition: ....

....

Dictionary: ....

Is your definition close? not so close?

8. .... (...........) Your definition: ....

....

Dictionary: ....

Is your definition close? not so close?

9. .... (..........)   Your definition: ....

....

Dictionary: ....

Is your definition close? not so close?

10. .... (..........)   Your definition: ....

....

Dictionary: ....

Is your definition close? not so close?

Practice Exercises

EXERCISE 1

In these passages relation words are left out. For each numbered blank space you have a choice of four words that might fit in the space and demonstrate the relations within the sentence. Circle the word that best completes the sentence. Only one of the words will be an appropriate fit even though all the choices may fit grammatically. The first one is done for you.

In the United States, as in England, Victorian morality was the public norm during the nineteenth century. A recently discovered study,   (1)   raises some doubt as to whether the private lives of Victorian women corresponded to their public image. Historian Carl Degler discovered in the Stanford University Archives a study of 45 women. Most of these women were born before 1870 and   (2)   grew up, married, and had children in the nineteenth century. The study was conducted via questionnaire by Dr. Clelia Mosher (1863–1940), a physician who devoted her life to destroying myths about the inferiority of women. She provided the earliest systematic study of the sexual attitudes and behaviors of American women.   (3)   she did not have a representative sample, she found that at least some women defied the Victorian stereotype of the passionless female.   (4)   of these women reported engaging in sex with neither reluctance nor distaste. Most expressed a desire for sexual intercourse and used some form of birth control.   (5)   most of the women believed that the primary purpose of sex was reproduction,   (6)   also felt that mutual pleasure was a worthy purpose in itself.

—From Allgeier and Allgeier, *Sexual Interactions*.

1.   a. although   b. next
      c. however   d. may be due to

246

2. a. while   b. thus
        c. now   d. means

3. a. In other words   b. For example
        c. On the contrary   d. Although

4. a. Most   b. In like manner
        c. Thereupon   d. At last

5. a. Although   b. Immediately
        c. Shortly   d. Also

6. a. for instance   b. in conclusion
        c. more than half   d. in short

   (7)   the planters regarded the slaves as investments, into which they had
sunk nearly $2 billion of their capital by 1860. Slaves were the primary form
of wealth in the South, and as such they were cared for as any asset is cared
for by a prudent capitalist.   (8)   they were sometimes, though by no
means always, spared dangerous work   (9)   putting a roof on a house. If a
neck was going to be broken, the master preferred it to be that of a wage-
earning Irish laborer rather than that of a prime field hand, worth $1,800 by
1860 (a price that had quintupled since 1800). Tunnel blasting and swamp
draining were often consigned to itinerant gangs of expendable Irishmen
   (10)   the labor was "death on niggers and mules."
       —From Bailey and Kennedy, *The American Pageant.*

7. a. Shortly   b. Above all
        c. The same as   d. Likewise

8. a. Immediately   b. Second
        c. Accordingly   d. At last

9. a. thereupon   b. like
        c. to illustrate   d. at the same time

10. a. thus   b. in comparison with
        c. in like manner   d. because

EXERCISE 2

In this exercise, circle the word that fits each numbered blank. The first one is
done for you.

Many people,   (1)   do not listen to science. They associate learned
behavioral characteristics with inherited physical characteristics and believe

that "whites are more intelligent than blacks,"   (2)   "blacks have more rhythm than whites,"   (2)   "yellows are craftier than both blacks and whites." As far as we can tell, there is no genetic relationship between the color of one's skin and the amount of intelligence, rhythm, or craftiness that a person possesses. Traits   (3)   intelligence, rhythm, and craftiness are believed to be acquired   (4)   experience and,   (5)   no one has been able to show that acquired characteristics can be inherited. Race,   (6)   cannot be used to explain acquired characteristics of people.   (7)   acquired characteristics, we must focus our attention on another concept—culture, which is the subject of the following three chapters. Before doing that,   (8)   , we must first examine the physical characteristics that make culture possible.

> —From Mendoza and Napoli, *Systems of Society: An Introduction to Social Sciences.*

1.   a. can be defined as   b. since
     c. may be due to   d. however

2.   a. next   b. in conclusion
     c. or   d. as a matter of fact

3.   a. such as   b. to sum up
     c. as a result   d. also

4.   a. however   b. as a result
     c. to illustrate   d. on the other hand

5.   a. after   b. as we pointed out
     c. shortly   d. immediately

6.   a. results   b. reasons
     c. similar to   d. therefore

7.   a. Next   b. For an explanation of
     c. For instance   d. May be due to

8.   a. however   b. after
     c. during   d. now

The Mehinaku of Brazil think of fathering children through sexual intercourse as a collective project by the males. The *number* of ejaculations into a woman's vagina is considered important in conception. The Mehinaku believe that one sexual act is insufficient to conceive a child,   (9)   the semen of a woman's husband forms only a portion of the infant.   (10)   moderation is also important—a woman who produces twins has had too many lovers. These anomalous offspring are immediately buried alive.

> —From Allgeier and Allgeier, *Sexual Interactions.*

9.   a. after   b. like
        c. for   d. thereupon

10.   a. To illustrate   b. However
        c. The same as   d. Immediately

EXERCISE 3

In this exercise, first circle the word that fits each numbered blank. Then, on the line following, write the name of the organizational pattern (definition, summary, comparison, and so on) that the clue word indicates. Be ready to discuss the reasons for your answers. The first one is done for you.

     (1)   most socialists, who believed in progress by peaceful evolution, Marx believed the transition from capitalism to communism would follow a particular pattern and would be accompanied by a violent revolution. Communist theoreticians have   (2)   this process in four stages.

     The   (3)   stage is marked by the workers' overthrow of capitalism and is followed by their seizure of the government.

     The second stage is characterized by the establishment of a *dictatorship of the proletariat*. A centralized authority is necessary   (4)   the majority of workers are not capable of ruling; direction by a small group of intelligent leaders—the Communist party—is required. Under the dictatorship, destruction of the capitalist class is completed and society is reorganized along socialist lines, with private ownership and profit abolished. The state   (5)   owns and operates the means of production.

     In the third stage, the dictatorship of the proletariat is replaced   (6)   the establishment of a "socialist" society. The political state still exists, and,   (7)   there may still be opposition, it has considerable power; economic production,   (8)   , is controlled by the workers.   (9)   production is still limited, output and payment are "from each according to his ability, to each according to his work."

     The fourth and highest stage is that of the true "communistic" society. Production is in such abundance that work and payment are made "from each according to his ability, to each according to his need." The political state is no longer necessary   (10)   there is no longer any antagonism between classes. Administrators are needed, however, to supervise industrial complexes.

          —From Gordon and Dawson, *Introductory Economics*.

1.   a. Next   b. Means
        (c. Unlike)   d. Conversely

               Contrast

2.   a. similarly   b. classified
       c. on one hand   d. hence

3.   a. first   b. in short
       c. for instance   d. too

4.   a. on the whole   b. consequently
       c. because   d. evidently

5.   a. in fact   b. to illustrate
       c. same as   d. now

6.   a. through   b. can be defined as
       c. type   d. on one hand

7.   a. to illustrate   b. because
       c. to summarize   d. as demonstrated

8.   a. although   b. during
       c. because   d. however

9.   a. Because   b. Shortly
       c. The same as   d. Various elements

10. a. also   b. may be due to
       c. because   d. can be defined as

EXERCISE 4

Circle the *one* choice that *could not be correct*. Three of the choices might fit in each blank. The first one is done for you.

Eating Disorders. The concern girls have over achieving the figure of a fashion model has an extreme form of expression in the problem of *anorexia nervosa.* Anorexia nervosa   (1)   an eating disorder which occurs largely among young adolescent girls,   (2)   it is also found among some young women, and   (3)   , among boys. It is   (4)   self-induced starvation, bizarre attitudes toward food, and distorted body image.   (5)   they are often severely emaciated, anorexic girls believe they are fat and become preoccupied with dieting. So distorted are their perceptions of their own bodies that they do not see themselves as emaciated but,   (6)   , as fat. Most victims of anorexia lose 25 percent or more of their normal body fat. Anorexia   (7)   causes its victims to stop menstruating, they become weak and they suffer muscle deterioration. From 5 to 15 percent of anorexics literally die of starvation.

Anorexia, which means "without food," seems to be an epidemic among young girls,   (8)   it was hardly a problem two decades ago. The cause of anorexia is not known,   (9)   researchers are investigating the possibility that it is related to a psychological need. One theory is that the need is to avoid becoming an adult, since starvation can impede physical growth and the onset of puberty.   (10)   theory is that anorexia is related to a rejection of the mother figure or to the experience of being the daughter of an overly protective and controlling mother.   (11)   by being anorexic, the girl demonstrates her ability to control at least one aspect of her own life.   (12)   , researchers note that the problem may stem from a faulty body image, which many adolescents have, given the societal ideal of feminine beauty of being very thin.   (13)   so much exposure is given to the tall, thin, almost emaciated female body in magazine ads and on television, it can be difficult for adolescents to accept their own body type.

—From Zigler and Finn-Stevenson, *Children: Development and Social Issues.*

1. a. is
    c. consequently
    b. may be
    d. could be

2. a. however
    c. as a result
    b. although
    d. yet

3. a. in some cases
    c. likewise
    b. similarly
    d. to sum up

4. a. however
    c. associated with
    b. in common with
    d. characterized by

5. a. Afterward
    c. At the same time
    b. Although
    d. Nevertheless

6.   a. rather   b. on the contrary
      c. conversely   d. at last

7.   a. also   b. likewise
      c. can be defined as   d. similarly

8.   a. however   b. although
      c. yet   d. the same as

9.   a. but   b. first
      c. however   d. yet

10.   a. Another   b. On the whole
      c. One more   d. A further

11.   a. Speculation is that   b. It is theorized that
      c. On the whole   d. It could be that

12.   a. In addition   b. Thereupon
      c. Finally   d. May be due to

13.   a. since   b. because
      c. to sum up   d. just because

What Are Your Thoughts?

1. Glance back over the reading passages in the exercises. Which of the ten patterns of organization seem to be used most frequently? Why do you think that is?

....

....

....

2. Again, glance over the same passages. Which of the ten patterns do you think is easiest to identify? Why is that pattern easy for you?

....

....

....

3. Describe what you believe your thinking goes through as you recognize the relationships within sentences: a sudden flash of insight? a gradual awareness? What occurs?

....

....

....

4. Which pattern seems most frequent in the sentences and paragraphs of the reading selections in the exercises in this chapter?

....

....

....

5. How did selecting and defining ten unfamiliar words (Words to Read by) affect your comprehension of those passages when you read them and answered the comprehension questions?

....

....

....

Answers to Selected Exercises

EXERCISE 1

1. c	2. b	3. d	4. a	5. a
6. c	7. b	8. c	9. b	10. d

EXERCISE 3

1c. unlike
2b. classification
3a. simple listing
4c. cause and effect
5d. time order
6a. generalization and example
7b. cause and effect
8d. contrast
9a. cause and effect
10c. cause and effect

Chapter 11

Recognizing Relations Between Sentences

> I've just found out what makes a piece of writing good ...: it is making the sentences talk to each other as two or more speakers do in a drama.
>
> —Robert Frost

This chapter will help you to:

1. see the similarity between skill in recognizing relations *within* and *between* sentences, which you have just learned.
2. understand why you need to acquire this comprehension skill.
3. know what to look for to spot relations between sentences.
4. see why it helps to know clue words.

The reading competency practiced in this chapter is very similar to the one you have just studied, except that instead of concentrating on relations *within* sentences, you concentrate on relations *between* sentences. Once again you rely on the expressions and clue words that you learned on page 153 and have used for recognizing both the author's overall organization and relations within sentences.

What Are Your Thoughts?

1. Why do writers even *think* about relations between their sentences, let alone *plan* those relations when they write? What are they trying to accomplish?

....

....

....

2. Do you, as a student writing many papers, ever think about relations between the sentences you write? If not, why not?

....

....

....

3. At what grade level do you think instruction should begin to develop skills in reading comprehension such as recognizing relations between sentences, recognizing relations within sentences, and recognizing the organizational pattern in a work?

....

....

....

4. Are these skills in reading comprehension, once learned, easily forgotten? Why or why not?

....

....

....

Writing to Comprehend

1. How does recognizing relations *between* sentences differ from recognizing relations *within* sentences, and from recognizing the *overall* pattern of organization? In a few sentences, summarize each of these comprehension skills, explaining why each is essential for achieving that "reading edge."

....

....

....

....

....

2. Which of these three relation skills is easiest for you to master? Why?

....

....

....

....

....

3. Have you ever had the experience of believing that your comprehension was better than a test score indicated? How is that discrepancy possible? What does it suggest?

....

....

....

....

....

Why Work at This Technique?

Writers use many devices and organizational patterns to make their presentation more interesting and more persuasive, to create stronger effect, to reveal special relationships, to make clearer the ideas presented, and for many other reasons. Often the relation *between* sentences is crucial to clear understanding of the author's purpose. As readers we can learn to recognize these relations between sentences when we encounter them, giving us an idea of how the author is attempting to convince and influence us. Thus equipped we will be able to read much more efficiently, faster, and with greater understanding and retention.

What to Look for

As with the other skills in reading comprehension you have been studying, improving in this technique takes more of your attention as you read. But what relations specifically should you be aware of?

1. A sentence that *contradicts* an earlier sentence.
2. A sentence that *summarizes* something said in an earlier sentence.
3. A sentence that gives a specific *example* of a statement in an earlier sentence.
4. A sentence that *alters the meaning* of an earlier sentence.
5. A sentence indicating that a fact, event, or idea has been *added* to an earlier sentence.
6. A sentence indicating the *place* or order of something referred to in an earlier sentence.
7. A sentence specifying clearly the *meaning* of a word or phrase mentioned in an earlier sentence.
8. A sentence indicating a subsequent *effect* of something discussed in an earlier sentence.
9. A sentence in which something is analyzed to see where it *fits in* with similar things mentioned in an earlier sentence.
10. A sentence in which the writer discusses the *similarities* between something and something else discussed in an earlier sentence.

Now look back at descriptions 1 through 10. See if you can identify each of these descriptions as one of the relations you learned back in Chapter 6. The first one is done for you.

1. *contrast* ....
2. ....
3. ....
4. ....
5. ....
6. ....
7. ....
8. ....
9. ....
10. ....

Well, how do you think you did? Check your answers against the correct answers listed at the end of this chapter. Any that you failed to identify correctly, look at again on page 153.

Clue Words

Remember, knowing and spotting your "clue words" will be a big help in identifying relations between sentences, and ultimately will greatly strengthen your understanding of passages you read. Reading your assigned texts will take on new significance as you acquire your improved skill in reading comprehension. From now on, you will be reading with a questioning mind, not just turning pages to complete an assignment.

Recognizing-Relations-Between-Sentences Margin Mark △

A triangle marked in the margin will indicate clue words telling you relations between the sentences. Remember to practice margin marking on everything—even the exercises that follow.

Words to Read by

For each of these words we list four possible choices for a definition. Only one of the four choices, though, is a definition of the word as it is used in the reading selection in this chapter. Be sure to refer to the passage (page number in parentheses) to establish the context for each word. If you do not know the meaning of a word, including answer choices, look it up in the dictionary. Circle the correct definition.

1. *ritualized* (261)
customary procedure
dependable
religious phrases
tasteful

2. *concise* (262)
dependable and candid
slang
brief and clear
clout

3. *utilitarian* (262)
harmful to others
having unlimited power
taking in everything
emphasizing usefulness

4. *proponents* (263)
synonyms
adversaries
advocates
compliances

5. *precipitating* (264)
raining
arranged in time sequence
unpretentious
causing to happen

6. *pollster* (266)
one who takes polls
one who uses polls
one who makes polls
one who dislikes polls

7. *neutered* (267)
mild, nonmalignant
neither masculine nor feminine
having one colored
nonliving things

8. *transgressions* (267)
belief in more than one god
disconsolate
irrelevant
a violation of the law

9. *phenomenon* (269)
being everywhere at once
bibliophobic
an unusual fact or occurrence
variant

10. *subtle* (271)
not obvious
good to others
having many colors
to decimate

Compare your answers with those at the end of the chapter.

Anticipate the Topics

These words suggest the content in the reading selections in this chapter's exercises. If these are the subjects, what might the authors be considering in the passages? Jot down a few possibilities for each topic.

genderism ....

vigorous writing ....

adrenalin ....

courtesy ....

double-blind ....

the depression ....

penny stocks ....

a person's build ....

polls ....

flappers ....

television journalists ....

adultery ....

drug and alcohol abuse ....

socialism ....

infant mortality ....

smoking ....

Practice Exercises

EXERCISE 1

In these questions circle the letter of the choice that best describes the relationship between the sentences indicated. Be ready to discuss the reasons for your choices. The first one is done for you.

1. [1] Anthropologist Erving Goffman (1977) analyzed the composition of photographs used in popular advertising. [2] He noticed that the composition of the photographs often contained "genderisms," that is, subtle stereotyped themes. [3] As an example, men were almost always shown with their heads higher in the photograph than women's, even when both the man and the woman were seated or in some other situation in which height should make little difference. [4] According to Goffman's analysis, this positioning reflects a ritualized subordination of women. [5] Typically one lowers one's head when in the presence of a person of superior authority and power, as when bowing to a king. [6] Thus the lower position of women may reflect their subordinate status to men.
   —From Hyde, *Half the Human Experience: The Psychology of Women.*

   What is the relation between sentence 2, beginning "He noticed ...," and sentence 3, beginning "As an example ..."?
   a. contrast
   b. summary
   c. generalization and example
   d. statement and clarification

2. [1] Before proceeding, some terms need to be defined. [2] First, it is worth noting that in our language the term "sex" is sometimes used ambiguously.
   —From Hyde, *Half the Human Experience: The Psychology of Women.*

   What is the relation between sentence 1, beginning "Before proceeding ...," and sentence 2, beginning "First, it is ..."?
   a. simple listing
   b. comparison
   c. cause and effect
   d. summary

3. [1] Vigorous writing is difficult to describe. [2] Although in most contexts "vigor"

implies forcefulness, all vigorous business writing is not forceful. [3] It can be tactful, matter-of-fact, descriptive, and even technical. [4] It can be formal or informal, and it can deal with matters that are important or routine, complex or simple. [5] Although a more vigorous writing style can often be achieved by editing or conciseness, vigorous writing is not always concise. [6] Vigorous writing is inevitably clear, and yet clarity and vigor are not synonymous.

—From Newman, *Communicating in Business Today.*

What is the relation between sentence 1, beginning "Vigorous writing ...," and sentence 3, beginning "It can be ..."?

a. contrast
b. simple listing
c. cause and effect
d. statement and clarification

4. [1] Adrenalin is what they call it, of course; the cause of all this anxiety. [2] Adrenalin, a rush of energy nature equips us with to protect us in perilous situations. [3] It brings on a readiness to fight or flee, the anthropologists tell us, depending on what the circumstances seem to warrant.

—From Newman, *Communicating in Business Today.*

What is the relation between sentence 1, beginning "Adrenalin is what ...," and sentence 2, beginning "Adrenalin, a rush ..."?

a. classification
b. comparison
c. definition
d. summary

5. [1] Consider the following sentence, taken from the first draft of a consultant's report to a client:

> [2] The introduction of new products appears to be inadvisable during the current period of time.

[3] Here is a pared-down version:

> [4] Introducing new products appears inadvisable at this time.

[5] As you can see, no part of the idea is lost in the revised version; it is merely less wordy.

—From Newman, *Communicating in Business Today.*

What is the relation between sentence 2, beginning "The introduction of ...," and sentence 3, beginning "Here is a ..."?

a. cause and effect
b. comparison
c. time order
d. summary

6. [1] Perhaps it seems a little hardnosed to underscore the utilitarian value of courtesy, but in the rush of a busy day it can be tempting to postpone or completely overlook small, gracious acts that take thought and effort. [2] This temptation is easier to resist if you understand the practical effects of courtesy. [3] A story about a certain vice president of operations make this point well. [4] Several senior executives are discussing some new theories about how important the quality of the work environment is for maintaining high worker productivity. [5] Questioning the value of praising his subordinates, the vice president argues, "I don't see the point. [6] I mean, after all, do I thank my tires for not being flat?" [7] To which one of his colleagues quickly responds, "You would if that's what you had to do to keep them from going flat!"

—From Newman, *Communicating in Business Today.*

What is the relation between sentence 1, beginning "Perhaps it seems ...," and sentences 3–7, beginning "A story about ..."?
a. generalization and example   b. time order
c. simple listing   d. definition

7.   [1] The technical procedure that is generally used to guard against observer effects is the "double-blind." [2] It simply means that observers are kept unaware of (blind to) which experimental group subjects are in, so that the observers' expectations cannot affect the outcome. [3] Unfortunately, the double-blind method is virtually impossible in gender differences research, as the gender of a subject is almost always obvious from appearance, and therefore the observer cannot be "blind" to it or unaware of it.

—From Hyde, *Half the Human Experience: The Psychology of Women.*

What is the relation between sentence 1, beginning "The technical procedure ...," and sentence 2, beginning "It simply means ..."?
a. comparison   b. cause and effect
c. statement and clarification   d. definition

8.   [1] If your words and ideas are ready to leap onto the page, let them come.
[2] Otherwise, one of the following techniques might help you get started.
    [3] Begin by telling your audience how you feel about the problem or issue at hand. [4] You might describe what went wrong or project future consequences. [5] If you don't have strong feelings about the issue, picture yourself talking to someone who does. [6] Or if you are of a divided mind, attempt a one-person debate about the pros and cons (picture yourself actually speaking the words of each of the opposing proponents).

—From Newman, *Communicating in Business Today.*

What is the relation between sentence 2, beginning "Otherwise, one of ...," and sentences 3–6, beginning "Begin by telling ..."?
a. definition   b. simple listing
c. classification   d. contrast

9.   [1] There's a lesson here. [2] Nervousness, it seems, is an emotion we can all do without. [3] The heck with that candy-box assortment of staring faces.

⁴ People are rather like chocolates, when you think about it: not everybody can be a fudge cream. ⁵ Some are licorice-macaroon nougats.
> —From Newman, *Communicating in Business Today*.

What is the relation between sentence 3, beginning "The heck with ...," and sentences 4 and 5, beginning "People are rather ..."?
a. simple listing
b. statement and clarification
c. cause and effect
d. definition

10. ¹ The misery and gloom were incalculable, as forests of dead chimneys stood starkly against the sky. ² Over five thousand banks collapsed in the first three years of the depression, carrying down with them the life savings of tens of thousands of widows and retired citizens. ³ Countless thousands of honest, hardworking people lost their homes and farms to the forecloser's hammer. ⁴ Bread lines formed, soup kitchens dispensed food, and apple sellers stood shivering on street corners trying to peddle their wares for five cents. ⁵ Families felt the stress, as jobless fathers nursed their guilt and shame at not being able to provide for their households. ⁶ Mothers meanwhile nursed fewer babies, as hard times reached even into the nation's bedrooms, precipitating a decade-long dearth of births. ⁷ As cash registers gathered cobwebs, the song "My God, How the Money Rolls In" was replaced with "Brother, Can You Spare a Dime?"
> —From Bailey and Kennedy, *The American Pageant*.

What is the relation between sentences 2–4, beginning "Over five thousand ...," and sentence 7, beginning "As cash registers ..."?
a. summary
b. contrast
c. definition
d. classification

EXERCISE 2

In these passages, determine the relations between the sentences identified. Circle the letter of the correct answer. Be ready to discuss the reasons for your choices. The first one is done for you.

1. ¹ A stock broker will often encourage a client to purchase hundreds or thousands of expensive stocks. ² But for investors who like to deal on a smaller level, there are penny stocks. ³ Penny stocks are those that sell on the Over the Counter market for less than five dollars.
> —Source unknown.

What does sentence 3 ("Penny stocks are ...") do in relation to sentence 2 ("But for investors ...")?
a. It contradicts the earlier sentence.
b. It defines something in the earlier sentence.

    c. It summarizes what was said in the earlier sentence.

    d. It gives a specific example of something said in the earlier sentence.

2.   [1] All university students experience stress, not just new students. [2] This is caused by high performance demands, Hammond said.

    [3] "There are so many ways you're expected to achieve—in each class, in your department, for your B.S. or B.A. degree and eventually for a job or acceptance into graduate school," she said. [4] "Each one requires hard work."

    —Source unknown.

What does sentence 2 ("This is caused ...") do in relation to sentence 1 ("All university students ...")?

    a. It alters the meaning of what was said.

    b. It indicates the order of what was said.

    c. It indicates a cause for an effect mentioned earlier.

    d. It limits the meaning of what was said.

3.   [1] Knowing how difficult it is for students to raise capital to realize business ventures, the founders of "I Can't Believe It's Yogurt" stores—Julie and Bill Brice—sponsored a contest for young entrepreneurs. [2] The Brices, who began their franchise when they were in college, offered the contest to students who could create a business that can be franchised. [3] The idea doesn't need to be new; it can be an improvement on an existing product or service. [4] First prize is $10,000, to be used to fund the start-up costs of the winning entry. [5] Last year 573 entries from 203 colleges in 48 states were received.

    —Tony Smithson, *Indiana Statesman*, Indiana State University.

What does sentence 2 ("The Brices, who ...") do in relation to sentence 1 ("Knowing how difficult ...")?

    a. It indicates the results of an effect in the earlier sentence.

    b. It indicates the place of something said in the earlier sentence.

    c. It expresses the similarities of something in the earlier sentence.

    d. It clarifies something said in the earlier sentence.

4.   [1] A person's build can be classified into three basic types, determined by a combination of variations in skeletal frame and muscular development.

    [2] Endomorphs are people with wide trunks and short arms and legs which make them look fat.

    [3] Ectomorphic people seem to be trim and thin. [4] They have long, thin arms and legs and a narrow trunk.

    [5] Those with an athletic physique characterized by "broad shoulders with well-proportioned muscular extremities" are called mesomorphs.

    —Source unknown.

What do sentences 2, 3, and 5 ("Endomorphs ...") do in relation to sentence 1 ("A person's build ...")?

    a. They summarize what was said in the earlier sentence.
    b. They contradict what was said in the earlier sentence.
    c. They indicate a simple listing of something said in the earlier sentence.
    d. They alter the meaning of what was said in the earlier sentence.

5.   In the same passage, what does sentence 4 ("They have long ...") do in relation to sentence 3 ("Ectomorphic ...")?
    a. It adds a fact to what was said in the earlier sentence.
    b. It contradicts something said in the earlier sentence.
    c. It alters the meaning of something in the earlier sentence.
    d. It gives an example of something in the earlier sentence.

6.   [1] Waterbed owners beware! [2] It can cost up to $300 a year to heat your luxurious sleeping contraptions. [3] The Southeastern Development Association of the Council of Governments recently released a report finding that the estimated 20 million waterbeds in the U.S. are incredible energy wasters. [4] Electric waterbed heaters sometimes run eight hours a day and use as much electricity as a large self-defrosting refrigerator. [5] Leaving a bed unmade every day can increase energy consumption by about 32 percent through heat loss, according to the report.
        —Source unknown.

What does sentence 4 ("Electric waterbed heaters ...") do in relation to sentence 1 ("Waterbed owners beware!")?
    a. It defines a word or phrase stated in the earlier sentence.
    b. It alters the meaning of what was said in the earlier sentence.
    c. It summarizes what was said in the earlier sentence.
    d. It provides an example of a general statement made in the earlier sentence.

7.   [1] A professor warned his class to beware of both polls and pollsters. [2] "They can get any answer they want with loaded questions," he cautioned.
    [3] He cited the case of the voters who replied "No" when asked if they approved of smoking while praying [4] "The vote turned to 'Yes' when the same people were asked if they approved of praying while smoking," he told his class.
        —From Outdoor Power Equipment.

What does sentence 4 ("'The vote turned ...'") do in relation to sentence 3 ("He cited the ...")?
    a. It indicates the time order indicated in the earlier sentence.
    b. It serves as a contrast to the earlier sentence.
    c. It indicates the order or place of something referred to in the earlier sentence.
    d. It provides an example of what was stated in the earlier sentence.

8.   [1] Even before the war, one observer thought the chimes had "struck sex o'clock in America," and the 1920s witnessed what many old-timers regarded as a veritable erotic eruption. [2] Advertisers exploited sexual allure to sell everything from soap to car tires. [3] Once-modest maidens now proclaimed their new freedom as "flappers" in bobbed tresses and dresses. [4] Young women appeared with hemlines elevated, stockings rolled, breasts taped flat, cheeks rouged, and lips a "crimson gash" that held a dangling cigarette. [5] Thus did the "flapper" symbolize a yearned-for and devil-may-care independence (some said wild abandon) in American women. [6] Still more adventuresome females shocked their elders when they sported the new one-piece bathing suits.
          —From Bailey and Kennedy, *The American Pageant.*

What does sentence 5 ("Thus did the ...") do in relation to sentences 2–4 ("Advertisers exploited sexual ...")?
    a. It serves as an example of what was said in the earlier sentences.
    b. It contradicts what was said in the earlier sentences.
    c. It adds to the earlier sentences.
    d. It summarizes what was said in the earlier sentences.

9.   [1] Lately a new breed of "journalists" has surfaced, talk show journalists. [2] Their goals are the same as those of most journalists: to find stories where none exist. [3] Their methods are, at best, tabloidal. [4] Still, they have garnered a respect and a salary that writers for *The National Enquirer* could never expect.
          [5] Having no ideas of their own, except a neutered respect for all of god's creatures no matter how incestuous, obese or lost, these men and women lead daily public meetings in which the most perverse aspects of private life are revealed for public consumption.
          —Source unknown.

What does sentence 5 ("Having no ideas ...") do in relation to sentence 1 ("Lately a new ...")?
    a. It is about the similarities of something said in the earlier sentence.
    b. It shows the cause of an effect stated in the earlier sentence.
    c. It provides an example of what was said in the earlier sentence.
    d. It alters the meaning and tone of what was said in the earlier sentence.

10.   [1] Among the ancient Hebrews (who flourished after about 1,000 B.C.), women were also portrayed as more "sexual" than men, and their status was inferior to that of men. [2] Sexual expression was supposed to be confined to one's spouse, but transgressions by females were dealt with more severely than those by males because women were considered to be the property of men. [3] In the Jewish law of that period, *adultery*, which was punishable by death, was defined differently than it is today. [4] Among the Hebrews, only married

women could be guilty of adultery; that is, adultery referred only to a married woman's having sexual intercourse with a man other than her husband.
[5] A man who had intercourse with a woman who was married to someone else was charged with the violation of the husband's property rights. [6] Although the punishment for this violation was severe, the man was not condemned to death.

> —From Allgeier and Allgeier, *Sexual Interactions*.

What does sentence 4 ("Among the Hebrews, ...") do in relation to sentence 3 ("In the Jewish ...")?

a. It contradicts the earlier sentence.

b. It indicates the place or order of whatever was said in the earlier sentence.

c. It discusses where a point fits in the classification indicated in the earlier sentence.

d. It gives a specific example of what was stated in the earlier sentence.

EXERCISE 3

In this exercise are several long passages with their sentences numbered. After carefully reading each passage, see how many relations between sentences you can find. Identify those relations on the lines following each passage. The first one is started for you.

1.   [1] The widespread use of alcohol, marijuana, and other illicit drugs not only among adolescents but among adults as well represents one of the most striking instances of social change in the last decade. [2] Drug and alcohol abuse among adolescents, however, is of particular concern not only because the use of drugs can have devastating emotional and physical consequences for a developing mind and body, but also because among adolescents, the use of one drug, marijuana, for instance, is associated with extensive use of other drugs as well. [3] In studies on drug and alcohol abuse, researchers found that there are stages in drug involvement. [4] At first, children and adolescents drink beer and wine. [5] At a slightly older age they supplement these with cigarette smoking and/or hard liquor, followed by marijuana. [6] Eventually they use not only these combinations of drugs and alcohol but other illicit drugs as well.
[7] Drug and alcohol abuse takes its toll on the physical and emotional health of adolescents and subjects them to other dangers as well. [8] It is the leading cause of automobile accidents, which account for the deaths of many adolescents and other people; it interferes with school work; and it creates social problems with family and friends. [9] Although the research on drug and alcohol abuse has thus far yielded only partial answers regarding the

possible effects of drug use, researchers do know that the effects of drugs and alcohol differ among individuals depending on their biological makeup, personality, and extent of drug abuse. [10] For some adolescents, the use of some drugs for short periods of time may not be associated with any devastating consequences.

—From Zigler and Finn-Stevenson, *Children: Development and Social Issues.*

Sentences ...*3*... and ...*4*...: *statement and clarification*

Sentences .... and ....: ....

Sentences .... and ....: ....

2. [1] As an example, let us consider a fairly well-documented phenomenon of psychological gender differences. [2] A class of students takes its first exam in Introductory Psychology. [3] Immediately after taking the exam, but before getting the results back, the students are asked to estimate how many points (out of a possible 100 points) they got on the exam. [4] On the average, males will estimate that they got higher scores than females will estimate they got. [5] At this point, the data have been collected and analyzed statistically. [6] It can be stated (neutrally) that there are statistically significant gender differences, with men estimating more points than women. [7] The next question is, how do we interpret that result? [8] The standard interpretation is that it indicates that women lack self-confidence or have low confidence in their abilities. [9] The interpretation that is not made, although it is just as logical, is that men have unrealistically high expectations for their own performance.

—From Hyde, *Half the Human Experience: The Psychology of Women.*

Sentences .... and ....: ....

Sentences .... and ....: ....

Sentences .... and ....: ....

3. [1] The communists seek to end capitalism by revolution, whereas the socialists wish to do it through the ballot box, adhering to constitutional procedures. [2] In socialism, education and persuasion are substituted for the militant class struggle the communists advocate. [3] For the most part, socialists believe in an orderly transfer of the means of production from private to public ownership. [4] This changeover can be accomplished by gradually increasing the size of the public sector, thereby allowing capitalism and socialism to live side by side during the transition.

[5] One of the important differences between socialism and communism may be seen in the treatment of nationalized property. [6] Under socialism, fair payment is made to the owners. [7] Because communists look with disdain

on capitalists, considering the property they own to be stolen from the people, they expropriate private property without any compensation.
[8] Furthermore, they do not accept a mixed economy (although they did in practice in Russia between the years 1921 and 1927) and they believe in total nationalization.
[9] Finally, socialism has a high regard for the political freedom of the individual. [10] It does not seek to control the total way of life of the people; instead, it is responsive to the popular will expressed through elections.
[11] Communism, on the other hand, is totalitarian, seeking to subject not merely economic affairs but all individual thought and activity to the good of the state.

—From Gordon and Dawson, *Introductory Economics.*

Sentences .... and ....: ....

Sentences .... and ....: ....

Sentences .... and ....: ....

4.   *No National Effort Can Save the Babies.* [1] The USA's high infant mortality rate is caused by sociology and culture. [2] It has little to do with economics and even less to do with the quality of our health-care system.

[3] Utah has one of the lowest infant mortality rates in the world, primarily because of the Mormon culture. [4] Florida's rate is three times higher than Utah's rate, even though people in Florida have higher incomes and better access to physicians than people in Utah.

[5] In the cultural underclass, many pregnant women (often themselves children) smoke, drink, take drugs and refuse to see doctors. [6] Even when medical treatment is free, many of these mothers avoid it. [7] We've set up clinics in high-risk neighborhoods, often to no avail.

[8] None of this is any reflection on our health-care system. [9] Once in hospitals, pregnant women and their babies have access to the best medical care anywhere. [10] We are willing to spend more than $1 million to save the life of one premature baby. [11] In almost any other country, that child would die.

[12] We stand ready to pay almost any price to fix any problem. [13] Almost all our spina bifida babies live; in England, most spina bifida babies die.
[14] To save the lives of young children, we routinely perform liver transplants, heart transplants and remove brain tumors—even if the parents can't pay the bill. [15] In other countries, these operations on children are virtually unheard of.

[16] Despite our enormous generosity, some say we are not generous enough. [17] "Let's make maternity and child care free for everyone," says the Institute of Medicine. [18] It's not hard to read between the lines. [19] Like congressional liberals, they've given up on poor people and opted for one more middle-class entitlement program.

[20] First there was free day care (routinely avoided by the black commu-

nity). [21] Next was paid maternity leave (of little use to women who don't already have a job). [22] Then there was free preschooling (of little value in areas where the schools are rotten anyway). [23] What other handouts will the middle class demand? [24] Free cooks? [25] Free maids? [26] Free yard service?

[27] In our inner-city slums, infant mortality rates are disgracefully high. [28] But the answer is not free medical care for the affluent suburbs. [29] Under socialized medicine in Europe, the children join the elderly at the end of the rationing lines. [30] They are denied access to medical advances that Americans take for granted. [31] And despite free maternity care, infant mortality rates in Europe parallel our own experience: Infant mortality is high in poor neighborhoods and low in wealthy ones. [32] In case anyone hasn't noticed, the federal government doesn't have a lot of spare change. [33] If we have some extra money, there are better things to do with it than providing free maternity care to middle-class women.

> —From *USA Today*, October 21, 1988, page 10A. Copyright © 1988 by *USA Today*. Excerpted with permission.

Sentences .... and ....: ....

Sentences .... and ....: ....

Sentences .... and ....: ....

5. *Beating Smoking Slander.* [1] As we reach the end of the Reagan revolution, many draw parallels between the '80s and the '50s. [2] But there is one subtle difference.

[3] In 1988, you go into a convenience store and say loudly, "I'll have a pack of condoms,"—but then whisper, "and a pack of cigarettes."

[4] Smokers are the lepers of the '80s, banished to the rear of airplanes (if smoking is allowed at all) and destined to sit at restaurant tables which always seem to be in the back by the kitchen.

[5] To make ourselves feel better after several of the '80s crusades flopped, we're treating smokers like second-class citizens. [6] Never mind that one-fourth of all American citizens smoke. [7] Never mind that the U.S. government receives a much-needed $10 billion per year from excise taxes on tobacco products. [8] Never mind that there are serious global and domestic problems like the arms race, the deficit, poverty and crime. [9] Just don't let us breathe their second-hand smoke. [10] Cigarette smoking is an unhealthy habit. [11] It is, however, a legal habit and should be treated as such. [12] The 1986 Surgeon General's report on "The Health Consequences of Involuntary Smoking" was in no way conclusive, yet this study fueled the massive second-hand smoke hysteria we have today.

[13] A continuation of the current, and sometimes violent, hostilities can only lead to more heated confrontations. [14] Perhaps Uncle Sam should spend a portion of the tobacco "sin" tax on providing adequate ventilation in public buildings.

[15] Separate smoking and non-smoking sections will help the private sector take care of itself, but for now, there needs to be more friendly and tactful communications between opposing forces.

[16] Many smokers do not—and should not—mind putting out their cigarettes or directing their smoke to an alternate direction when politely asked. [17] Likewise, non-smokers should be more tolerant and diplomatic, and realize second-hand smoke will not cause the ruin of society as we know it.

—Kate Jeffrey, *The Daily Texan*, University of Texas, Austin.

Sentences .... and ....: ....

Sentences .... and ....: ....

Sentences .... and ....: ....

EXERCISE 4

Read this passage on "Plankton and Nekton." Then take a few minutes to analyze this passage and come to some conclusions about how difficult or easy it would be in an examination. Answer these questions.

1. Would this passage be potentially easy or difficult to be tested on?

    ....

2. What elements in this passage might cause you some difficulty?

    ....

3. Can you identify the main idea?

    ....

4. Does the passage have topic sentences? Stated or unstated?

    ....

5. Any unfamiliar words? Any context clues?

    ....

6. Does it have many supporting details? Are most of these details important or unimportant?

    ....

7. Which skills in reading comprehension that you have studied so far would be *unlikely* to be tested in a passage such as this?

    ....

Finally, and very important—

8.   What happens to your comprehension and retention on this passage when you answer the preceding questions? Why?

....

....

9.   What did this exercise teach you about successfully analyzing technical or scientific reading materials?

....

....

PLANKTON AND NEKTON

Nearly all of the marine invertebrates that have been discussed depend wholly or partially on plankton. Most planktonic organisms are microscopic but a few are surprisingly large. The one characteristic they all share is an inability to swim faster than one knot. Thus they are at the mercy of even moderate currents.

The planktonic fauna of the Texas bays is highly seasonal. Many of the species are sensitive to relatively minor changes in temperature, salinity, oxygen level or toxin in the water. The species composition may change markedly during a heavy rain or drought. Moreover, the larvae of most marine animals are planktonic, and these are usually seasonal in their appearance. Such organisms, which spend only a portion of their life cycles in the plankton, are collectively called meroplankton; those that are planktonic during their entire lives are called holoplankton. The most frequently encountered forms of holoplankton in the bays are copepods, medusae, ctenophores, chaetognaths, mysids and sergestid shrimp.

Perhaps the most common of our holoplanktonic species are the copepods of the genus *Acartia. Acartia tonsa* is the best known of these copepods. It is a small, short-lived filter-feeder. During the summer, when the water is warmest, it completes its life cycle in less than two weeks. Its swimming motion is very jerky; it flits through the water propelled by its long antennules. It is a euryhaline species, i.e. it can tolerate a wide range of salinities. It is found in habitats ranging from the lower ends of the bayous to the hypersaline lagoons of the southern Texas coast.

The chaetognath, *Sagitta tenuis,* is a copepod predator which is sporadically abundant. This chaetognath or "arrow-worm," as it is sometimes called, uses its long fins to glide through the water. Its large hooks flanking the mouth are used to capture copepods and other small crustaceans. Its size permits it to subdue even small fish larvae.

Among our most exotic animals are the sergestid shrimps *Lucifer faxoni* and *Acetes americanus louisianensis.* These small shrimps have their eyes mounted on long stalks—the ultimate in peripheral vision. Like many other plankters their presence is sporadic. *Acetes* is an estuarine species most abundant in low salinity bays. *Lucifer* is an oceanic species that moves into the bays during the summer. *Acetes* has minute claws on the last three pairs of legs on the first body section; *Lucifer* has only a rudimentary claw on the last pair of these legs.

—From Fotheringham, *The Beachcomber's Guide to Gulf Coast Marine Life.*

Answers to Selected Exercises

WHAT TO LOOK FOR

1. contrast
2. summary
3. generalization and example
4. statement and clarification
5. time order
6. simple listing
7. definition
8. cause and effect
9. classification
10. comparison

WORDS TO READ BY

1. customary procedure
2. brief and clear
3. stress on usefulness
4. advocates
5. to cause to happen
6. one who takes polls
7. neither masculine nor feminine
8. a violation of the law
9. an unusual fact or occurrence
10. not obvious

EXERCISE 2

1. b   2. c   3. d   4. c   5. a
6. d   7. b   8. d   9. d   10. d

Chapter 12

Recognizing
Valid Arguments

The venerable tradition of respectful argumen-
tation, based on evidence, conducted with courtesy, and leading to the exposition of truth, is a
precious part of our heritage in this land of
freedom. It is the duty of educated men to
understand, appreciate and perpetuate this
tradition.

—James P. Shannon

This chapter will help you to:

1. recognize a valid argument.
2. recognize the twelve common invalid arguments.
3. learn the two questions to keep in mind when you wish to recognize valid arguments.

In all your reading in college and for the rest of your life, you will want to read
with a questioning mind. One great reason for this questioning approach is
that it will enable you to recognize a valid argument (it's more likely to be
an *invalid* argument) in your reading material.

What Is a Valid Argument?

A valid argument is a statement which fits into a logical pattern of reasoning
and which includes *relevant, verifiable* proof supporting a conclusion. Can you
prove it? That is all you have to decide.

Invalid arguments are often used unintentionally by writers who are intent
on making a specific point or gaining support for their conclusions and who are

not careful to follow logical reasoning in doing so. With just a few exceptions, all you will need to recognize valid arguments is to be *aware* of the passage you are reading, use a healthy dose of common sense, and acquire experience in identifying valid (and especially, *invalid*) arguments.

Two Vital Questions

Always keep in mind these two questions when a writer presents an argument supporting a conclusion.

1. Is this argument *logical?*
2. Are these reasons (given to support the conclusion) *true?*

Common Invalid Arguments

Recognizing valid arguments is often difficult to do. Recognizing *invalid* arguments is much easier, especially if you are familiar with the twelve common fallacies, one of which is usually used to make the argument invalid. Once you understand these fallacies and can spot them when they are employed in writing, you will be able to assume that the writer's argument is invalid. If these fallacies *do not* appear in the writing, you should lean toward assuming the argument is valid. Remember, with this comprehension skill your best help is your own *common sense.* These twelve fallacies are suggested by Jean Wyrick's *Steps to Writing Well* (Holt, Rinehart and Winston, 1984).

1. *The stated conclusion is not necessarily a* logical result *of the facts presented* (*non sequitur*, "it doesn't follow").

An example of this fallacy occurs when a writer concludes, "Ron Sharp has been an excellent high school principal, and so he will make an excellent mayor for our city." As you may realize, that a person has been successful in one administrative position does not automatically mean that person will be successful in a different position. Common sense and your experience tell you that.

2. *An* irrelevant *point is introduced to divert the reader's attention from the main issue* ("red herring").

The label *red herring* comes from the old practice resorted to by escaping slaves or prisoners, who would drag a smoked (reddish) herring or other strong-smelling fish across their trail to confuse or divert the tracking dogs. If a writer is discussing the merits of television ministries and their influence on viewers and suddenly begins to condemn *Enquirer*-like newspapers and their sensationalism, such a condemnation would be considered a red herring. The sensationalist newspapers have nothing to do with an evaluation of how the ministries affect the audience.

3. *The writer evades the real issues by appealing to the reader's emotions* (argument *ad populem,* "to the people").

This fallacy plays upon the reader's emotional responses to such negative words as *fag* and *communist* or to positive words such as *honesty, American,* and *freedom.* A writer who says "Only a communist would see the merit in electing him to office" is avoiding discussion of the candidate's strengths and weaknesses and merely substituting an appeal to the emotions.

4. *An* extended comparison *is used as proof of a point* (faulty analogy).

Sometimes if you look closely at metaphors and extended comparisons you will see that the two things being compared are not really similar. For example, arguing that a new law making it illegal to drink alcoholic beverages while piloting a boat is wrong because, if the state can prohibit that, it can just as easily outlaw drinking alcoholic beverages while fishing off a dock, is faulty analogy. The two situations are not at all alike. Even though the analogy might suggest similarities (water, alcohol, law), that analogy *proves* nothing.

5. *The writer attempts to convince the reader that the issue has* only two sides—*one right, one wrong* (either/or).

The statement that "If you don't vote to build the nuclear power plant, you won't have any electricity" is irrational because it neglects several other ways of generating electricity. One of the best-known (and popularly accepted!) examples of this either/or oversimplification was the 1960s bumper-sticker slogan on thousands of cars during the Vietnam war: "America: Love It or Leave It." As we now see so clearly in hindsight, other choices were available.

6. *An argument is based on* insufficient or unrepresentative evidence (hasty generalization).

Suppose you have owned two parrots and both have bitten you frequently. If you declare that all parrots are vicious birds, you are making a hasty generalization, because thousands of parrots never bite anyone. If the generalization is drawn from an inadequate or unrepresentative sample (your own experience, for instance), your conclusion is invalid.

7. *An attempt is made to validate a point by suggesting that "everyone else believes this"* (bandwagon appeal).

This technique is merely an attempt to evade discussing the issue itself. We are especially familiar with this tactic in advertising. "Discriminating men use

POW! cologne." If they are "discriminating men" (like me, of course), POW! must be good. Right? Wrong. Whether POW! is good or bad hasn't even been addressed.

8. *An attack is made* on a person's character *rather than on his or her argument* (argument *ad hominem,* "to the man").

"Professor Goldsworthy can't be a good psychology teacher because she's divorced." This claim is invalid because, in itself, Professor Goldsworthy's marital status has nothing to do with her ability to teach her psychology classes.

9. *Something is* presented as truth *that is supposed to be proven by argument* (begging the question).

When a writer tries to get something from nothing (like a beggar), such as merely asserting something and giving no argument for facts that first must be argued, the writer is using an invalid presentation. In the statement, "All useless city property, such as the building on the corner of 9th and Oak, should be sold," the writer has already decided that the building is useless but has not taken responsibility for proving the point.

10. *A statement is used as proof that simply* repeats *in different words what a writer is trying to prove* (circular thinking).

"There aren't enough seats in the auditorium because there are too many students." Really—.

11. *The writer implies that because one event follows another in time, the first event* caused *the second (post hoc ergo propter hoc).*

This Latin phrase means "after this, therefore because of this." Occasionally we are fooled and mistake a *time* connection for a *direct-cause* connection. Lending your car to your roommate did not cause your water pump to quit; lending the car merely preceded the failure in time. If you had been driving your car at that time, the pump would still have given out. Rely heavily on your common sense.

12. *An abstract concept is used as if it were concrete reality* (hypostatization).

Be very cautious if a writer uses statements like "Sociology shows us ...," "Literature illustrates ...," or "Science proves ...." The suggestion here is that each of these abstractions speaks with one voice, and that it agrees with the argument the writer is making. On the contrary, sociology, literature, and science hold varied opinions, often with much disagreement.

Errors in reasoning take many forms, but these are the ones you are most likely to run into. They should give you a good idea of what to watch out for.

Writing to Comprehend

1. These twelve common fallacies are always interesting to study becaus each of us can think of so many examples. See if you can think up your own examples for each of the twelve. Write them down so that they can be shared with the rest of the class. If time permits, read your examples to the class and let them identify each fallacy.

   a. ....

   ....

   b. ....

   ....

   c. ....

   ....

   d. ....

   ....

   e. ....

   ....

   f. ....

   ....

   g. ....

   ....

   h. ....

   ....

   i. ....

   ....

   j. ....

   ....

   k. ....

   ....

1. ....

....

2. Why is common sense so necessary in **recognizing invalid arguments**?

....

....

....

....

....

What Are Your Thoughts?

1. When does an argument become a *valid* argument?

....

....

....

2. In this chapter we identify twelve common fallacies that invalidate arguments. Which are most often used by your friends when they talk with you? Which are commonly used in the things you read—including tabloids? Are the fallacies that you and your friends use the same ones used by the writers whose work you come in contact with? Why or why not?

....

....

....

3. Can you recognize invalid arguments even if you never receive training in spotting them? How?

....

....

....

4. Outside of this class, when will this comprehension skill be useful?

```
...........................................................................................
...........................................................................................
...........................................................................................
```

An Important Bit of Advice

When it comes to valid or invalid arguments, you really have only two choices; treat the argument (and any test questions) as you would a true-false question. Is it true, or is it false?

Recognizing-Valid-Arguments Margin Mark ∧

The margin mark that indicates an invalid argument is an inverted V. No need to attempt to spot and mark valid arguments; just mark the invalid ones.

Words to Read by

Locate these words in the reading passages on the pages indicated. On the lines following, suggest a definition for each word as it was used in the passage. If you cannot come up with a definition based on the context and use of a word, look it up in the dictionary and write the dictionary definition on the lines. Be ready to discuss how you arrive at your definition for each word.

1. trafficking (282) ....
....

2. nitwit (283) ....
....

3. representative (283) ....
....

4. deterrent (284) ....
....

5. prohibit (285) ....
....

6. screening (284) ....

....

7. pricey (288) ....

....

8. deadbeat (289) ....

....

9. sex appeal (288) ....

....

10. discriminating (288) ....

....

Compare your definitions with those at the end of the chapter.

Practice Exercises

EXERCISE 1

Circle the letter for the correct answer. Remember, you are really being asked if what is said is true or false. The first one is done for you.

1. I visited Portland last year for two weeks and it rained every day. I could never live in a city where it rains every day.

Is the argument logically valid or invalid?
a. valid   (b.) invalid

2. Eight city police officers were arrested for trafficking in cocaine. The whole police department is corrupt from top to bottom.

Is the argument logically valid or invalid?
a. valid   b. invalid

3. Some students should take an extra course each semester so that they can graduate early.

Is the argument logically valid or invalid?
a. valid   b. invalid

4. Every student should take an extra course each semester in order to graduate early.

Is the argument logically valid or invalid?

a. valid   b. invalid

5. Whenever I don't get caught in a traffic jam on the way to work, I know it will be a great day.

Is the argument logically valid or invalid?

a. valid   b. invalid

6. The members of the city council are all nitwits and fools who can't even keep awake during the meeting. Most of the time they appear to be drunk or stoned.

Is the argument logically valid or invalid?

a. valid   b. invalid

7. Because she got such low grades on her exams she is in danger of failing the course.

Is the argument logically valid or invalid?

a. valid   b. invalid

8. Because he got such low grades on his exam he will either have to drop the course or fail it.

Is the argument logically valid or invalid?

a. valid   b. invalid

9. Colonel Ron Nelson, the nation's original "Top Gun," says that we should reelect Senator Smith. "He is my kind of elected representative," he said in an interview.

Is the argument logically valid or invalid?

a. valid   b. invalid

10. Question: What is your telephone number?

   Answer: It is impossible to get through at our house. My sister is on the phone all the time. And so is my mother.

Is the argument logically valid or invalid?

a. valid   b. invalid

EXERCISE 2

In these passages circle the correct answer and then on the line following indicate the name of the fallacy that makes the statement invalid. Select your fallacy name from the list. If you do not remember what each means, turn back to pages 276–278 and quickly review.

    a. not a logical result (*non sequitur*)
    b. an irrelevant point ("red herring")
    c. appeal to emotions (argument *ad populem*)
    d. an extended comparison (faulty analogy)
    e. only two sides (either/or)
    f. insufficient or unrepresentative evidence (hasty generalization)
    g. everyone else thinks or does it (bandwagon appeal)
    h. character attack (argument *ad hominem*)
    i. presented as truth (begging the question)
    j. repeats in different words (circular thinking)
    k. it follows, therefore it caused (*post hoc ergo propter hoc*)
    l. abstract is concrete (hypostatization)

The first one is done for you.

1. The death penalty is an effective deterrent to crime because people will stop and think about what might happen to them if they commit a crime.

   Is the argument logically valid or invalid?
   a. valid   (b.) invalid

   a. not a logical result (non sequitur)

2. He must start eating differently or prepare to die at an early age.

   Is the argument logically valid or invalid?
   a. valid   b. invalid

   ....

3. President Reagan was one of the presidents who made effective use of radio and television.

   Is the argument logically valid or invalid?
   a. valid   b. invalid

   ....

4. He would make a great treasurer for our rock-climbers club. He has attended all the meetings and has been on three of our trips.

   Is the argument logically valid or invalid?
   a. valid   b. invalid

   ....

5. Overly large kindergarten classes cause a problem in education because too many children are in these classes.

Is the argument logically valid or invalid?

a. valid   b. invalid

....

6.   There are reasons for the laws that prohibit children from attending public screening of pornographic movies.

Is the argument logically valid or invalid?

a. valid   b. invalid

....

7.   I know I don't deserve to pass this course, but I've been sick, my car broke down, and my father had a heart attack.

Is the argument logically valid or invalid?

a. valid   b. invalid

....

8.   If you can't come up with some good reasons why I'm wrong, that proves I'm right.

Is the argument logically valid or invalid?

a. valid   b. invalid

....

9.   My wife and my daughter are the two sweetest people I know. Women are much more considerate than men.

Is the argument logically valid or invalid?

a. valid   b. invalid

....

10.   I take drugs because all my friends do, and they got me started.

Is the argument logically valid or invalid?

a. valid   b. invalid

....

11.   Women are working as capable and efficient firefighters in many American cities.

Is the argument logically valid or invalid?

a. valid   b. invalid

....

12. Former President Ronald Reagan should be considered an excellent president. President Nixon was not only a poor president, he was a criminal.

Is the argument logically valid or invalid?

a. valid   b. invalid

....

13. The best pizza in the world is made in Boston because of the strong Italian community there. All the food cooked by Italians is great.

Is the argument logically valid or invalid?

a. valid   b. invalid

....

14. All the Civil Liberties Union does is protect Nazis, perverts, child molesters, and communists.

Is the argument logically valid or invalid?

a. valid   b. invalid

....

15. Some of Mohammed's teachings were not original; they had been around for centuries.

Is the argument logically valid or invalid?

a. valid   b. invalid

....

16. Science shows us that improved quality of life comes through research and invention.

Is the argument logically valid or invalid?

a. valid   b. invalid

....

17. Last week I had to buy new tires. This week my brakes had to be replaced. Next week I'm sure something else will go wrong.

Is the argument logically valid or invalid?

a. valid   b. invalid

....

18. All deadly weapons designed for killing people, such as handguns, should be prohibited from being sold.

Is the argument logically valid or invalid?

a. valid   b. invalid

···

19.   Everyone we know has a microwave oven. We shouldn't be the only ones who don't own one.

Is the argument logically valid or invalid?
a. valid   b. invalid

···

20.   Reverend Johnson can't be a good minister. I saw him buying a bottle of wine in the grocery store.

Is the argument logically valid or invalid?
a. valid   b. invalid

···

EXERCISE 3

In this exercise you are asked to determine if an argument is invalid and, if it is, to rewrite it so that it is valid. The first one is done for you.

1.   Everyone worried about unemployment in the future will support me in the coming election.

If the argument is invalid, rewrite it here so that it is valid.

People worried about unemployment in the future will want to consider my position on unemployment and think about voting for me in the coming election.

2.   I enjoy going to the dentist because he is handsome and always treats me courteously.

If the argument is invalid, rewrite it here so that it is valid.

···
···
···

3.   A vacation in the Virgin Islands is the good life.

If the argument is invalid, rewrite it here so that it is valid.

···

....

....

4. This is the only sports car in today's market with power, economy, great handling, and sex appeal that is also affordable.

If the argument is invalid, rewrite it here so that it is valid.

....

....

....

5. A golf pro and a tennis pro both own condos here—you should, too.

If the argument is invalid, rewrite it here so that it is valid.

....

....

....

6. Discriminating beer drinkers always choose this beer.

If the argument is invalid, rewrite it here so that it is valid.

....

....

....

7. Animal lovers who *really* love animals always get their pets from the animal shelter, never from pricey pet stores.

If the argument is invalid, rewrite it here so that it is valid.

....

....

....

8. We should give to the poor all the clothing which we don't wear regularly or which is out of fashion, such as most of the skirts in your closet.

If the argument is invalid, rewrite it here so that it is valid.

....

....

....

9. The restaurant business seems to attract criminals and deadbeats who rip off owners regularly.

   If the argument is invalid, rewrite it here so that it is valid.

   ....

   ....

   ....

10. Losing weight is an easy task for any person who has character and determination, and who is willing to move beyond the needs of the flesh.

    If the argument is invalid, rewrite it here so that it is valid.

    ....

    ....

    ....

Answers to Selected Exercises

WORDS TO READ BY

Definitions will vary.

1. trafficking: carrying on trade
2. nitwit: a stupid or silly person
3. representative: a typical example
4. deterrent: something that deters or restrains
5. prohibit: to forbid or prevent by authority
6. screening: showing films
7. pricey: fashionably expensive
8. deadbeat: one who does not pay his debts
9. sex appeal: quality of looking attractive to another person
10. discriminating: fastidiously selective

EXERCISE 2

1b. a. not a logical result (*non sequitur*)
2b. e. only two sides (either/or)
3a.   (valid)
4b. a. not a logical result (*non sequitur*)
5b. j. repeats in different words (circular thinking)
6a.   (valid)
7b. c. appeal to emotions (argument *ad populum*)
8b. e. only two sides (either/or)

  9b. f. insufficient evidence (hasty generalization)
10b. g. everyone else does it (bandwagon appeal)
11a.   (valid)
12b. b. an irrelevant point ("red herring")
13b. d. an extended comparison (faulty analogy)
14b. h. character attack (argument *ad hominem*)
15a.   (valid)
16b. l. abstract is concrete (hypostatization)
17b. k. it follows, therefore it caused (*post hoc ergo propter hoc*)
18b. i. presented as truth (begging the question)
19b. g. everyone else does it (bandwagon appeal)
20b. h. character attack (argument *ad hominem*)

Chapter 13

Drawing Logical Inferences and Conclusions

Life [and reading] is the art of drawing sufficient conclusions from insufficient premises.

—Samuel Butler

I am no athlete—but at one sport I used to be an expert. It was a dangerous game called "jumping to conclusions."

—Eddie Cantor

This chapter will help you to:

1. read between the lines.
2. see that drawing logical inferences is not as tough as it may sound.
3. recognize why writers use inference.

You have learned how to read the ideas stated on the printed page and determine the author's literal meaning, but not all meaning is clearly stated. Most authors expect readers to *draw inferences* to get a clearer understanding of their meaning.

All writing holds information that is clearly stated ("He was hot.") and material which is not specifically stated but which is still there in *implied* form ("He was dripping with sweat."). You can answer questions about stated information by simply recalling or locating the words in the passage where the author addresses the subject and refreshing your memory about it. *Implied* information, however, is information that is not directly stated but is only *suggested* or *hinted* at by the writer's choice of words. *When you use the information collected in a passage to come to a conclusion about additional facts and information that are not specifically stated, you are drawing logical inferences.*

Reading Between the Lines

One of the skills that efficient readers strive for is drawing logical inferences and conclusions, and determining the meaning in a phrase, sentence, or idea when not all the information is clearly stated. Authors don't always use devices such as topic sentences to clearly express their main ideas. Often they expect you to infer important ideas as well as minor details. Skillful readers develop the ability (mostly it's just a heightened sensitivity to ideas being stated) to put facts and information together in such a way—"reading between the lines"—as to lead to logical conclusions. Readers add their own knowledge and understanding to the facts and ideas stated by the writer. When readers combine all this information they are able to infer or *conclude* about material they are reading.

It's Not as Tough as It Sounds

Drawing inferences from your reading is less difficult than it may sound to you at the moment. In fact, it is really quite simple because you are already highly skilled at it. All your life you are daily drawing conclusions about people you meet, things that are said to you by friends—and enemies, and things that you see and hear in the media. You don't even think about it, but you are coming to conclusions about these people and ideas without having specific facts to back up your conclusions. You just do it. Often you may infer something about a person by simply glancing at that person. You might get a "feeling," an inference, from conversation—how someone said something, or didn't say something. You may conclude something about someone by thinking over a person's actions, character, or moods. All these thoughts, feelings, and facts are combined with everything you already know from experience and from making logical associations, and then are analyzed—most often instantly—and you come to a conclusion. You have inferred ideas that you believe are correct and factual.

Why Is Skill at Inference
Necessary in Reading?

Often the author "doesn't come right out and say it," and so you the reader must be willing and able to identify correctly the message the author is presenting. But why don't writers just say what they want to say, clearly and plainly? They have several reasons.

1. Writers usually cannot (often because of limited space) include all the infor-

mation that might be relevant to their purposes. Thus, they must rely on the reader's ability to infer.

2. Writers sometimes leave out information because including it would divert the reader's attention from the essential point being made or from the train of thought.
3. Writers sometimes leave out information because they reasonably assume their readers are already familiar with it.
4. Writers often rely on inference to create or sustain emotional power and artistic value. This technique is often applied in creative writing such as poetry or fiction. Leaving something unstated often creates humor, fear, irony, or a climax when the reader has to infer a point or draw a conclusion.
5. Writers sometimes leave out information they don't want the reader to know when they want to present a one-sided argument, hoping that the reader will not be aware of the facts left out. This is questionable writing at worst, editorial writing at best. Be aware of calculated evasions.
6. Writers sometimes must trust the reader's inferential skills because including specific information may be illegal or dangerous (in some countries), or it may leave the writer open to a lawsuit.

These reasons, and many others, mean that readers must constantly be aware that they need to exercise inference.

Inference Questions to Ask

Ask these two questions about all the reading you do.

1. What can I conclude from the ideas the writer stated?
2. What *feeling* do I get about what the author said?

Logical-Inference Margin Mark

We need no margin mark for inferences, because if something is inferred it is not written.

Writing to Comprehend

1. How would you explain the phrase, "read between the lines," and how i is accomplished, to a student newly arrived from another country who had never heard the expression?

....

....

....

....

....

2. Think about the subject of inference for a few minutes and then write a brief opinion paragraph about its place as an important (or unimportant) skill in reading comprehension for college students.

....

....

....

....

....

3. It has been suggested that the three levels of reading comprehension are:

a. reading the lines,
b. reading between the lines, and
c. reading beyond the lines.

What does each of these three levels mean?

....

....

....

....

....

What Are Your Thoughts?

1. What is a "logical inference" and how do you arrive at it?

....

....

....

2. Several reasons were given for writers' leaving out information and thu requiring the reader to infer something. Which seems textbook authors' major reason for relying on inference? Why do you think that? What does that cause you to conclude about your textbooks?

....

....

....

3. Does gaining skill at inferring correctly when you read benefit you when you are not reading? When? Where? How?

....

....

....

4. Which skill in reading comprehension in this textbook did you most benefit from this semester? In what way?

....

....

....

Words to Read by

Answer these questions by looking up the key word from each sentence in your dictionary. The page numbers in parentheses indicate the passages that include each key word. You may wish to read that key word in its context. Write the answer on the lines provided. How do you determine which words to look up?

1. Why is *intervention* not always appreciated? (301)

....

2. If you are *vanquished,* have you won or lost? (301)

....

3. How certain is a *dubious* theory? (301)

....

4. What do you do when you *initiate* plans? (302)

5. What does *indeterminate dimension* mean? (302)

....

6. An *incursion* usually means what? (302)

....

7. What does *critical* mean in this passage? (302)

....

8. What are the *dregs*? (303)

....

9. What does *NIMBY* mean? (304)

....

10. Can a train be *shunted*? (304)

....

11. Name one or more television *temptresses*. (305)

....

12. Does *preliterate* mean you can or cannot read? (305)

....

13. What does *prototype* mean? (305)

....

14. From what language does *accelerate* come? (306)

....

15. Are there *vocational programs* that don't require specialized training? (306)

....

Compare your answers with those at the end of this chapter.

Anticipate the Topics

These are the topics in the reading passages used in the exercises in this chapter. Anticipate the content in these passages by writing a main-idea sentence for each of the topics. After you have finished the exercises, come back to these main-idea sentences and see how close you were to guessing the content in the passages correctly. How have these Anticipate-the-Topics activities affected your comprehension?

Reconstruction ....

Little Red Riding Hood ....

fat ....

business failure ....

army ....

fake IDs ....

AIDS ....

waste ....

geography ....

women ....

B-1 bomber ....

racetrack ....

accelerated educational program ....

Practice Exercises

EXERCISE 1

Circle the letter for the inference that appears to be most reasonable and logical from the information given. The first one is done for you.

1. That lady always sits in the very first row whenever she comes to the movies.
   a. The lady can't hear very well.
   b. The lady can't see very well.
   c. The lady feels comfortable in the front row.
   d. The lady doesn't like the crowd toward the rear.

The correct answer is *C*. From the little information we are given, we can only infer that for some reason the lady feels comfortable up front. The other answer choices would require us to have more information about *why* she sits up front.

297

2. A man walked out of a hardware store carrying a *For Sale* sign.
   a. He is for sale.
   b. The store is for sale.
   c. The man's house is for sale.
   d. The man has purchased a *For Sale* sign.

3. Inside the abandoned house were sleeping bags, potato-chip bags, and soft-drink cans.
   a. Some people were staying there, at least briefly.
   b. Kids were partying there.
   c. Vagrants were living there.
   d. The people who abandoned the house didn't take all their things.

4. Snow is on the roads and lawn but not on the sidewalk.
   a. The sidewalk was shoveled.
   b. The snow fell in a weird pattern.
   c. The sidewalk is heated by under-the-surface heaters.
   d. The snow always melts faster on hard surfaces.

5. Three soldiers in uniform were walking along at the side of the road.
   a. We have been invaded and are at war.
   b. Three soldiers were going somewhere.
   c. The soldiers were lost.
   d. The soldiers were probably absent without leave.

6. A sign in the window of a dormitory says, "Save the whales: date a fat chick."
   a. A "fat chick" lives there.
   b. A guy who dates overweight girls lives there.
   c. Someone is trying to be funny.
   d. The owner of the sign loves whales.

7. My neighbor enjoys possum and squirrel hunting.
   a. The neighbor enjoys hunting.
   b. The neighbor hates possums and squirrels.
   c. The neighbor needs the food.
   d. The neighbor likes the taste of possum and squirrel.

8. Three really beautiful young women were sunbathing nude on a deserted stretch of beach.
   a. The women were trying to attract men.
   b. The women enjoy nude sunbathing.
   c. Only beautiful women are brave enough to sunbathe nude.
   d. The women were violating the law.

9. My roommate got home at 4:30 A.M.
   a. He had a really "hot" date.
   b. His car broke down.
   c. Something kept him out late.
   d. He enjoys coming home very late.

10. My grandmother always sits in a rocking chair.
    a. She enjoys the rocking chair.
    b. It is the only chair available.
    c. It is the only chair big enough for her.
    d. It is in the right location so that she can see television easily.

EXERCISE 2

Circle the letter for the inference that appears most logical. On the lines following the answers, briefly explain the reason for your choice. The first one is done for you.

1. The plants on the patio are all dying.
   a. They were killed by the frost.
   b. They didn't get enough water.
   c. They got too much sun.
   d. They were not cared for properly.

   The plants are dead. Someone didn't provide what they needed to live.

2. The interior of the apartment was a mess; clutter was everywhere.
   a. The apartment was vandalized.
   b. The residents like living in a messy apartment.
   c. The apartment was a mess for some reason.
   d. The people who live there have children and pets.

   ....

   ....

3. The walls in his office were covered with paintings of sailing ships.
   a. He likes paintings of sailing ships.
   b. He is a painter of sailing ships.
   c. He is a sailor.
   d. He is a yacht broker.

   ....

299

....

4. He uses a manual typewriter to type his manuscript.
   a. He doesn't own an electric typewriter.
   b. He is comfortable typing with a manual typewriter.
   c. He doesn't have electricity.
   d. He can't afford an electric typewriter.

....

....

5. A lady with a gallon of wine walked out of a liquor store at 8:00 A.M.
   a. She has been partying all night.
   b. She has to bring the wine to a party at work.
   c. The lady has a drinking problem.
   d. It was a convenient time to go to the liquor store.

....

....

6. Pieces of a surfboard washed up on my beach the other day.
   a. A surfboard got smashed up somehow.
   b. "Jaws" is at it again.
   c. A surfer has probably drowned.
   d. The waves must have been enormous recently.

....

....

7. A man carrying a violin case and a brown paper bag rushed out of the bank and hurried down the street.
   a. The bank had just been held up.
   b. A musician with a bag lunch was in a hurry.
   c. A man with a violin case and a paper bag was in a hurry.
   d. The man had just deposited money on the way to work.

....

....

8. The car ahead of me had an auto-rental sticker on its bumper and rear window.
   a. A tourist was driving the car.
   b. The car probably was a rental car.
   c. The driver was probably returning the rental car.
   d. There must be a special rate this week on rental cars.

....

....

9. The woman in the grocery store had a cart loaded with baby food.
   a. She probably has a baby.
   b. She likes the taste of baby food.
   c. She is stocking up on baby food so that she will not have to go to the store for several weeks.
   d. She is a store employee stocking the shelves.

....

....

10. The two college professors wore corduroy jackets and smoked pipes.
    a. The professors were identical twins.
    b. Most professors dress in corduroy and smoke pipes.
    c. These two professors happened to dress similarly and smoke pipes.
    d. Casual style is in this year for college professors.

....

....

EXERCISE 3

Which *two* of these statements for each passage would the writer of the passage support? Circle the two letters for the correct inferences. Be ready to discuss your choices. The first one is done for you.

1. Many white Southerners regarded Reconstruction as a more grievous wound than the war itself. It left an angry scar that would take generations to heal. They resented the upending of their social and racial system, the humiliation of being ruled by blacks, and the insult of federal intervention in their local affairs. Yet few rebellions have ended with the victors sitting down to a love feast with the vanquished. Given the explosiveness of the issues that had caused the war, and the bitterness of the fighting, the wonder is that Reconstruction was not far harsher than it was.
   —From Bailey and Kennedy, *The American Pageant.*

   a. All white Southerners hated Northerners and blacks.
   b. The anger of the white Southerners would not easily disappear.
   c. Southern whites would forget the problems quickly.
   d. The Reconstruction period was very difficult for white Southerners.

2. A dubious theory, if you ask me. A lot of good I'd be for either fighting *or* fleeing. Picture yourself, coming at your enemy squeaking and gibbering.

Or attempting to flee him on legs made of Playdough, all the while yodeling dryly.

—From Newman, *Communicating in Business Today.*

a. The person writing pictures himself more as a lover than a fighter.
b. The person writing probably would not make a good choice for group spokes-man.
c. "Squeaking and gibbering" and "yodeling" are all good forms of defense.
d. Self-confidence isn't oozing from the writer now, but eventually will be.

3. Once upon a point in time, a small person named Little Red Riding Hood initiated plans for the preparation, delivery and transportation of foodstuffs to her grandmother, a senior citizen residing at a place of residence in a forest of indeterminate dimension.

In the process of implementing this program, her incursion into the forest was in mid-transportation process when it attained interface with an alleged perpetrator. The individual, a wolf, made inquiry as to the whereabouts of Little Red Riding Hood's goal as well as inferring that he was desirous of ascertaining the contents of Little Red Riding Hood's food basket, and all that.

—From Newman, *Communicating in Business Today.*

a. The storyteller has a purpose other than entertainment.
b. This story is likely to impress older children.
c. Parents will enjoy telling this story to their children.
d. This story isn't being told to small children.

4. Did you know that the fats in our bodies, which we try so hard to get rid of through exercising and surgery, have a function? That the fat cells fight and never die? That exercising is better than dieting? That 70 percent of your calories are burned while you rest?

—Source unknown.

a. Fat is increasingly harmful to your health as you age.
b. There is more to fat than meets the eye (pun sort of intended).
c. Understanding our bodies is important for good health.
d. The more you rest, the faster your calories will be burned off.

5. Another cause of business failure is lack of capital. Typically, owners of small businesses start out using all their own savings and borrowing as much as they can; still they often have too little money to carry them through the first critical year, when sales are likely to be small. Banks are not eager to lend money to new and unproved firms. When they do, interest rates are likely to be high. Suppliers are seldom willing to advance much merchandise or raw materials until good credit ratings have been built.

—From Gordon and Dawson, *Introductory Economics.*

    a. Play it safe and don't go into business.
    b. Running your own business is a risky business at best.
    c. You can never have enough capital reserves.
    d. Borrowing as much as possible is a good way to protect your new business from failure.

6. I went into the Army like a lot of people do—a young scared kid of 17 told he should join the Army to get off probation for minor crimes. At the time the Army sounded real fine: three meals, rent-free home, adventure and *you would come out a man.* (It's amazing how many parents put this trip on their kids.)

    In basic training I met the dregs of the Army. (Who else would be given such an unimportant job as training "dumb shit kids"?) These instructors were constantly making jokes such as "don't bend over in the shower" and encouraging the supermasculine image....

    —From Hyde, *Half the Human Experience: The Psychology of Women.*

    a. The army was not a pleasant experience.
    b. Parents don't really know what effect the army has on their kids.
    c. Being a "man" means to be tough and hard.
    d. A way to become a "man" is to go through the experience of being in the army.

7. *On Guard For Fake IDs.* The surge of fake identification (ID) among college students has prompted the South Carolina Department of Highway and Public Transportation (SCDHPT) and businesses to clamp down on their ID policies, said Kenneth Reed, special investigator for the SCDHPT. Methods to deter fake IDs include cameras that take pictures of people requesting new drivers licenses, clerk training programs and fines of up to $2,500. Wendel Guyton, manager of Crazy Jacks, said his club has taken more than 30 fake IDs during one weekend. One USC fake ID user said, "I have one because I figure if I can be sent to some god-forsaken land or be executed in the chair and vote for a politician who can pass such laws, then why can't I drink?"

    —Lisa Pyle, *The Gamecock,* University of South Carolina.

    a. The penalties for using fake IDs are going to get more severe.
    b. The penalties for using fake IDs are going to get easier.
    c. It is getting increasingly difficult to use a fake ID.
    d. It is getting easier to use a fake ID.

8. *AIDS Decline Forecast.* The annual number of AIDS cases in the U.S. will decrease in the 1990s according to a mathematical model designed by a visiting mathematics professor at Clemson U., S.C. Professor Marc Artzrouini, who based his model on statistics from the Centers for Disease Control, said, "The annual number of new AIDS cases in the U.S. will reach a maximum of 20,000 to 30,000 during the early 1990s and decline slowly thereafter." Artzrouini believes the decline will occur because he feels the AIDS virus has been contained to two high-risk groups—homosexual/bisexual men and intravenous drug users—and people are changing their behavior. However, Artzrouini said that reporting delays and the number of unreported cases could change the projected statistics by 10 to 20 percent.

—Amy George, *The Tiger,* Clemson University, South Carolina.

a. AIDS will decline because a cure will be found.
b. We can stop worrying so much about the spread of AIDS.
c. High-risk groups will still be in grave danger of contracting AIDS.
d. Drug usage will not decrease because of AIDS.

9. Estimates are that the world's industries produce 400 million tons of waste each year, 60 percent of which comes from the United States. And as the NIMBY ("Not In My Back Yard") movement spreads here and in Western Europe, more and more of it is being shunted off to poor countries which desperately need hard currency.

—Source unknown.

a. Other countries don't mind disposing of our industrial wastes.
b. Poor countries will continue to act as waste dumping grounds until those countries become economically sound.
c. It is better to dump our waste in other countries than in our own.
d. The waste in our country will continue to increase in the next few years.

10. For years we've heard that Johnny can't read. According to a recent international survey by the National Geographic Society, it seems that Johnny also has no idea where he is.

The society tested the geographical knowledge of 10,280 people, including 1,116 Americans. Adults in the United States tied for sixth place with Great Britain; only Italy and Mexico scored lower. Americans between the ages of 18-24 were more geographically ignorant than any other group in the survey.

—Source unknown.

a. People don't like geography.
b. We should stop teaching geography because no one learns it anyway.
c. We are teaching less geography in our schools.
d. There is less demand (need) to know geography nowadays.

EXERCISE 4

In these passages many facts can be inferred. For each passage suggest three inferences or conclusions that come to mind.

1. In the fourth century A.D. the Christian church (now Rome's official religion) insisted that women were temptresses who threatened men's spirituality. As late as the ninth century, serious debate arose over whether women had souls. Early medieval clergy blamed such ailments as impotence and loss of memory on women. These conditions were viewed as being caused by the devil and his allies, female witches (an attitude that is still widespread among preliterate and preindustrial peoples throughout the world).

    —From Allgeier and Allgeier, *Sexual Interactions*.

    a. ....

    b. ....

    c. ....

2. Robert J. Havinghurst and David U. Levine point out that in 1970 almost 90 percent of children from upper- and upper-middle-class families entered college, while fewer than 20 percent of children from lower-working-class families did.

    —From Mendoza and Napoli, *Systems of Society: An Introduction to Social Sciences*.

    a. ....

    b. ....

    c. ....

3. The supersonic B-1 bomber is now in the prototype stage. It can fly twice the speed of sound and can carry two and a half times the bomb load of the B-52 it is supposed to replace (about 100 megatons). The Air Force wants 540 of them, but the need for the B-1 is still being debated. We also have the "cruise" missile, which can fly at low enough altitudes to evade detection by enemy radar; it is a jet-powered, unmanned aircraft that can travel for thousands of miles and hit a target within ten yards.

    —From Mendoza and Napoli, *Systems of Society: An Introduction to Social Sciences*.

    a. ....

    b. ....

    c. ....

4. The setting is a racetrack. It is five minutes before the start of the seventh race. Your problem is to figure out which horse will win the race. You have

studied the racing form carefully and have determined that Dangerous Dan has better breeding, has posted faster workouts, and has performed better in past races than the other horses entered in the seventh race. You infer that a horse which has done all of those things should win the race; therefore, your logic tells you that Dangerous Dan will win. Furthermore, the last time you were at the racetrack, you bet on Dangerous Dan, and he won. Since you know he is a winner, you want to bet on him again. But suddenly you have a brilliant flash of insight, a hunch, that tells you that Rambling Ralph will be the winner.

> —From Mendoza and Napoli, *Systems of Society: An Introduction to Social Sciences.*

    a. ....

    b. ....

    c. ....

5. Since there are variations among students in their school performance and in their potential to excel academically, not all students pursue the same course of academic training. Some students are considered brighter than others and are placed in an accelerated educational program where they are challenged to study increasingly complex subjects that will prepare them for further education in college. Others are placed in a slower-paced academic program or in a vocational program which prepares them for the world of work.

> —From Zigler and Finn-Stevenson, *Children: Development and Social Issues.*

    a. ....

    b. ....

    c. ....

EXERCISE 5

This is an excerpt from John Updike's short story, "A&P." Read the passage and then, as if you were the instructor in the class, prepare a multiple-choice test on the passage with questions similar to those you have been answering in this textbook. Create one question for as many of these skills in reading comprehension as you are able.

1. recognizing the main idea
2. identifying supporting details
3. determining word meaning from context

4. recognizing the author's purpose
5. identifying the overall pattern of organization
6. distinguishing between statements of fact and statements of opinion
7. detecting bias
8. recognizing the author's tone
9. recognizing relationships within sentences
10. recognizing relationships between sentences
11. recognizing valid arguments
12. drawing logical inferences and conclusions

Make these questions as fair as you can, at the same time being sure to create questions that are clear. After you write your questions, be ready to answer in class the analysis questions that follow.

A & P

Now here comes the sad part of the story, at least my family says it's sad, but I don't think it's so sad myself. The store's pretty empty, it being Thursday afternoon, so there was nothing much to do except lean on the register and wait for the girls to show up again. The whole store was like a pinball machine and I didn't know which tunnel they'd come out of. After a while they come around out of the far aisle, around the light bulbs, records at discount of the Caribbean Six or Tony Martin Sings or some such gunk you wonder they waste the wax on, sixpacks of candy bars, and plastic toys done up in cellophane that fall apart when a kid looks at them anyway. Around they come, Queenie still leading the way, and holding a little gray jar in her hand. Slots Three through Seven are unmanned and I could see her wondering between Stokes and me, but Stokesie with his usual luck draws an old party in baggy gray pants who stumbles up with four giant cans of pineapple juice (what do these bums *do* with all that pineapple juice? I've often asked myself) so the girls come to me. Queenie puts down the jar and I take it into my fingers icy cold. Kingfish Fancy Herring Snacks in Pure Sour Cream: 49¢. Now her hands are empty, not a ring or a bracelet, bare as God made them, and I wonder where the money's coming from. Still with that prim look she lifts a folded dollar bill out of the hollow at the center of her nubbled pink top. The jar went heavy in my hand. Really, I thought that was so cute.

Then everybody's luck begins to run out. Lengel comes in from haggling with a truck full of cabbages on the lot and is about to scuttle into that door marked MANAGER behind which he hides all day when the girls touch his eye. Lengel's pretty dreary, teaches Sunday school and the rest, but he doesn't miss that much. He comes over and says, "Girls, this isn't the beach."

Queenie blushes, though maybe it's just a brush of sunburn I was noticing for the first time, now that she was so close. "My mother asked me to pick up a jar of herring snacks." Her voice kind of startled me, the way voices do when you see the people first, coming out so flat and dumb yet kind of tony, too, the way it ticked over "pick up" and "snacks." All of a sudden I slid right down her voice into her living room. Her father and the other men were standing around in ice-cream coats and bow ties and the women were in sandals picking up herring snacks on toothpicks off a big glass plate and they were all holding drinks the color of water with olives and sprigs of mint in them. When my parents have somebody over they get lemonade and if it's a real racy affair Schlitz in tall glasses with "They'll do It Every Time" cartoons stenciled on.

"That's all right," Lengel said. "But this isn't the beach." His repeating this struck me as funny, as if it had just occurred to him, and he had been thinking all these years the A & P was a great big dune and he was the head lifeguard. He didn't like my smiling—as I say he doesn't miss much—but he concentrates on giving the girls that sad Sunday-school-superintendent stare.

Queenie's blush is no sunburn now, and the plump one in plaid, that I liked better from the back—a really sweet can—pipes up, "We weren't doing any shopping. We just came in for the one thing."

"That makes no difference," Lengel tells her, and I could see from the way his eyes went that he hadn't noticed she was wearing a two-piece before. "We want you decently dressed when you come in here."

"We *are* decent," Queenie says suddenly, her lower lip pushing, getting sore now that she remembers her place, a place from which the crowd that runs the A & P must look pretty crummy. Fancy Herring Snacks flashed in her very blue eyes.

"Girls, I don't want to argue with you. After this come in here with your shoulders covered. It's our policy." He turns his back. That's policy for you. Policy is what the kingpins want. What the others want is juvenile delinquency.

All this while, the customers had been showing up with their carts but, you know, sheep, seeing a scene, they had all bunched up on Stokesie, who shook open a paper bag as gently as peeling a peach, not wanting to miss a word. I could feel in the silence everybody getting nervous, most of all Lengel, who asks me, "Sammy, have you rung up their purchase?"

I thought and said "No" but it wasn't about that I was thinking. I go through the punches, 4, 9, GROC, TOT—it's more complicated than you think, and after you do it often enough, it begins to make a little song, that you hear words to, in my case "Hello (*bing*) there, you (*gung*) hap-py *pee*-pul (*splat*)!"—the *splat* being the drawer flying out. I uncrease the bill, tenderly as you may imagine, it just having come from between the two smoothest scoops of vanilla I had ever known were there, and pass a half and a penny into her narrow pink palm, and nestle the herrings in a bag and twist its neck and hand it over, all the time thinking.

The girls, and who'd blame them, are in a hurry to get out, so I say "I quit" to Lengel quick enough for them to hear, hoping they'll stop and watch me, their unsuspected hero. They keep right on going, into the electric eye; the door flies open and they flicker across the lot to their car, Queenie and Plaid and Big Tall Goony-Goony (not that as raw material she was so bad), leaving me with Lengel and a kink in his eyebrow.

"Did you say something, Sammy?"

"I said I quit."

"I thought you did."

"You didn't have to embarrass them."

"It was they who were embarrassing us."

I started to say something that came out as "Fiddle-do-doo." It's a saying of my grandmother's, and I know she would have been pleased.

"I don't think you know what you're saying," Lengel said.

"I know you don't," I said. "But I do." I pull the bow at the back of my apron and start shrugging it off my shoulders. A couple customers that had been heading for my slot begin to knock against each other, like scared pigs in a chute.

Lengel sighs and begins to look very patient and old and gray. He's been a friend of my parents for years. "Sammy, you don't want to do this to your Mom and Dad," he tells me. It's true, I don't. But it seems to me that once you begin a gesture it's fatal not to go through with it. I fold the apron, "Sammy" stitched in red on the pocket, and put it on the counter, and drop the bow tie on top of it. The bow tie is theirs, if you've ever wondered. "You'll feel this for the rest of your life," Lengel says, and I know that's true, too, but remembering how he made that pretty girl blush makes me so scrunchy inside I punch the No Sale tab and the machine whirs "pee-pul" and the drawer splats out. One advantage to this scene taking place in summer, I can follow this up with a clean exit, there's no fumbling around getting your coat and galoshes, I just saunter into the electric eye in my white shirt that my mother ironed the night before, and the door heaves itself open, and outside the sunshine is skating around on the asphalt.

I look around for my girls, but they're gone, of course. There wasn't anybody but some young married screaming with her children about some candy they didn't get by the door of a powder-blue Falcon station wagon. Looking back in the big windows, over the bags of peat moss and aluminum lawn furniture stacked on the pavement, I could see Lengel in my place in the slot, checking the sheep through. His face was dark gray and his back stiff, as if he'd just had an injection of iron, and my stomach kind of fell as I felt how hard the world was going to be to me hereafter.

YOUR QUESTIONS

1. ....

    a. ....   **b.** ....

    c. ....   **d.** ....

2. ....

    a. ....   **b.** ....

    c. ....   **d.** ....

3. ....

    a. ....   **b.** ....

    c. ....   **d.** ....

4. ....

    a. ....   **b.** ....

    c. ....   **d.** ....

5. ....

    a. ....   **b.** ....

    c. ....   **d.** ....

6. ....

    a. ....   **b.** ....

    c. ....   **d.** ....

7. ....

    a. ....   **b.** ....

    c. ....   **d.** ....

8. ....

    a. ....   **b.** ....

    c. ....   **d.** ....

9. ....

    a. ....   **b.** ....

    c. ....   **d.** ....

10. ....
   a. ....   b. ....
   c. ....   d. ....

11. ....
   a. ....   b. ....
   c. ....   d. ....

12. ....
   a. ....   b. ....
   c. ....   d. ....

ANALYSIS

What was difficult about creating these questions?

Which was the most difficult question to create? Why was it so difficult?

What did this exercise teach you about these twelve specific reading-comprehension skills? Are you perhaps a little better able to read with increased awareness of how to answer these kinds of questions yourself, because you worked hard to create fair, clear questions?

Does creating questions give you an idea of how teachers create the questions you have to answer?

In your own words, what's the value of learning to write specific types of questions that test skill in reading comprehension?

Were some questions for this short-story portion difficult or impossible to create? Why? What does that tell you about how to analyze reading materials and texts that you are to be tested on?

Answers to Selected Exercises

WORDS TO READ BY

Answers will vary.
1. often done without permission
2. lost
3. not very
4. Think up, begin, or originate plans.
5. unknown size
6. an attack
7. requiring special care and attention

8. the least desirable
9. "not in my back yard"
10. Yes.
11. (Answers will vary.)
12. Cannot.
13. an original model
14. Latin
15. No. Vocational implies specialized training.

EXERCISE 2

1. d	2. c	3. a	4. b	5. d
6. a	7. c	8. b	9. a	10. c

EXERCISE 4

Answers will vary.

INSTRUCTIONS

Read the passages and the questions that follow each passage carefully but quickly. Circle the letter for the correct answer to each question.

PASSAGE 1

1 Women tend to smile more than men although, once again, it
2 is not clear how this difference should be interpreted. Smiling
3 has been called the female version of the "Uncle Tom shuffle"
4 —that is, rather than indicating happiness or friendliness, it
5 may serve as an appeasement gesture, communicating, in
6 effect, "please don't hit me or be nasty." Smiling seems to be a
7 part of the female role. Most women can remember having
8 their faces feel stiff and sore from smiling at a party or some
9 other public gathering at which they were expected to smile.
10 The smile, of course, did not reflect happiness, but rather a
11 belief that smiling was the appropriate thing to do. Women's
12 smiles, then, do not necessarily reflect positive feelings, and
13 may even be associated with negative feelings.
14   There is really very little research on smiling and its
15 implications for women and gender roles. There is one

313

16 interesting study, however, of smiling in interactions between
17 parents and children. When fathers were smiling they tended
18 to make more positive statements to their children, compared
19 with when they were not smiling. Mothers' statements, on
20 the other hand, were no more positive when they were smil-
21 ing than when they were not. Parents, and particularly
22 mothers, smiled more when they thought they were being
23 observed than when they thought they were not being
24 observed. This suggests that smiling is indeed part of a role
25 people play. Finally, it seemed that children had learned to
26 sort out the contradictory messages (smile accompanied by a
27 negative statement) they got from their mothers; they ig-
28 nored the smile and responded to the negative statement.

—From Hyde, *Half the Human Experience: The Psychology of Women.*

1.   The main idea in this passage is
a. The place and implications of smiling for women is a subject that needs further study.
b. Children learn to sort out contradictory messages from smiling mothers.
c. Smiles do not reflect happiness.
d. Parents, and especially mothers, smile more when they think they are being
observed.

2.   In developing this passage, the pattern of organization the author uses can be
described as
a. contrast   b. time order
c. statement and clarification   d. simple listing

3.   The author of this passage creates a tone that can be described as
a. detached   b. ambivalent
c. obsequious   d. outraged

4.   What does the sentence beginning in line 25 ("Finally, it seemed ...") do in
relation to the sentence beginning in line 15 ("There is one ...")?
a. It contradicts something that was stated beginning in line 15.
b. It indicates the order of something that was stated beginning in line 15.
c. It indicates an effect of something discussed beginning in line 15.
d. It summarizes something that was suggested beginning in line 15.

PASSAGE 2

1 My family and I recently returned from a trip to Alaska, a
2 place that combines spectacular natural beauty with a breath-
3 taking amount of tax-deductibility if you write a travel article

4 about it, which is what I'm doing. I'll start with some Facts at
5 a Glance:
6 WHERE ALASKA IS: Way the hell far from you. Beyond
7 Mars.
8 HOW YOU GET THERE: You sit in a variety of airplanes
9 for the bulk of your adult life (longer if you take a child).
10 WHAT THEY HAVE THERE THAT WILL TRY TO KILL
11 YOU: Bears. I am quite serious about this. Although Alaska
12 is now an official United State with modern conveniences
13 such as rental cars and frozen yogurt, it also contains a large
14 number of admitted bears, striding freely about the land-
15 scape, and nobody seems to be the least bit alarmed about
16 this. In fact, the Alaskans seem to be PROUD of it. You walk
17 into a hotel or department store, and the first thing you see is
18 a glass case containing a stuffed bear the size of Nigeria. Our
19 hotel had TWO of these. It was what we travel writers call "a
20 two-bear hotel." Both bears were standing on their hind legs
21 and striking a pose that said: "Welcome to Alaska! I'm going
22 to rip your arms off!"
23 This struck me as an odd concept, greeting visitors with a
24 showcase containing a major local hazard. It's as if the
25 Greater Miami Chamber of Commerce went around setting
26 up glass display cases containing stuffed cocaine smugglers,
27 with little plaques stating how much they weighed and where
28 they were taken. (Which is not such a bad idea, now that I
29 think of it.)
30 Anyway, we decided the best way to deal with our fear of
31 bears was to become well-informed about them, so we bought
32 a book, *Alaska Bear Tales*. Here are some of the chapter
33 titles, which I am not making up:
34 "They'll Attack Without Warning"
35 "They'll Really Maul You"
36 "They Will Kill"
37 "Come Quick! I'm Being Eaten by a Bear!"
38 "They Can Be Funny"
39 Ha ha! I bet they can. I bet Mr. and Mrs. Bear are a
40 bundle of hilarity as they tussle playfully over the remaining
41 portion of a former tourist plumped up by airline food. But
42 just the same, I'm glad that the only actual, non-stuffed,
43 practicing bears that we saw were in the Anchorage zoo.

—From *The Bradenton Herald*, Bradenton, Florida, July 3, 1988. Copyright ©
Dave Barry. Reprinted from *The Miami Herald*.

5. The first sentence in this passage ("My family and I ...") indicates that the author's purpose is to
   a. discuss something
   b. describe something
   c. analyze something
   d. defend something

6. The sentence beginning in line 11 of this passage ("Although Alaska is ...") is a statement of
   a. fact
   b. opinion

7. In this passage the author shows bias in favor of
   a. airline food
   b. cocaine smugglers
   c. bears in zoos
   d. bears

8. The author of this passage creates a tone that can be described as
   a. serious
   b. complex
   c. disapproving
   d. comic

9. The word or phrase indicating the relationship within the sentence that begins in line 1 ("My family and I ...") is
   a. statement and clarification
   b. cause and effect
   c. comparison
   d. contrast

PASSAGE 3

1 Although the eyes of all mammals are moistened and soothed
2 by tears, only human beings shed tears in response to
3 emotional stress; yet we know nothing about this uniquely
4 human behavior. A recent theory suggests that tears help to
5 relieve stress by ridding the body of potentially harmful
6 stress-induced chemicals. Thus far, it has been demonstrated
7 that emotionally induced tears have a higher protein content
8 than tears produced in response to eye irritation, such as that
9 caused by a cut onion. However, stress-related chemical
10 differences have yet to be identified.
11   Other provocative evidence supports this idea. For
12 example, one report found that people with stress-related
13 illnesses cry less than their healthy counterparts. In
14 addition, it is well known that people feel better "after a good
15 cry." In our society, it has been documented that men cry
16 much less frequently than women, and they appear more
17 susceptible to ulcers and some other stress-related problems.
18 In America, the most frequent triggers of crying episodes
19 involve interpersonal relations, such as arguments, and
20 movie or television scenes. Thus, the peak crying time is

21 between seven and ten in the evening, when people are likely
22 to be with others and/or watching television.

—From Feshbach and Weiner, *Personality.*

10. The details given in the sentences in lines 11–22 ("Other provocative evidence ...") do which of these?
    a. Add believability to the passage.
    b. Help us understand that crying is important to one's health.
    c. Provide evidence supporting a tentative conclusion.
    d. Explain how much tears need to be studied.

11. The sentence beginning in line 4 ("A recent theory ...") indicates that the author's purpose is
    a. to convince   b. to describe something
    c. to explain something d. to criticize

12. The sentence beginning in line 4 ("A recent theory ...") is a statement of
    a. fact   b. opinion

13. In this passage the author shows bias in favor of
    a. emotional stress   b. arguments
    c. emotionally induced tears d. men who cry

14. The word or phrase indicating the relationship within the sentence that begins in line 1 ("Although the eyes ...") is
    a. classification   b. contrast
    c. cause and effect d. generalization and example

15. The statements in lines 12–15 that "people with stress-related illnesses cry less than their healthy counterparts" and that "people feel better after a good cry" are
    a. valid   b. invalid

PASSAGE 4

1 You can see from even this brief discussion that the preven-
2 tion of child abuse is a difficult and multifaceted task. The
3 importance of preventing it, however, cannot be overempha-
4 sized, because the physical and psychological consequences of
5 abuse can be very serious. Child abuse can result not only in
6 physical handicaps but also in severe neurological problems.
7 Blows to the head can cause bleeding inside a child's skull,
8 ultimately leading to brain damage. What is particularly
9 surprising and disturbing is that infants, whose skull is much

317

10 larger than their brain (which is still growing) can suffer
11 hemorrhages throughout the brain simply by being shaken.
12 Known as the *shaken baby syndrome*, this form of abuse can
13 cause brain damage as well as visual problems and deficits in
14 language and motor skills.
15   Besides the neurological consequences of abuse, abused
16 children also suffer from disturbances in emotional and social
17 development. They have learned from their home life that
18 their involvement with other people carries with it a great
19 deal of pain, and they tend to be inhibited and socially unre-
20 sponsive, often backing away when a friendly caregiver or
21 another child approaches them. Such children have also been
22 found to be overly compliant or to exhibit violent and aggres-
23 sive behavior toward adults and peers. Some abused children
24 are "hypervigilant," meaning that they are constantly on the
25 lookout for danger, scanning the environment and ever-ready
26 to attack. A variety of underlying processes may account for
27 such behaviors among abused children. It may well be the
28 case that because of the ill treatment they have received,
29 these children failed to develop the social skills required to
30 engage in harmonious social interactions. Or, they may be
31 imitating the hostile interpersonal exchanges that they have
32 experienced.

        —From Zigler and Finn-Stevenson, *Children: Development and Social Issues.*

16. The main idea in this passage is that
  a. Abused children suffer from disturbances in social and emotional develop-
    ment.
  b. Abused children are constantly on the lookout for danger.
  c. *Shaken baby syndrome* is abuse characterized by brain damage and other
    problems.
  d. The physical and psychological consequences of child abuse are very serious.

17. In line 2, the word *multifaceted* means
  a. full of excitement   b. unusual
  c. having several parts   d. boring

18. The sentence that begins in line 2 ("The importance of ...") suggests that the
author's purpose is
  a. to evaluate   b. to present new information
  c. to tell a story   d. to analyze something

19. The word or phrase indicating the relationship within the sentence that begins
in line 23 ("Some abused children ...") is

a. definition
c. classification

b. time order
d. cause and effect

20. You could infer all of these except
a. Child-abuse victims are physically scarred but emotionally stable.
b. Child-abuse victims are not found just in the lower economic and social classes.
c. Child-abuse victims often need help for years.
d. Child-abuse victims don't always recover emotionally.

PASSAGE 5

1 Hurricanes form over the tropical oceanic regions where the
2 Sun heats huge masses of moist air. An ascending spiral
3 motion results, in the same manner as described in tornado
4 formation. When the moisture of the rising air condenses, the
5 latent heat provides additional energy and more air rises up
6 the column. This latent heat is a chief source of the hurri-
7 cane's energy and is readily available from the condensation
8 of the moist air of its source region.
9   Unlike the tornado, a hurricane gains energy from its
10 source region. As more and more air rises, the hurricane
11 grows, accompanied by clouds and increasing winds that blow
12 in a large spiral around a relatively calm, low-pressure center
13 —the eye of the hurricane. The eye may be 20 to 30 mi wide,
14 and ships sailing into this area have found that it is usually
15 calm and clear with no indication of the surrounding storm.
16 The air pressure is reduced 6–8% (to about 28 in of Hg) near
17 the eye. Hurricanes move rather slowly at a few miles per
18 hour.
19   Covering broad areas, hurricanes can be particularly
20 destructive. There are winds of at least 74 mi/h, but these can
21 be much greater, up to 120–130 mi/h, which are *very* danger-
22 ous. Mobile homes are particularly vulnerable to hurricane
23 winds. The greatest threat from a hurricane's winds comes
24 from their cargo of debris—a deadly barrage of flying missiles
25 such as lawn furniture, signs, roofing, and metal siding.
26   Hurricane winds do much damage, but drowning is the
27 greatest cause of hurricane deaths. As the eye of the hurri-
28 cane comes ashore or "makes landfall," a great dome of water
29 called a storm surge, often over 50 mi wide, comes sweeping
30 across the coast line. It brings huge waves and storm tides

319

31 that may reach 25 ft or more above normal. The rise may
32 come rapidly, flooding coastal lowlands. Nine out of ten hurri-
33 cane casualties are caused by the storm surge. The torrential
34 rains that accompany the hurricane produce sudden flooding
35 as the storm moves inland. As its winds diminish, rainfall
36 floods constitute the hurricane's greatest threat.
37   Once cut off from the warm ocean, the storm begins to die,
38 starved for water and heat energy, and dragged apart by
39 friction as it moves over the land. Even though a hurricane
40 weakens rapidly as it moves inland, the remnants of the
41 storm can bring 6–12 in. of rain or more to the areas they
42 cross. For example, Hurricane Diane of 1955 caused little
43 damage as it moved into the Gulf coastal area; but long after
44 its winds subsided, it brought floods to Pennsylvania, New
45 York, and New England that killed 200 persons and cost an
46 estimated $700 million in damage. In 1972, Hurricane Agnes
47 fused with another storm system, flooding creek and river
48 basins in the Northeast with more than a foot of rain in less
49 than 12 hours, killing 117 people, and causing almost $3
50 billion damage.

—From Shipman et al., *An Introduction to Physical Science.*

21. The subject in this passage is
   a. tornadoes   b. hurricanes
   c. winds   d. hurricane winds

22. In line 6 the word *latent* means
   a. potential   b. low
   c. high   d. extreme

23. In developing this passage, the pattern of organization the author uses can be described as
   a. time order   b. contrast
   c. statement and clarification d. classification

24. If the author were delivering this passage orally, his or her tone of voice would probably be
   a. objective   b. celebratory
   c. righteous   d. awestruck

25. What does the sentence beginning in line 32 ("Nine out of ten ...") do in relation to the sentence beginning in line 26 ("Hurricane winds do ...")?
   a. it contradicts what is said in line 26.
   b. it summarizes what is said in line 26.

c. it acts as a specific example of what is stated in line 26.

d. it alters the meaning of what is stated in line 26.

26. Which of these statements would the author support?

a. Hurricanes are merely big storms like tornadoes.

b. Hurricane winds aren't much of a problem unless you live on the coast.

c. Hurricanes are more of a problem for airplanes than for boats.

d. Hurricanes are destructive and dangerous across large areas.

PASSAGE 6

1 In 1969–1970, I spent a year living with the *So* tribe in the
2 semi-arid mountains of Northeastern Uganda in Africa. In
3 this polygynous tribe, the number of cows and goats owned by
4 a man is a measure of his wealth, and it is in cows and goats
5 that he pays for his wives.
6   We spent several months informally observing the *So*,
7 learning their language, and conducting a census. I then
8 conducted a series of interviews with a random sample of the
9 tribal members in the attempt to understand their sexual
10 attitudes and behavior. Did the women feel jealous of their
11 cowives? What coital positions were used? Who initiated
12 intercourse? What stimulation techniques were used? Were
13 masturbation, homosexuality, bestiality, and adultery prac-
14 ticed? What was the purpose of sexual intercourse? I also
15 wanted to learn their attitudes and behavior regarding
16 contraception, procreation, sterility, gender roles, intercourse
17 during menstruation and pregnancy, and other aspects of
18 sexuality.
19   Following a general principle for studying sensitive topics,
20 in the first interview I asked relatively innocuous questions
21 to give the informant and me some time to become acquain-
22 ted and at ease. In constructing the most intimate questions,
23 I tried to avoid wording that would imply any value judg-
24 ment.
25   There were some topics for which there were no *So* words.
26 For instance, there was no term for masturbation, and
27 although I was able to get the idea across to males through
28 appropriate gesturing, the practice seemed to be totally
29 unimaginable to females. Although adolescent males
30 occasionally masturbated, it was taboo for married adult
31 males to masturbate, because this was a "wasting of seed."
32 *Love* was another word for which there was no *So* term.

33 There was *apudori* (to have sexual intercourse), and there
34 were words for friendship, but no word for love per se.
35 Homosexuality was not practiced, falling into a category of
36 behaviors (including adult masturbation, intercourse during
37 menstruation, and bestiality) that were considered evidence
38 of witchcraft. In addition, contraception was totally unknown
39 to the *So*. My question "What can you do if you don't want to
40 have any more children?" was greeted with the same sort of
41 astonishment that you might express if someone asked "What
42 can you do if you no longer want your legs?"
43   The attitudes and experiences of men and women regard-
44 ing intercourse were very different. For men, intercourse was
45 very positive, both because they highly valued procreation
46 and because they enjoyed the activity itself. Those men who
47 were married to more than one woman spent an equal
48 amount of time with each wife, but avoided a particular wife
49 when she was menstruating. During intercourse they did not
50 engage in any sort of foreplay. Female breasts, which the *So*
51 women left exposed, had no erotic significance. And except for
52 the incidental contact that occurs during vaginal penetration,
53 to touch any portion of the vulva was forbidden.
54   In the absence of precoital stimulation, the negative
55 attitude of *So* women toward sexual intercourse was not
56 particularly surprising. I still have a vivid memory of one
57 very beautiful middle-aged woman describing with clenched
58 teeth and hands her first experience with intercourse. She
59 said that it hurt badly—it burned—but that she got through
60 it by telling herself repeatedly that she had to do this to get a
61 baby and that she had to have a baby to get cows. When
62 asked how she felt about sex now, she said that she wished
63 her husband had enough cows to take a "little wife," but that
64 it didn't hurt as much now as it had at first. In no instance
65 did a woman indicate ever having an orgasm; in fact, orgasm
66 was viewed as synonymous with ejaculation and as exclu-
67 sively a male phenomenon. In exploring the total absence of
68 female orgasm, I attempted to find out if *So* women were
69 aware of having a clitoris. I described it and drew pictures of
70 vulvas, but to no avail. I have considered at length these
71 gender differences in sexual attitudes, attempting to find
72 explanations. Perhaps the tribe's survival depended to some
73 extent on these attitudes. Given disease and constant
74 warfare with neighboring tribes, the tribe was in danger of
75 extinction. Because there were more females than males, the
76 population could be maintained as long as women gave birth
77 to as many children as possible. If women enjoyed sex, they

78 might not want to share their husbands with other women.
79 As it was, however, cowives tended to have rather close
80 relationships with one another. They did not compete for
81 men; rather, they shared the responsibilities of raising their
82 husband's children and providing him with food from their
83 gardens. Were wives to value sexual intercourse, other than
84 for reproduction, they might resent the time their husbands
85 spent with the others—three weeks out of four in the case of
86 a man with four wives.

—From Allgeier and Allgeier, *Sexual Interactions*.

27.   The detail sentence that best supports the subject in this passage (a survey of the sexual attitudes and behavior of the So tribe) is the sentence beginning on
a. Line 73. "Given disease and constant warfare ..."
b. Line 72. "Perhaps the tribe's survival ..."
c. Line 49. "During intercourse they did not ..."
d. Line 25. "There were some topics ..."

28.   In line 66 the word *synonymous* means
a. valuable   b. worthless
c. different from   d. the same as

29.   The first sentence in this passage ("In 1969–70 ...") suggests that the author's purpose is
a. to classify something   b. to describe an experience
c. to offer a solution   d. to criticize

30.   In developing this passage, the pattern of organization used by the author can be described as
a. cause and effect   b. simple listing
c. generalization and examples   d. definition

31.   In this passage the author shows bias in favor of
a. the present treatment of So women
b. general principles for studying sensitive topics
c. one man, multiple wives
d. the system of co-wives

32.   Which of these statements would the author support?
a. So women appear ready for feminist ideas.
b. Among the So, sexual intercourse for women was not something to anticipate with pleasure.
c. Falling in love among the So is full of romantic tradition.
d. Among the So, enjoyment is the major reason for sexual intercourse.

PASSAGE 7

1 A Department of Health, Education, and Welfare study found
2 that, if the total cost of America's driver education programs
3 is compared to the approximately 60,000 annual deaths on
4 the nation's highways, this approach to good driving "saves"
5 lives at a cost of about $88,000 per life. Other studies have
6 indicated that there is little correlation between whether a
7 person has taken a driver education course and later safe
8 driving behavior (as measured by arrests, involvement in
9 accidents, and the like). The one variable that does seem most
10 important is good or bad driving habits by members of a
11 person's family (father, mother, husband, wife, sister, brother,
12 and so on). In contrast to driver education, the introduction of
13 seat belts costs about $87 per life, and studies show that they
14 effectively save lives in automobile accidents. Furthermore,
15 some studies suggest that 10,000 or more lives may be saved
16 each year as a result of lowering the speed limit in order to
17 conserve energy. The major cost involved is new speed limit
18 signs. In summary, driver education courses are designed to
19 change the habits of individual drivers, whereas seat belts
20 and lower speed limits are designed to change the highway
21 context for all motorists, including drivers and passengers
22 alike.

—From Lowry and Rankin, *Sociology: Social Science and Social Concern.*

33. The subject in this passage is
   a. the value of seat belts and lower speed limits
   b. driver education saves lives
   c. the cost of saving lives on the road
   d. family driving habits

34. This passage contrasts with which of these?
   a. driving habits of husbands and wives
   b. cost of driver education with number of lives saved
   c. types of safety features in cars
   d. differing speed limits for different roads

35. The sentence beginning in line 1 of this passage ("A Department of Health …") is a statement of
   a. fact   b. opinion

36. In this passage the driver shows bias against
   a. driver-education courses   b. arresting driving violators

c. saving lives through driver training

d. Health, Education, and Welfare studies

37. What does the sentence beginning in line 12 ("In contrast ...") do in relation to the sentence beginning in line 1 ("A Department of Health ...")?
   a. It indicates an effect of something discussed beginning in line 1.
   b. It indicates similarities with something discussed beginning in line 1.
   c. It sets up a contrast with what is said beginning in line 1.
   d. It defines something mentioned beginning in line 1.

38. The statement in lines 13–14 that "seat belts cost about $87 per life" and "they save lives in automobile accidents" is
   a. valid
   b. invalid

PASSAGE 8

1 Modern banking had its origins in ancient England. In those
2 days, people wanting to safeguard their coins or gold had two
3 choices—hide it under the mattress or turn it over to some-
4 one else for safekeeping. The logical people to turn to for
5 storage were the local goldsmiths, since they had the
6 strongest vaults.
7   The goldsmiths accepted the gold for storage, giving the
8 owner a receipt stating that the gold could be redeemed at a
9 later date. When a payment was due, the owner went to the
10 goldsmith, redeemed part of the gold, and gave it to the
11 payee. After all that, the payee was very likely to turn around
12 and give the gold back to the goldsmith for safekeeping.
13   Gradually, instead of taking the time and effort to
14 physically exchange the gold, businesspeople began to
15 exchange the goldsmith's receipts as payment. Therefore, the
16 gold never left the goldsmiths' vaults. It wasn't long before
17 enterprising goldsmiths saw the potential for profit in this
18 arrangement. As long as the gold remained in the vaults, the
19 owners wouldn't miss it if it were loaned to someone else
20 —for a fee. The odds were overwhelmingly against all the
21 depositors' wanting their gold at the same time—and few
22 people would ever demand their very own gold coins back.
23   The circulation of goldsmiths' receipts was the beginning
24 of paper currency and of commercial banking. And the enter-
25 prising goldsmith who first lent somebody else's gold for a fee
26 was the first to make a bank loan for interest.

—From Megginson et al., *Business*.

39. The sentence beginning on line 13 ("Gradually, instead of taking ...") shows which of these?
   a. the difficulty in safeguarding and using gold coins
   b. people's unwillingness to care for their own gold
   c. the time and effort involved in dealing with hard currency
   d. the movement from storage of gold to developing banking services

40. In line 11 the word *payee* means
   a. person   b. person paying
   c. the payment   d. interest on the payment

41. The sentence beginning in line 1 of this passage ("In those days ...") is a statement of
   a. fact   b. opinion

42. The author of this passage creates a tone that can be described as
   a. apathetic   b. pleasant
   c. cruel   d. farcical

43. What does the sentence beginning in line 15 ("Therefore the gold ...") do in relation to the sentence beginning in line 13 ("Gradually, instead of ...")?
   a. It states an effect of something discussed starting in line 13.
   b. It analyzes where something fits in with something discussed starting in line 13.
   c. It discusses the similarities between something and something else discussed starting in line 13.
   d. It specifies clearly the meaning of something mentioned starting in line 13.

44. The assertion in lines 23–24 that "The circulation of goldsmiths' receipts was the beginning of paper currency and of commercial banking" is
   a. valid   b. invalid

PASSAGE 9

1 In September 1982, Americans were gobbling up over 130
2 million painkilling tablets, pills, or capsules daily, at a cost
3 of over $1.2 billion a year. Makers of the five major brands—
4 Tylenol, Anacin, Bayer, Bufferin, and Excedrin—were
5 spending over $130 million every year on advertising. It was
6 worth that much, though, for a 1 percent increase in their
7 market share meant more than $7 million in extra sales.
8   In 1955, McNeil Consumer Products Company, a subsid-
9 iary of Johnson & Johnson (J&J), the brilliant marketing

10 company, had introduced Tylenol as a prescription drug when
11 aspirin was found to be potentially harmful. In the mid-
12 1960s, J&J's marketing experts transformed Tylenol into a
13 consumer product to compete with Anacin, Bufferin, and
14 Bayer. It had 7 to 8 percent of the market by 1975, when
15 Datril, a copycat product, was introduced—at a lower
16 cost—by Bristol-Myers. J&J retaliated by reducing prices,
17 increasing advertising, and resorting to knuckle-dusting
18 lawsuits to beat down competition. In three years, Tylenol
19 had captured another 25 percent of the market and become
20 the best seller. After spending over $85 million on advertising
21 from 1978 to 1982, J&J had 37 percent of the market and was
22 increasing that share 2 to 3 percent each year.
23   Then, in October 1982, seven people in Chicago died from
24 cyanide-laced Extra-Strength Tylenol capsules. Although it
25 was proven that the tampering was done on retail store
26 shelves and not at the factory, Tylenol's sales dropped 80
27 percent, and its share of the market dropped to 12 percent in
28 November 1982. J&J immediately stopped production,
29 recalled 22 million bottles of capsules, offered a $100,000
30 reward for information leading to the arrest of the guilty
31 party or parties, and opened up toll-free lines to answer
32 customer concerns. Since 80 percent of its customers bought
33 Tylenol on the recommendation of their doctors, J&J also
34 used telegrams, telephone calls, and visits by sales
35 representatives to reassure physicians and pharmacists all
36 over the country.
37   J&J had three alternatives: do nothing and hope that
38 people would buy the product again after the crisis was over,
39 bring the product out under another name, or do everything
40 possible to protect the brand and recover its lost customers.
41 Since sales totaled $500 million a year and profits were $80
42 million, 17 percent of J&J's earnings, the company made an
43 absolute commitment to rebuilding Tylenol's name.
44   A three-way tamperproof package was designed. Then the
45 chairmen of McNeil and J&J demonstrated to the public at
46 news conferences and on TV talk shows how safe and secure
47 the new product was. They explained that Tylenol would cost
48 no more because of the new packaging, and that the U.S.
49 Food and Drug Administration had cleared J&J of any
50 wrongdoing. Retailers and customers were reimbursed for
51 any capsules thrown away, and a 25 percent discount was
52 given to retailers for Tylenol purchases at or above pre-crisis
53 levels. Also, $1.00 customer coupons for purchasing the new

54 safety-sealed capsules appeared in newspapers, magazines,
55 and mailboxes. These coupons went out before customers had
56 had a chance to replace their discarded Tylenol with a
57 competing brand. The company paid the entire cost of these
58 activities—over $100 million—but the effort paid off. Tylenol
59 had recaptured over 30 percent of the total market by early
60 1984.

—From Megginson et al., *Business*.

45. The details given in lines 18–22 ("In three years ...") illustrate which of these?
   a. the extent of Tylenol's market
   b. just how many painkillers Americans "gobble"
   c. the superiority of Tylenol over Anacin and Bufferin
   d. the power of advertising in selling painkillers

46. In developing this passage, the pattern of organization the author uses can be described as
   a. classification   b. time order
   c. summary   d. cause and effect

47. The word or phrase indicating the relation within the sentence that begins in line 44 ("Then the chairmen ...") is
   a. statement and clarification   b. contrast
   c. simple listing   d. cause and effect

48. The statement in lines 32–33 that "80 percent of its customers bought Tylenol on the recommendation of their doctors" is
   a. valid   b. invalid

49. You could infer all these *except*
   a. Tylenol captured the market in a variety of ways.
   b. J&J's commitment to Tylenol was profit motivated.
   c. The writer feels J&J acted inappropriately following the Tylenol tampering incident.
   d. Painkillers will continue to be a major product for J&J.

50. The subject in this passage is
   a. how J&J successfully marketed Tylenol.
   b. the medical superiority of Tylenol.
   c. how tamperproof packaging was introduced.
   d. the importance of discount coupons.

Skill Analysis Guide

Directions: Circle the numbers of the test questions you got wrong and record the number of minutes you spent on each test.

Chapter and Comprehension Skill	Pre Test	Mid Test	Post Test
2. Main idea	1, 29, 36, 41, 45	5, 16,	1, 16, 21, 33, 50
3. Details	19, 24, 30, 42, 46	1, 6, 17	10, 27, 34, 39, 45
4. Word meanings	2, 31, 37, 47	7, 18	17, 22, 28, 40
5. Author's purpose	3, 13, 32, 48	8, 21	5, 11, 18, 29
6. Pattern of organization	4, 14, 20, 38	9, 19	2, 23, 30, 46
7. Fact or opinion	8, 21, 25, 43	2, 22	6, 12, 35, 41
8. Bias	9, 15, 33, 49	3, 11	7, 13, 31, 36
9. Tone	10, 22, 26, 44	12, 23	3, 8, 9, 42
10. Relations within sentences	11, 16, 27, 39	4, 13	9, 14, 19, 47
11. Relations between sentences	5, 17, 28, 40	14, 24	4, 11, 25, 43
12. Valid or invalid argument	6, 12, 34, 50	20, 25	15, 38, 44, 48
13. Inference	7, 18, 23, 35	10, 15	20, 26, 32, 49
Test time	.... minutes	.... minutes	.... minutes

If you have two or more questions wrong in any one comprehension skill on either the Pre Test or the Post Test, or if you miss more than one in any one comprehension skill on the Mid Test, you will want to read and review that chapter's instructions. Also, review that chapter's exercises carefully. The more you practice the exercises for each chapter, the more skill you will gain in these types of comprehension.

Also, compare your Post Test score with your Pre Test score. On the Post Test, did you have fewer errors? Did you improve your ability to correctly answer questions in the types of comprehension skills on which you were weak in the Pre Test?

Look at the number of minutes you spent on each test. Is your reading getting faster?

Index